SEARCHING THE LIMITS OF LOVE

SEARCHING THE LIMITS OF LOVE:
AN APPROACH TO THE SECULAR TRANSCENDENT: GOD

DAVID J. HASSEL, S.J., PH.D.
ASSOCIATE PROFESSOR OF PHILOSOPHY
LOYOLA UNIVERSITY OF CHICAGO

A Campion Book

LOYOLA UNIVERSITY PRESS
CHICAGO 60657

LIBRARY OF CONGRESS CATALOGING IN PUBLICATION DATA

Hassel, David J., 1923–
     Searching the Limits of Love

     Includes index.
     1. Love.   2. Absolute, The.   I. Title.
BD436.H335 1985   212'.7   85-266
ISBN 0-8294-0461-9

Design by Jean Hollman

To
MY MOTHER, CATHERINE ELIZABETH,
AND TO MY FATHER, DAVID,
WHO SHOWED ME WHAT LOVE COULD BECOME

CONTENTS

PREFACE

Those who have tried searching the limits of love know only too well that this is no easy enterprise. It is not like a walk along the pleasurable sun-drenched beaches of Florida nor even like a climb into the romantic majesty of Colorado mountains. The enterprise, if rewarding, is always tortuous and occasionally agonizing. Yet every man and every woman must sometime take this exploratory journey or forever be bored with life.

This book attempts to face honestly the question whether the other-centered love which we all crave to give and to receive is actually possible. It tries to be faithful to a person's daily experience of life as lover and as beloved. Yet it also tries to discover beneath this experience the mysterious powers and influences which give love its strength, meaning, surprise, hope, and liberty. Such an endeavor eventually demands philosophic probing, which uses indirectly the statistical discoveries of sociology and the explanatory schemes of psychology but goes beyond them. Yet the philosopher must always return to the everyday experience of men and women and check out his conclusions. Again, although we live off each other's observations of life and love, still only the individual person can look deeply into personal experience and know whether or not the phenomena which reveal the unmistakable presence of other-centered love are truly present within this experience.

When one undertakes such a personal search, one almost unwittingly discovers or denies the presence of a secular transcendent: a central value within and yet beyond the world—a value which enters into and steadily supports all one's thoughts and decisions as they shape one's world. Here a person does metaphysics without fully realizing it. For then one searches out the ultimate presence and meaning within one's life and world. If reading this book stimulates and illumines any such search, the author's highest hopes would be achieved.

But the friction of much disciplined thinking is needed to strike the spark of philosophical light. Thus I am writing for persons who are searching for the ultimate meaning of life and are willing to pay the price to discover it. I hope that professional philosophers will also find some fresh insights and new questions to ponder. For much recent writing tends to undermine confidence in the ability of human intelligence to discover any absolute, any transcendent being. Perhaps students of such philosophers will enjoy the opportunity to confront some evidence for the existence of a secular transcendent, of an all-provident, all-loving, all-present God. I hope at some later time to explore five other approaches to God, by way of evolution, heroic decision, intelligent freedom, interplay of individual and social responsibilities, and human survival of evil.

I also hope—fondly, perhaps—some day to thank with more than these few words the following people who have encouraged me to continue the sometimes surprisingly joyful work of putting this book together. Their love was not only loyal, but intelligent; not only trustworthy but liberating and expansive.

First of all, I am indebted to Mr. Michael Stanfa whose insightful response to an examination question in April, 1971, and whose discussion of it with me during the student rioting that same month got me thinking along the basic lines of this book. I am especially grateful to Fr. Edmund Fortman, S.J. and to Fr. Robert Harvanek, S.J., who thoroughly read and critiqued this book at the expense of their own writing time and who have encouraged me year after year as they patiently go over almost everything I write. The same may be said of Fr. Frank Oppenheim, S.J. whose friendship has long supported me in much more than writing. My colleagues in the philosophy department of Loyola University of Chicago have been patient with my second semester absences as I tried to complete this book. Among these, Dr. Louise French, B.V.M., showed a grasp of the whole project; Dr. Benjamin Llamzon took particular issue with my treatment of Sartre; Dr. William Zanardi raised pertinent questions of method; Fr. Leo Sweeney, S.J., brought his background of Thomism to bear on the book; and Fr. Robert Schmidt, S.J., and Fr. Murel Vogel, S.J., have been my mentors for three decades. Dr. Elizabeth Drugan, S.H.C.J., offered me the advice of one challenging the book with experiences as teacher, administrator, educational researcher, and friend. Two faithful typists brought this book into shape with crucial and high competence: Mrs. Mary Ellen Hayes and Mrs. Natalie F. Hector. Mr. Michael Albers, when a graduate student at Loyola University, read the manuscript critically in order to research bibliography and incidentally gave me a sense of how the younger philosophers might look at this book.

I have also whole communities to thank. My Jesuit community at Loyola University, Chicago, supported me financially and, more importantly, fraternally. A student community through ten years underwent my throes of creation with kindness and with an occasional smile of condolence. Among the students, Sr. Teresa Cole, S.H., was remarkable for the perceptiveness of her extended written comments. Finally, may I thank the Jesuits attached to Loyola University Press, namely Fr. Daniel Flaherty, Fr. George Lane, and Fr. Robert Clark, for graciously accepting and editing this book. The Lord knows how much I have depended on them.

Many people enter into a book started back in 1971; I feel sure that I have failed to mention some of these people who have been so generous with their time, thought, and support. May their unfortunate (for me, at least) hiddenness be well rewarded by the Lord who forgets no deed done for his *anawim*. All these people tried their best to help me escape foolish statements and other mistakes.

DAVID J. HASSEL, S.J.
Feast of the Assumption, August 15, 1984

INTRODUCTION

The Mystery
and the Problem
of Love

PRELUDE

The seed of this book was a remark made in a test paper by a student, Mr. Michael Stanfa, in a philosophy of religion class at Loyola University, Chicago. He asked whether strong human love did not make superhuman demands upon a person—demands which would appear absurd (impossible to fulfill) in a godless world, but which would be possible and understandable (although mysterious) in a God-created world.

Ironically, during the protests against the Vietnam War (1969–71) across the country and at Loyola University, Michael Stanfa and I met one day to talk over this insight. As the shouting outside the window of our conference room grew more strident with partisan conflict, he and I talked of other-centered love and its healing (wholing) qualities. He wondered aloud whether we or the rioters were the wild ones; we managed a small laugh at ourselves.

Later in the year, I developed this insight broadly enough to offer it as a symposium paper. In it I contrasted the absolute freedom of the Sartrean person with the total unfreedom of the Herbert Spencerian person to show that the factual practice of other-centered love was impossible for either of them to explain but that a description of humankind lying between these two extremes yielded not only an explanation of other-centered love but also a discovery of God within this love. To some the paper appeared like a slow-moving dirigible, a hardly challenging target for the tracer bullets of their criticism. A few others thought that the central idea of the paper, though charred by the critique, was nevertheless worthy of salvage. I was able to blame the original idea on Mr. Stanfa who bravely sat in the symposium audience, though I accepted full guilt for its much larger development in the paper.

During a sabbatical (in September, 1972–June, 1973), I worked the ten-page paper into a full-length book. I solicited criticism from colleagues, and revised it. I then watched it bounce from publisher to publisher—mainly because it was not exciting enough. It seemed that it demanded too much work of the reader who was not expected to be much interested in this problem of whether or not interpersonal relations would yield knowledge of the secular transcendent, often called God.

3

This estimate struck me as strange. Love songs have not gone out of fashion; intimacy is still considered a great prize of life; the terrible failures of human intimacy called *divorces* are prevalent in western society; the wonder of sacrificial living in our contemporaries—Ghandi, Martin Luther King, Jr., Mother Teresa of Calcutta, Dietrich Bonhoeffer, Dorothy Day, and Maximilian Kolbe—to name but a few, and in the past lives of such people as Teresa of Avila, Thomas More, George Wesley, Vincent de Paul, and Florence Nightingale still stirs our hearts.

Nor is self-sacrifice limited to great figures of the past and present. Each of us knows families in which great sacrifices have been made with love: a widower struggles to raise a family alone, or a wife and children provide twenty-four hour care of a retarded child while the husband holds down two jobs to cover the extraordinary expenses, or the eldest son in a family goes to work right out of high school and puts off marriage in order to send his younger sister and brother through college—hackneyed examples because they are not rare. Such quiet heroism occurs also in business, when an industrialist, out of a sense of integrity, risks heavy financial loss to indemnify clientele for a faulty product. It occurs in science when researchers risk health and reputation to produce a life-preserving machine or an antibiotic. It occurs within government service with the CIA, the diplomatic corps, the cabinet of the president, or an advisory body of the senate, when men and women sacrifice safe careers and lives to take on thankless jobs and dangerous missions.

All such people, and even those who refuse to sacrifice for others, must face the great questions of life more than once: Why should I stretch myself taut for anyone—except, of course, myself? What right have people—my wife, my daughter, my boss, my country, my pastor—to demand this of me? All must ask themselves the question: is sacrificial or other-centered love anything more than masochism? Is it just a futile pouring of one's life down a drain? Why should a person waste energy, beauty, ambition, health, and possessions so that another can thrive? What can possibly come from constant other-centered love but eventual exhaustion and defeat? If such questions burn into us long enough and receive only the faintest response, then a cynicism begins to corrode even the firmest devotion to those we love.

Yet part of the mystery of human love is that we will still love, still sacrifice; at times we eagerly undergo apparent self-diminishment for the sake of another's growth. Thus no event of life is more filled with mystery than love. Nor is any event more thoroughly analyzed in problematic fashion. The complex conceptualizations of modern day Freudians and Jungians are matched in abundance by those of medieval philosophers and Graeco-Roman essayists. The search for the meaning of love goes on not only behind ivy-clad university walls and in psychiatrists' chrome-furnished suites but also on park benches and at morning-after breakfasts. For these reasons, it will be initially necessary to outline the problem of love and to take a first glance at the mystery of love before one attempts to probe for their deeper meaning and, perhaps, for the underlying life of the secular transcendent.

1. The Mystery of Love

Anyone who tries to approach the secular transcendent, or God, through love-relationships but does not first consider the mystery of love risks much. One may underestimate the rich complexity of this mystery or overestimate the ability of human reason to map the depths of love through literature or philosophy or psychology or theology.[1] This is particularly true when a person seeks to discover the so-called divine within this mystery of love since one seeks to understand transcendent mystery by way of the deepest human mystery. Thus this approach incurs a double chance of error. To illustrate this, a number of instances will be given of merely the mystery of love—with no attempt to extricate the transcendent element possibly present. This simple approach will show how hard it is to take even the first philosophic baby step towards the secular transcendent, whom we call God.

Essential Reciprocity of Love

One of the basic insights driven into the human heart and mind rather early in life is that love is either reciprocal or nonexistent. Each of us along life's way has tried to love someone dearly, even idolized him or her, but felt this attempt at love die from lack of response. Each of us has also gone through the opposite experience. Another reached out toward us in the hope of affectionate return. But this plea for a return of love left us cold, perhaps antagonistic, maybe even disgusted. A thousand reasons can be offered for our refusal. But one fact remains: no love occurred because no reciprocal response took place. On the other hand, if one honestly responds to another's overture for friendship, some mysterious spark leaps across between the persons to warm their hearts, to strengthen their confidence in themselves and in the other, and eventually to lift them into the deep peace and security of mutually acknowledged union.

Because of traumatic rejection, however, some never attempt love again—so precious and powerful is the reciprocity of love. Others who once felt a gracious response in the beloved never tire of attempting other loves. Still others never feel worthy of love yet always want it. They elaborate defenses against rejection or betrayal; their response to another's overture is loaded with provisos (if you do this, I'll. . .) and is sometimes crushed by the weight of these conditions. And then there are those who try to fake a loving response in the vain hope that love will eventually happen if they fake it hard enough and long enough; the only result is empty self-mockery. Yet all these types of lovers, no matter what their success or failure, share a fascination with the mystery of love. None of them ever doubts that love must be mutual to be love, that reciprocity is the essential element for love's existence.

The Start and Stop of Love

It is exactly this mysterious reciprocity of love which makes us wonder how love can ever get started. If love is a reciprocal or mutual act, then it demands simultaneity of offer and of response to the offer. But how to achieve such simultaneity? How does the young lover ever get the courage first to reach out to the beloved? What makes this an act of love when as yet the accepting response does not exist? In other words, what mysterious element starts the dance of approach and response which is the reciprocity of love?

A quick answer could be that the young lover has a basic self-trust which enables him or her to initiate this love relationship. But what is the source of this self-trust? Previous loves of parents, brothers and sisters, and school friends may well be the basis for this trust. Yet how did these first loves start? Further, if they are the basis for self-trust, how can they—so different from this new extra-familial and peer love—support it? For this new love draws the young person out of the family in seeming disregard of previous loves. As Genesis says: A man shall leave father and mother and cleave to his wife so that they may become one flesh. Can this new love at one and the same time need a certain distance from previous loves and yet use them as a basis to entrust the self to another?

Foreverness

Even if a young person could explain how a love first starts, this is no guarantee that one would know how this love grows. One could advance the previous explanation and declare that the first act of love becomes the self-trust which enables both lover and beloved to grow into a second deeper stage of love. An objector to this explanation would not want to deny that love grows out of love. But the objector might reply that each stage of love's growth is actually a new start and is more difficult than the previous stage since it takes on more responsibility for the beloved and for the latter's other relationships of love, such as the in-laws of married love. Something more is needed than merely a good beginning.

Indeed, at exactly this point of new growth, many a love falters and dies. How does the self-trust expand sufficiently to start the second stage of growth? And how can this happen simultaneously in lover and beloved so that the reciprocity which founds every act of love can come to be?

Here we touch the mysterious continuity of deep love—its foreverness. Without much thought, a person generally takes for granted that a healthy love relationship will grow indefinitely, that it will last as long as the two lovers live. Certainly, there are moments of doubt when conflict occurs. Yet over the years, as the conflicts, one after the other, resolve in further growth of love, a deep security grows that this love will never end. But can the basis of this security be only the love relationship itself? Given human fragility and the shattering power of events beyond human strength, can this foreverness be based on human love alone? Is such love totally self-guaranteeing? Or is some mysterious 'more' required to make the foreverness of human love a real hope, not a fond delusion?

Perdurance of Love in Absence and Loss

A mother's love for her growing children reveals another mysterious facet of human love since it seems to deny the theorem that reciprocity is essential to love. A mother may have to wait twelve to thirty years before a child is ready to respond to her love, for example, when he first notices some evening in the kitchen that she is very tired or very lonely and needs him there. Where does the mother get the courage to wait so long for this response and, in the instance of a large family, to wait again and again for each child? Can this possibly be love if the children cannot respond with love? Is it, then, merely instinctive affection? How can a mother's love begin and perdure under such condi-

8

tions? And yet how can she long support such a demanding life without the love of her children?

Some answer that the love of her husband and, later, the love of her mature children, somehow come to her through her immature unloving children so that she receives a substitute response adequate to establish the reciprocity essential to love. Such a substitute response, however, could hardly exist for the widow or the divorced woman raising three youngsters under ten years old. Nor does this account explain well how a mother can turn against a husband or against the whole family if she thinks a child must be protected. Lastly, substitute love would here appear to be an unreal projection upon the unloving child so that the latter is not seen and therefore not valued as an autonomous person. Are we, then, to say that a mother cannot love her children until they can make a mature response to her love-overtures? Is this demanded by the reciprocity of love?

The mystery of love is deepened when love is found to perdure even though the beloved offers less and less to be loved. The wife struggling to raise a family despite an alcoholic husband and the husband endeavoring to support a spendthrift wife are prime examples of the strange perdurance of love despite the diminishment of its object. In such married loves, one wonders why total collapse does not occur more often. Within such tortured loves, some sovereign, yet gratuitous, demand for continued support of the weakened partner, for compassion beyond normal human powers, seems to be at work. Somewhere and somehow, the spouse finds a perduring worth in still loving although the partner becomes less and less capable of adequate response. Occasionally, in these cases the offended spouse is driven by a neurotic need to be a martyr or by a stubborn desire to keep up appearances. But more often he or she is as realistic about the spouse as a Maine farmer about the fickle weather. Within such a person operates a strong, though much buffeted, conviction that continued love of the mentally sick or irresponsible spouse is something needed and very desirable. What could be the source of such devotion—if it is not merely a false sense of responsibility or simply a fear of society's reprisals? What or who could make such sovereign demands upon another person? Certainly, not the spouse, nor the children, nor the in-laws. What or who, then? This is the mystery.

Multiplying Loves

In stressing the dependency aspect within the reciprocity of love, one calls attention to the somewhat negative side of the mystery of love. But when a person glances at the independence generated in the lover by the love, one glimpses a more positive side. It is no secret that the lover who rejoices in one deep love becomes more sensitive to other persons and consequently more capable of other loves. To the lover's surprise, the new loves do not diminish the original love; indeed, they feed it in a benevolent, enriching cycle. For example, grandparents find that their original love opens out not only to their own children but also to their grandchildren, not only to these but also to the neighbors' children. The beautiful skill of loving, developed as much by suffering as by joy, is not diminished but increased by use.

The supposed distraction of other loves seems to deepen the commitment to the beloved of the first love. In contrast, some couples fear that their original love would be cramped by other loves. So they choose to be childless and very selective in acquaintances. But then they find it hard to keep their own love alive, discovering that their very concentration on the one love cramps and smothers it. What is it about love which impels us to offer it to others, and not hug it to death? The newly engaged couple discovers new beauty in older people, in plants, in previously bothersome younger brothers and sisters, in animals, and in blue-green seas or red dawns; they want to show their discovery to these others by offering them a new tenderness and attention. Yet how can such loves be multiplied out of the original love without seeming to diminish it, if only by distraction?

The experience of grandparents and of the newly engaged has its counterparts in the lives of a psychological counselor, a politician, and a clergyman. Each must operate within a professional framework; still the love for a wife or husband, or for a close friend, enables each to peer more deeply and to be more compassionate within every client. Further, the more healthy loves such a professional has, the more he or she can offer respect, loyalty, and affectionate support to the people served. Here the original love is recognized as creative and communitarian in a remarkable way. For though the number and depth of a person's loves are limited by sheer physical energy, time, and location of opportunities, still the loves allowed by limiting circumstances do multiply and enhance each other in a benevolent circle of mutual enrichment. Yet how is this seeming fact possible? For love's growth is dependent on reciprocation; while the multiplication of loves and their deepening would seem to diminish the opportunities for such reciprocation in the original love. Does not the doctor's or the lawyer's devotion to clients often leave his or her spouse and children starved for affection and their love for him or her stunted? Is not this multiplication of loves by the original love very mysterious if not very ambivalent?

Love's World of Meaning

If a person's original love is a center from which other loves may radiate, gather strength, and mutually interrelate, then a world of meaning develops around this type of lover.[2] This is the person's community with its various intersecting rings of friends and acquaintances, of influences and affections, of desires and hopes, of service and play.

This lover may be a bachelor uncle supporting his widowed sister's four children by his work as a fireman. In taking the place of the father, he has gradually centered his life in the growing lives of the children although he still spends much time with his friends at the firehouse, at the office of the Firemen's Benevolent Association, and at his church's gymnasium where he coaches basketball. But slowly the central meaning and value of his life has moved from the camaraderie of the firehouse to the family life of his sister's home—especially as her two boys entered their teens.

This is the world of meaning which love gives to the bachelor uncle. But it is a mysterious world which he would never have predicted nor, perhaps, have chosen for himself. Is it all a mere accident and can it evaporate just as easily as it materialized? If the central love is lost, does the whole world of meaning collapse? How does one go on living when this occurs? Should not a lover, therefore, hedge his or her bets so that more than one central love and more than one world of meaning are available to the lover in the event that one of the worlds of love collapses? But how many people are capable of one world of love, much less of two or three? Does deep love condemn a person to final despair at the collapse of his or her world? Or is there a wider world of meaningful love at once encompassing and permeating each lover's smaller world of love—a wider world which offers support, continuity, and additional meaning to the smaller world so that even if the latter should die, the lover would have reason to continue to live and love in hope of a future community of loves?

Love's Liberation through Responsibility

The world of meaning offered by the multiplication of loves out of a central and deep love carries within it a strange paradox; the lover's personality appears to expand with liberty even while taking on more and more obligations to others. At first glance, one would expect that the gathering of obligations would eventually so bind the lover that even breathing would become impossible. But this does not always happen. For example, take the woman social worker in the slums or the American priest-missionary in Tanzania. In both cases, the lover is moving into a strange culture to serve the needs of a suspicious people. For the social worker there is a central meaningful love in marriage to a socially conscious husband and for the priest-missionary there is his warm comradeship with Christ. In both instances a central love not only lures them into the strange culture but also offers them the strength to endure its first shocks. Over the years, the lovers each enter intimately into the lives of the people they serve. The deeper the intimacy with the individuals and families served, the more each lover takes on responsibility for them.

One cannot deny that often a missionary or a social worker will feel crushed by these responsibilities and, in hope of greater freedom and joy, will give up the profession by leaving the people. But not always. Sometimes a lover finds a new liberty through the intimacy and its resultant obligations, a new dedication to people, a stronger ability to suffer inconvenience and pain for those loved. It seems that this lover's personality grows in intelligence not only of the cultural situation but also of life's deepest rhythms, takes on a deeper tenderness and compassion for all people and not just for those immediately served, and grows in hopeful joy because of growing trust in people's innate goodness. Indeed, through willingness to suffer for people, the lover becomes more aware of people's weakness, more prudent in evaluating it, and more patient in adjusting to it. In other words, out of this loving service arises a beautifully balanced personality centered in love. Liberty takes on a human shape and presence.

In such a liberated person, there is a willingness to sacrifice the whole world of success for the people served. Ironically, sacrifice or the willingness to be depleted for the beloved has produced a remarkable fulfillment. Supposed self-exhaustion has turned out to be full self-development; the death of the self, loss of ambition for self-aggrandizement, has brought stronger life. Are we entering here the deepest area of mystery in love? And is this why so many give up on love and bargain for the more cozy existence of a slowly narrowing and gradually more homogeneous circle of friends and acquaintances? Is it possible that a growing and liberated love demands that the lover continually stretch herself or himself out to encompass ever widening circles of friends and ever more various experiences? Does liberty, beautiful as it is, demand a constant suffering for its growth? Is this why the human heart sometimes feels itself ambivalently shrinking at the very moment that it opens itself wide to accept another person and another situation to itself? Who or what can sustain the human heart over so many years and so many shrinkings and openings? Certainly the central human loves of one's life. But are they enough? Is something more needed and, if so, what could it be? If this is not the mystery of love, what is the mystery?[3]

Evidently, it is time to consider the problem of love so that some partial intelligible grasp of this mystery of love becomes possible. Otherwise, we are left totally baffled and simply shrugging at this mystery.

2. THE PROBLEM OF LOVE

Yes, it is agreed—love is not simply a problem but is much more a mystery. So, why bother to discuss the problem of love? First of all, though the mystery of love is not the problem of love, yet they are related and do influence each other. Mystery is a reality challenging us with its opaque richness. A problem, on the other hand, is a person's reaction to the mystery; it is one's struggle to understand and to live with that mystery. Furthermore, diverse understandings occur at different levels of a mystery and thus there are as many ways of living with the mystery as there are diverse understandings of it. For example, one's problematic understanding of a certain friendship may be from the standpoint of everyday experience with one's closest friend on an assembly line, at the Friday evening poker game, and on short fishing vacations. But this understanding, if educated, could be also from the standpoint of psychology or religion or sociology or poetry or philosophy or from all these standpoints converged on the one friend. On this score, the dense mystery of friendship can be approached from different levels of understanding and thus can present us with diverse problems of understanding it.

Usually these problems arise from the ways we live out a friendship. It may be that a young woman is befriended by a much older woman and, in the richness of the growing friendship, meets

1. the psychological problem of bridging between conservative and radical mentalities,
2. the social problem of integrating this older friend with her other younger friends,
3. the philosophical problem of distinguishing the essential and nonessential elements of friendship, and
4. the everyday, experiential problem of letting the strong-willed older woman know that her dominating ways can create hostility within the friendship.

The rich reality of the friendship, its very mystery, causes problems of understanding and of loving for both the younger and the older woman.

Strangely enough, the partial solution of these problems augments the mystery, since a new understanding often lights up

14

hitherto unsuspected depths yet to be explored. In fact, the growing wonder at the mystery can at times present terrible problems for the human mind. Because of the reciprocal relationship between mystery and problem, it is then easy to mistake the one for the other although they are quite distinct. Here philosophy distinguishes problem from mystery and proceeds to reflect on this mystery at the level of philosophy, though aware of other kinds of understanding such as the psychological and the sociological.

The Philosophical Problem of Love

When the philosopher speaks of the problem of love, he or she is not trying to give experience of the mystery of love, though he or she may never safely ignore the experience while talking about the problem of love. Rather, one is concerned here with ways of conceptualizing this experience already enjoyed so that the resultant concepts may reflect light back on the dark mystery itself. Although one's conceptualization enters into the experience of the mystery, it is not the mystery itself but a means of better understanding and more thoroughly living it. Conceptualization of love, then, is simply an interpretion of its mystery at the philosophical level of understanding.

This interpretation can hardly encompass the whole mystery of love, even if all the philosophical understandings of love from the Pre-Socratics to Gabriel Marcel could be integrated to converge a single beam of light into this mystery. Instead, the individual philosopher is quite content to narrow his or her gaze to a particular facet of the vast philosophic problem of love, to delineate this facet with some clarity, and to return to the mystery of love with this new insight in order to see the latter slightly better than before. In so doing, one hopes to avoid depreciating too badly the total problem of love and considering too abstractly one's particular facet. Thus this book approaches the secular transcendent through the interpersonal relations of love; attention will be limited to the problematic facet of other-centered love. Within this facet, evidence of a transcendent presence will perhaps reveal itself. Here we face a double problem. The first is the problematic object: is there such a thing as other-centered love? The second is the methodological problem: how does philosophic insight into the mystery of other-centered love reveal transcendent presence within this love? This latter problem is the object of section three of this introduction: the search for philosophic understanding of the mystery of love.

Is Other-centered Love Possible?

Let us consider at once that first part of the problem of love on which our search for the secular transcendent focuses: is other-centered love possible? Is it not true that every self is dependent on the response of the beloved and wants that response for oneself? If love is reciprocal by its very structure, how can one give oneself lovingly to another without requiring a return gift from the other? Would this not make every act of love like a lasso which is cast only to draw its defenseless prey into the lassoer's power? Can love as essentially reciprocal ever be other-centered? In other words, would not the wholesomeness of an act of love be measured by the success of its return from the beloved? Indeed, the better the lover's advance of trust the more consciously sure one would be of the beloved's significant response. Does not this very assurance of successfully induced return make other-centered love rather self-centered?

A second difficulty presents itself: how does a person ever break out of the circle of self-centered love? Children are notoriously self-centered because of their preponderant physical needs; yet the fulfillment of these needs makes possible a later psychological growth and some consequent freedom from purely physical living. Still, the tendency to self-centeredness has been set and transfers itself to the developing psychological level of the child who will ingeniously orchestrate conflict between the parents in order to get its pleasure of an ice cream cone, an increased spending allowance, or a second-hand car.

If someone should try to answer this difficulty by claiming that mature love is precisely the breakthrough from self-centered to other-centered living, the retort is: But would not this mature love be simply a more complex and subtle form of self-centeredness like that of the Epicureans who took great self-satisfaction in the aesthetic pleasure of nonmaterialistic friendships or like that of social do-gooders who pride themselves on their unselfish endeavors to aid the poor and the outcast? Does not the prevalence of self-centered adults render suspect any practice or theory of other-centered love? Indeed, the followers of Sartre are convinced that other-centered love is a living contradiction. It is a contradiction, they feel, because it is an attempt to erase the self by its own act of love; it is a living contradiction because people are drawn strongly to attempt other-centered love again and again by their absurd natural desire to play God. How, then, could other-centered love ever be possible?

The Chosen Absolute—Is it Other-centered Love?

If other-centered love is a mirage luring the human into self-contradiction, then this present approach to the secular transcendent is headed for a cliffside since it has other-centered love as its main directive thrust. We should, then clarify at once what we mean by other-centered love. Such clarification will give us a provisional working definition which can then, throughout the rest of this essay, be tested and further refined by our experiences of other-centered love.

One way to investigate other-centered love—a way which may at first seem to be a long detour—is to observe how a person discovers, develops, and sometimes changes an ultimate life goal or basic priority or greatest life value. For the latter is a chosen absolute which governs a person's every decision and, therefore, all acts of other-centered love.

For example, a young actress may be convinced that the most important thing in her life is stardom—until she falls in love with a movie director who demands that she give up her career to raise a family. For a time he becomes the center of her life. Her desire to please him determines her every decision; all other values and desires yield to his needs. After a while, continual restlessness begins to seize her, and she returns to her first desire: an acting career, which will make her a star. The night comes when she must choose between her husband and her career. Her choice to seek stardom establishes this goal as her chosen absolute by which all else is measured and made subordinate. Even her two children and finally her Baptist religion are so measured. Stardom is the inexorable demand which gives to her life continuity, central meaning, freedom to reject anything less than stardom. It even provides a community of friends and acquaintances of like tastes and ambition. This is the chosen absolute for her; for a lawyer it could be reform of the national court system, for an ambitious young executive it could be the presidency of Sears Stores, for a lonely girl it could be an ideal husband whom she pursues—at least in her dreams. Does the actress's shifting among chosen absolutes indicate self-centered love or could her love still be other-centered?

This ultimate value of one's life can go underground for a while, as in the marriage of this actress. But it will eventually surface to full consciousness no matter how deeply it hides. For it is present to form every decision.[4] As these decisions accumulate, it structures the person's personality; the chosen absolute comes to full possession of the person's life. This does not mean that the actress, for example, cannot change her absolute. She can do so, but with excruciating pain, if her chosen absolute deeply forms her personality. For she must change all her ways no matter how deeply ingrained. This may demand that she uproot herself from family, friends, long-time job, and favorite pastimes. All subordinate values shift to secondary importance in total conversion; all other values bow before the actress's ultimate value. Thus her basic ability to love may be measured by her devotion to her chosen absolute. Indeed, would the way in which she loves this absolute determine whether her love is self-centered or other-centered? Or is there another major factor to be considered?

The Absolute beyond Chosen Absolutes

At this point it appears that each person chooses a highest value or absolute to ultimately guide one's life. In fact, a husband may change his chosen absolute a number of times during his life and for this reason be called unstable. He may at first consider his own pleasure his absolute, later he may make his wife and children the absolute, still later he may find his absolute to be God, and finally he may revert back to his own pleasure.[5] Does all this shifting of absolutes mean that the chosen absolute is merely a matter of arbitrary choice and not really an absolute in any sense at all? The answer to this question is yes, if the mere restless changing of absolutes is considered the absolute, that is, if change is mistaken for freedom and therefore sought for itself as an ultimate value. The answer is maybe if pursuit of the absolute becomes the sole chosen absolute as when people claim that the pursuit of happiness is the only happiness. For it cannot be denied that, no matter whether I fight against my chosen absolute or pursue it madly or try to ignore it, I find it entering all my decisions inescapably.

At this juncture I can go in either of two directions (thus the *maybe*):

1. I can declare that the pursuit of an absolute, chosen or not-chosen, is foolish since no absolute can ever be more than my own desire projecting the impossible ahead of me as a deluding lure; or

2. I can discover that this lure is a reality distinct from myself, that it is the continuing reason why I am changing my chosen absolutes in order to reach it.

Thus the very changing of chosen absolutes can indicate an absolute beyond my chosen absolutes and it need not mean simply that all absolutes are arbitrary or that one's very nature absurdly demands pursuit of that sheer fantasy called an absolute. This absolute, underived from any chosen absolutes and yet attracting one into choice of these absolutes, would evidently be the ultimate source of all one's loves. Is this underived and unchosen absolute necessary for the giving of other-centered love? Does this mean that all other absolutes, because they are chosen, lead inevitably to self-centered love?

How would this absolute beyond any chosen absolute be experienced? Is it the experience of strength and worthwhileness which the young widow feels within the crushing sorrow of her husband's death? Her husband was racked by pain of incurable bone cancer. Their two young children were mystified and scared. The young wife found herself praying for the death of her husband lest he suffer beyond his endurance. Having expected to be torn apart by his death, instead she now finds herself at peace in the recognition that her husband's suffering is over and that during the last three weeks she and he had grown very close as they waited for his death together. Somehow, deep within her, she feels that his death is not wasted, that their suffering together has been worthwhile, that all is not ended. She can explain this to no one; it is simply her experience. She has a new tenderness for her bewildered children, for the people who come to console her, for all sufferers. Is this mysterious, perduring assurance of something worthwhile, this strong peace, actually an experience of the absolute beyond all chosen absolutes of lover, family, security, recognition, and career? Are the new strength and understanding more than the simple operation of a psychological defense 'mechanism'? And do they not seem to blend into other-centered love?

Parents, too, watching at the deathbed of a beloved child, have experienced, amid the piercing bitterness, the deep worthwhileness of their love for this child. They have even discovered themselves capable of turning this love to the other children of the family with new warmth, strength, and understanding after the death of the child. The other-centeredness of the love does not allow them an embittering self-pity. Nor did their love let them yield when the child rejected more painful operations offering some hope of recovery and when she demanded their twenty-four hour attendance to the neglect of their other children. Their child's good was more important than the child's desires or willfulness.[6] Does the mysterious strength and understanding which they experience within their love indicate that an absolute beyond all their chosen absolutes of a secure future is present to them? Is this an experience of the absolute beyond all absolutes, the secular transcendent? Would this be the source of all loves—particularly of other-centered loves—since it draws all lovers to love generously?

If there should be an absolute beyond all absolutes, is it personal? People have consistently found that any value less than person eventually humiliates them when they put it first in their lives. Don Juan's concentration on the pleasure of seducing the most beautiful and noble women of Europe eventually exhausted him; the exultant exercise of dominion over the nations of Europe filled Napoleon with a hollow restlessness; the monomanic desire to control all the match factories of Europe led Ivar Kreuger to suicide.[7] Only on another human can a person center all energies without inevitable humiliation and with some hope of final exaltation. The beloved indeed has the power to humiliate and dishearten, but does not always use this power. Often enough, the great gamble of the lover's whole self on the beloved's person is warranted. Could the absolute beyond all chosen absolutes, if it exists, be anything but personal?

But is not the centering of one's life on another person an enslaving subordination of the lover's self to the beloved? It certainly is slavery if the offering of the self is meant to buy the return of love, or if the offering is made absolutely as though the beloved were a despotic god to be pleased at any cost. For these reasons, centering one's life on the beloved should not debase the lover. For then the very attempt to love renders the lover less loveable; love becomes suicide. If other-centered love truly is love, it should increase, rather than diminish, the lover's sense of liberty and of manliness or womanliness. Even after failure, the lover should be able to say: I'd do it again this way if I had a second chance. Could it be that the absolute beyond all chosen absolutes liberates the lover from the idolatry of chosen absolutes and thus enables other-centered love?

Paradox: Healthy Self-love Is Basis for Other-centered Love

Before we attempt to define other-centered love and to search out the absolute beyond all chosen absolutes, one matter needs resolution. Previously we emphasized not only the other-centeredness between lover and beloved but also the beloved's total acceptance of the lover's total gift. We may thereby overlook the fact that, paradoxically, a healthy self-love pervades the other-centered love between lover and beloved. Indeed, if this were not true, their other-centered love would quickly deteriorate. Unless the loving wife knows that her self-gift is worthwhile and that she herself is worthy of her beloved's trust, then her gifting will lack confidence and be enfeebled. Unless the beloved husband knows that he has within him the attractive talents which make his loving wife's self-gift worth her while, his response to her self-gift will be doubting and therefore forced or uneasy or somewhat guilt-ridden. Such a response will spread the contagion of doubt to the lover-wife, in a reciprocal round of ever-weakening gift and response.

Healthy self-love, then, is basically self-respect and self-trust engendered first of all when as a child one receives unquestioning attentive love that demands little but expects the best. Later, the child's adolescent self-respect and self-trust mature through the experience of peer-trust and respect. At this point the young person is ready to offer and to receive other-centered love.

Looked at philosophically, even the most heroic other-centered action is filled with healthy self-love. For the most unselfish love expects and hopes for a return of love since other-centered love is essentially reciprocal and since the lover respects the warm generosity of the beloved. On the other hand, if the lover imperiously demands a response from the beloved and thus restricts the latter's freedom, then this self-love is truly selfish and unhealthy because the lover is more intent on receiving from the beloved than on giving.

The most heroic act of love is selfish in another sense. One's every good deed strengthens and enhances one's personality. Men and women delight in loving others because the more other-centered the act of love is, the more human and self-fulfilling it is. For, as we have seen, other-centered love can be deeply trusting and giving, liberating and expansive, filled with meaning and hope, ready to create and to sacrifice loyally. Paradoxically, the lover best loves himself or herself in totally concentrating love on the beloved. The most selfless of all persons encouraged us to love our neighbor as we love ourselves.[8]

Consequently, the more healthy the self-love in lover and beloved, that is, the more deep the self-respect and the self-trust of each, the more other-centered their love can be since the security of fuller self-trust enables each to concentrate more totally on the other in self-forgetfulness. Respect for one's self turns out to be the power to respect others. This is one more paradox hidden in the mystery of other-centered love. The presence of healthy self-love in other-centered love makes us suspect that an absolute beyond all absolutes is also present. For selfishness would seem to be more natural to man and woman in their relativity, yet their deepest joy is to love other-centeredly and absolutely. Thus healthy self-love seems to encourage the complementarity of the absolute and the relative in other-centered love. Far from turning the self into a hermetically sealed chosen absolute, the self-respect and self-confidence of healthy self-love open the lover to that support of the unchosen absolute which enables other-centered love to occur.

Other-centered Love—a Provisional Working Definition

The preceeding observations allow us to develop a working definition of other-centered love which we can later modify as additional evidence requires and which we can explore as a way to the absolute beyond all chosen absolutes. Other-centered love is love which does not debase the lover's self, yet subordinates the lover to the beloved's good, the ultimate value of the lover. Note that the lover is not subordinated to the mere desires or will of the beloved; the first could be enslavement of the lover and the second could result in evil for the beloved. Other-centered love is, then, a trustful focusing of the lover's life on the good or ultimate happiness of the beloved although the lover's very growth in manliness or womanlinesss through that love may entail the seeming self-diminishment of sacrifice. Such love may be romantic, familial, sisterly, fatherly, friendly, or communal. It may enter into any deep interpersonal relationship—as the previous examples have indicated—so long as the lover gives the self totally to the beloved without, paradoxically, diminishing the lover's self-respect, humanity and liberty.

Given this working definition, we can ask: does other-centered love actually exist in this self-serving world of ours or is it an impossibility? How this factual mystery could be possible is precisely the first part of the philosophic problem of love. Secondly, we will explore philosophically the question: if other-centered love should exist, is it ultimately meaningful? Is it the carrier of humankind's fullest nobility? Is it interiorly supported by an absolute beyond all chosen absolutes? Or is it the ultimate revelation of man's basic self-contradiction and, if taken seriously, the sign of his deepest silliness?

These problematic questions challenge us to a philosophic search for some answers to love's mystery. But what is this search and according to what principles or guidelines do we pursue it? In other words, how do we develop the problematic concepts by the light of which we can peer back into the mystery of love so that we may live it more fully and creatively?

3. Search for Philosophic Understanding of the Mystery of Love

What precisely is the intent of our present approach? To answer baldly: we undertake a philosophic search for the secular transcendent within the mystery of love. More specifically, our search will enter into other-centered love with the hope of possibly touching upon the absolute beyond all one's chosen absolutes: the unchosen absolute. Actually this search responds to the deepest drive within a person to achieve utopia, to find a real Shangri-la, to arrive at the communion of saints. Out of this drive have issued the most intimate and soaring of human colloquies: the *Symposium* of Plato, the *De Amicitia* of Cicero, the Last Supper narrative of John the Evangelist, the *De Trinitate* of Augustine, the literary tradition of the medieval troubadours, Heloise's letters to Abelard, St. Bernard's *De Diligendo Deo*, Kierkegaard's *Either/Or*, Marcel's *Creative Fidelity*.

Search within Mystery

To probe within mystery, as we must do here, is to risk a crippling discouragement—unless one plots beforehand the limits of one's search. These limits are dictated by the nature of mystery. For mystery is a reality whose inexhaustible being is never adequately conceptualized into neat maneuverable ideas no matter how long and cleverly one works. Mystery has a value and an existence which are not answerable to the searcher. It has a stubborn independence, yet it gives central meaning to the searcher's life so that without it the searcher becomes bored, later paralyzed of initiative, even moribund. Despite its autonomy, mystery tends to unite person with person in ever higher communities from family to United Nations, from study clubs to noösphere, from prayer groups to international church. Though mystery is deeply appreciable by people, its independence of their ingenuity and their brutality enables it to grow more, not less, mysterious as they explore it.[9] Among such mysteries are energy, friendship, God, hope, existence, novelty, heroism, evil, human destiny, and the unity of the universe.

Other-centered love is one such mystery. The more psychologists, philosphers, poets, and novelists attempt to express this love in neat ideas, concise aphorisms, lush metaphors, austere systems of thought, and clever personality diagrams, the more elusive it seems to become for the pincers of their ideas and techniques. Yet without it, life becomes dull, the world's meaning becomes threadbare, the value of persons is dwarfed, and hostility turns society barbaric. The mystery of other-centered love is not beyond the scope of reason; yet thought alone simply cannot control it, just as muscle alone cannot win it. Still it lures us on, century after century, to build empires as well as to cultivate friendships, to risk death as well as to seek more life. And now it entices us to find out whether or not within its riches is hidden the unchosen absolute beyond all our chosen absolutes, the secular transcendent or God.

This mystery, having provoked problems of understanding, must be investigated methodically. For the methodic development of concepts will enable us to achieve understanding for illumining and, thus, for living well the mysteries of other-centered love and of the transcendent.

Outline of Search

Our search within other-centered love for the underived or unchosen absolute will advance in four stages. First, because this mystery is so vast, we will explore it according to the three different worlds of Jean-Paul Sartre, Herbert Spencer, and moderate realism. Sartre's psychological human being, we find, enjoys such an independent freedom that he or she can give the self to the beloved only by domineering. For the same reason, he or she cannot admit to a lordly God. At the other extreme, Spencer's sociological human being, as a simple focus of environmental factors, exhibits such total dependence that he or she cannot freely give the self to the beloved. Thus a moderate realism discovers that the lover must be both independent and dependent in order to give self freely to the beloved and, in turn, to accept freely the beloved's gift of self. This the moderate lover does without domineering, or being dominated by, the beloved.

In a second stage of this search, we explore the biological, psychological, moral and metaphysical levels of the moderate lover in order to discover how a person's independence works within dependence, that is, how an absolute can operate within a person's relativity, so that other-centered love is possible.

In a third stage, we view the human experience of this mystery, and find that other-centered love manifests its independence or absoluteness in six characteristics: foreverness, perduring self-trust, sovereign demand, liberating expansiveness, healing wholesomeness, and freedom for total sacrifice. These characteristics both demand and reveal a supportive unchosen absolute beyond all chosen absolutes, that is, a secular transcendent which makes possible one's other-centered love.

Lastly, in a fourth stage of this search, we analyze the six characteristics to determine what or who the absolute beyond all absolutes is, namely, the secular transcendent supporting and revealing unconditional love.

Because our search must be methodic to be philosophic, because we must distinguish our resultant conceptions from the mystery which they illumine, and because we never exhaust this mystery of love and of the secular transcendent but always find it deepened by these concepts, we must first consider the mystery, problem and methodic search of love before beginning our approach to the unchosen absolute beyond all chosen absolutes. Otherwise, false expectations would cloud our vision or distract our minds from the great reality of the mystery.

Appendix to the Introduction

(For Those Seeking More Detail Concerning the Method to Be Used in This Approach)

Embrace of Method and Object

The type of search depends on two factors: the object of the search and the searcher. The two should modify each other. For example, one reaches out differently for a hot coal and for a cool mushroom; the counsellor proceeds in two different ways with the nightclub dancer and with the lady-senator from Nebraska. Clearly, the object of the search determines partially the method of the searching. But it is equally true that the object discovered is, in turn, modified by the method used to find it. The wrong pair of tongs can turn the hot coal into gritty dust and the cool mushroom into mangled pulp. The counsellor's technique of quiet gentleness can enable the nightclub dancer's inner drive for integrity to break throught the hard shell of fears and facade. The same counsellor's humorous shock-technique may help the lady-senator's relaxed spontaneity to surface through her crisp, almost mechanical professionalism.

In this philosophic search for the unchosen absolute or secular transcendent, how do we let the object determine our method of search and how can we expect our method to delimit its object? Certainly the defining of expectations determines the method of search and yet we must fit these expectations to the object we seek. The object of our search here is precisely a person's experience of other-centered love at the heart of human mystery. A descriptive phenomenology helps us to establish the facts of this experience within mystery. For this phenomenology does not attempt to set up a heavy structure of conceptual explanation which would cramp the existence of mystery and thus give the searcher a warped awareness of the facts. Rather, its delicate openness restrains it from substituting its static concepts for the living mystery.

But before the phenomenologist can describe the phenomena with care and fidelity, he or she must become conscious of the alternative presuppositions to one's discovered facts and to one's method. For such awareness alerts one to one's implicit expectations which define and, hence, control one's methodic results. For

27

this reason, an early procedure will be the description and analysis of the various types of world in which other-centered love could or could not exist. For example, can this love survive in a Sartrean world of absolute interior freedom or in a Spencerian world of unfree total relativity? Must it live in a world lying between these two extremes? The contrast of these diverse 'worlds' uncovers presuppositions and offers new views of old facts. In this way, it alerts the phenomenologist to implicit presuppositions underlying his or her method of exploring the experience of other-centered love.

When phenomenologists realize the implicit expectations behind their questioning of experience, they and perhaps those who follow their steps become more alert to the riches within their experience of other-centered love. This deepens the sense of mystery. For questions always lead to more questions and thence to more insights into the mystery. This process slowly convinces us that there will always be more to know the longer we ask questions. The opposite of this is to feel that one's conceptualization of the mystery has made the mystery totally explicable, routine, exhausted of intelligibility. Such depreciation of the unlimited riches of a mystery is a mark of trivialization. Thus the phenomenological moment in our searching should make us more aware of love's mystery, not less aware; more sure of never exhausting its riches. Yet at the same time, it may well establish the fact of other-centered love and the factual presence of an absolute beyond all absolutes within the experience of this love. Further, it will yield the data out of which demonstrative analysis can fashion more precise concepts capable of further illumining the mystery of love.

Thus the philosopher can employ demonstrative analysis to establish the conditions which make these data possible. Demonstrative analysis is an attempt to get behind the phenomenological facts to their causes. By eliminating alternative causal explanations of these facts, the analysis illumines their meaning so that the philospher can back into the lone causal explanation remaining. This gives no X-ray knowledge of other-centered love or the unchosen absolute. Rather, it yields a very humble type of limit knowledge which enables one to focus upon the reality without grasping it directly. Thus, like a road map, demonstrative analysis brings us to our destination which is so much more than the map.

In this way, demonstrative analysis is adapted to mystery since it claims no exhaustive knowledge of the mystery but merely an indication of its existence and of its basic contours. Further, this limit type of knowledge makes demonstrative analysis properly sensitive to the fact that its concepts are not the mystery but simply tools for focusing one's understanding upon the mystery.

Our Approach Put Briefly

This adjusting of method and object to each other within the mystery of other-centered love can be illustrated by the following outline of our approach to the unchosen absolute or secular transcendent. Let us first put the approach in one sentence: within one's experience of other-centered love is discovered a mysterious independence characterized as continuous self-trust, foreverness, sovereign demand, creative unifying, expansiveness of world-meaning, freedom for total sacrifice—qualities demanding and revealing the personal immanent presence of a supporting unchosen absolute (Existence Itself) within the human act of other-centered love.

Let us expand this description of the present approach (our philosophic search) into four stages so that we can examine the method and its object more easily. Then we will also get a bird's-eye view of the whole terrain of this book. According to a demonstrative analysis employing a logic of exclusion and working with the facts garnered by descriptive phenomenology:

1. From a comparison of world views, it becomes clear that a person cannot love with other-centeredness, if he or she is totally absolute (Jean-Paul Sartre) or totally relative (Herbert Spencer) in freedom. Either one's absolute interior freedom would demand that one dominate the beloved or one's total relativity would prevent one's free gift of oneself to the beloved—any self-gift would be voluntary slavery. Thus these two world views deny the very possibility of other-centered love. Yet their dual attempts to account for the human experience of love point up the fact that this other-centered love must be both absolute and relative.

2. Through descriptive phenomenology, we discover that humankind is factually capable of other-centered love insofar as people live well the tension between the absolute (the

independent) and the relative (the dependent) which operate biologically, psychologically, morally and metaphysically in their being and loving. Demonstrative analysis shows that such tension is possible only if an immanent yet distinct absolute beyond all chosen absolutes supports one's existence as lover. For the denial of such an absolute inevitably drives us back to either a Sartrean or a Spencerian world, both of which are impossible because both, of their very nature, yet for opposed reasons, falsely imply that other-centered love is impossible to humankind.

3. Phenomenologically, this unchosen absolute is found within a person's act of other-centered love insofar as this love includes a continuously developing self-trust, a foreverness, a sovereign demand, a creative unity, an expansiveness of central world meaning, and a freedom for total sacrifice (that is, total liberation).

Demonstrative analysis then shows that these factual qualities enable a person to act absolutely even though his or her existence is not absolute, and therefore that the source of the absolute qualities is an absolute immanent to the human being—an absolute beyond, yet within, all chosen absolutes. This is the unchosen absolute, the secular transcendent or God.

4. In turn, these qualities reveal that this unchosen absolute is a personal and compassionate former of community, the initiator of all loves, the center of all personal communication, the guarantor of the 'forever', the expander of liberty, the ultimate total object of human love, and basically Existence Itself (because this absolute is total giver forever in creative fidelity). This unchosen absolute is actually the sole unqualified absolute of the whole universe, the transcendent being secularly initiating and supporting all human loves.

With these four steps we enter into the mystery of other-centered love to discover the secular transcendent whose mystery is not dispelled but rather is enhanced by the philosophic problematic approach and whose mystery makes other-centered love more alluring than ever. Again, these four steps can develop problematic concepts to send accurate light into these two related mysteries. In this way, the never-ending philosophic search within other-centered love and within the secular transcendent can be a constant fulfilling of the human person's deepest hungers.

FIRST STEP

HUMANKIND AS
ABSOLUTELY FREE
AND TOTALLY RELATIVE

A s we have seen, other-centered love is impossible to understand even partially, unless one first studies the various absolutes which could make such love first possible and then actual
by luring it into operation, that is, into being. But crucial to any
approach to these absolutes are their provisional working definitions offered at the outset. It is so easy to define *absolute* in such a
way that it refers only to the transcendent and becomes an abstrac-
tion unusable for sounding experience or for challenging interpretations other than the definer's. To avoid this trap, it would
help to survey various meanings for *absolute* along the spectrum
of philosophic opinion.

With a broadly serviceable definition of absolute, one can proceed to provisionally evaluate the meanings of *absolute* in the
various philosophers' different interpretations of the universe, of
the human, and of love. In the second part of this first step, consideration of the doctrines of Jean-Paul Sartre and Herbert
Spencer, who are at opposite ends of the spectrum of interpretations, offers a convenient means of centering in upon a more
moderate meaning of the human and absolute. It would help,
then, first to discover a provisional definition for *absolute* so that
we can later deal with Sartre's and Spencer's meanings for absolute, the human, and love. We do this by exploring three different worlds, namely, those of the godless universe, the godless
human, and the transcendent being within and beyond both man
and universe.

A. PROVISIONAL DEFINITIONS OF ABSOLUTES

The Godless Universe

If the universe is self-perpetuating and if the human is only one subordinate part of this world, then the universe as a whole itself is the ultimate value; it is the norm by which all of its parts are compared and evaluated. In the philosophy of Baruch Spinoza, the great proponent of pantheism, the single and sole substance that is all of reality gives meaning and value to all its modes of being; the human being and its reactions to this world compose merely one of these modes. Directly opposed to the single-substance world of Spinoza is Herbert Spencer's world of converging and diverging atoms dominated by the relativistic principles of evolution and dissolution.[10]

In Spencer's universe, human purpose has no effect on world development because human actions are merely the result of atomic physical forces beyond a person's power to resist or to mold. All activity is physical motion following the lines of least resistance. Consequently, the ultimate value or absolute for Spencer is the evolution of the universe. Hence one's value consists in one's ability to contribute to this evolution solely by physical presence and activity. Though Spencer speaks of the Unknowable or God as the only absolute, such a reference to God indicates the irrelevancy of this absolute to the fact of the evolving universe.

Thus Spinoza and Spencer effectively give us an absolute universe and a human being which is a derivative part of this universe. If the reader should define God as a being distinct from the universe yet immanent within it, then the absolute universe of Spinoza is theoretically godless, and that of Spencer is practically godless. Their universes run without any influence from a secular transcendent.

Godless Human

Other thinkers completely invert this system of values. They make the world derivative from the human for they find that humankind remakes the world to its own image. For Freud, psychological person tries to build the world to the image of his or her own inner life. Marx's economic human remolds the whole world according to the dynamics of a collectivist economy. Nietzsche's superman, in coming to dominate the world, fashions the self out of its self-created morality. Out of one's constructed society, Dewey's person intelligently structures himself or herself and hence restructures society. For Sartre, existential man or woman is responsible for all the events of the world because the self is totally free in its interior decisions to fashion the world to its own uses according to its freely chosen values. Amid these five diverse approaches, one theme is constant: humankind makes the world subservient to itself and thus establishes itself as its supreme value since humankind owes nothing to any superior being. Human society is truly the measure of all things. Even though this society is growing and varying, it remains the absolute since its inherent betterment is the continuous value to which all other values cede and from which they derive their meaning and impact.

The Transcendent

Some feel that they have discovered within human experience a distinct presence which permeates the whole universe and yet goes far beyond the latter. This presence, divine in its immensity and majesty, is somehow independent of humankind and of the world even though dedicatedly working within them. In the judgment of Augustine or of Aquinas: this presence has brought the world into existence out of nothing and fashioned humankind out of the world to direct the latter's development. Humans are asked to finish the work begun by God. Whitehead would add to this that humans also fashion God insofar as God cooperates with them and is modified by this cooperation. Kant strongly suspects that God communicates to people a divine dedication to the world's process and a divine respect for the autonomous person—despite the fact that God hides behind the world's phenomena. Still, all four philosophers find the world and human beings to be derivative from God in a continuing dependence. Thus, for them, God is the supreme, perduring value that antedates the universe, provides for the latter's growth, and offers himself as humankind's final destiny.

Definition of the Absolute

What characteristics of the absolute can we gather from this brief survey so that we can draw a generic picture true of all three worlds? Such a generic definition should enable us to begin our search for the absolute in other-centered love. It would seem that an absolute must be an ultimate value against which all other values are measured and to which they all cede at any point of conflict. In this way the absolute assures continuity, stability, and unity to the life of the one making the evaluation; it is the center of meaning and of action for him or her. If this absolute is relevant, it cannot escape being active deep within the world. Furthermore by its immanence, it naturally unifies society. Yet it is not under the control of the individual person even if evolving mankind be the absolute within a godless world. For chance happenings are always at hand to derail the individual's planned destiny for herself or himself; evil is never absent, never insignificant, always seemingly about to overwhelm one and one's world.

An absolute, then, is that immanent supreme value which gives continuity to all life, community to all humans, central meaning to every intelligence, and hope to each action. It would seem that one cannot live without some absolute even if one has to invent it. This would seem to be the clear conclusion of Viktor Frankl's experience of logotherapy.

At this point it may be well to sketch quickly how the absolute beyond all chosen absolutes may well differ from the chosen absolutes. For although both of these types of absolute fulfill the provisional definition of absolute, nevertheless they fulfill the definition diversely. In other words, although both types of absolute operate in a person's experience, they reveal themselves with different characteristics. A chosen absolute, such as career, family, friendship, or business, is freely selected and inventively fashioned by the human person; just as freely, one can discard it for another chosen absolute.

But the absolute beyond all chosen absolutes cannot be chosen in this way: it is simply there to be recognized or ignored within all chosen absolutes. Even when ignored, it is not discarded, but remains there, and reappears in each chosen absolute. Nor can one fashion it according to one's needs and whims; it resists all such attempts to redo it. for example, if 'happiness' should be the un-chosen absolute—*unchosen* here means that people constantly seek it, no matter how they deny the pursuit of it—it will be within and yet beyond every chosen absolute of the person seeking happiness. Indeed, it will refuse to be defined simply by any or all chosen absolutes but will set its own conditions in such a mysterious way that no seeker can define happiness totally, or own it securely, or be unamazed by its multiplying facets or natural characteristics. It is always in, and yet beyond, us and our chosen absolutes—far beyond.

Consequently, one must carefully distinguish a chosen from an unchosen absolute. Failure to do so makes other-centered love most difficult to understand—especially since one's chosen absolute may be the 'self' as in Ayn Rand's philosophy of hyper-individualism. If the self is mistaken for the unchosen absolute, then self-centered love becomes the only and highest love possible to the individual.

We have concentrated on defining the unchosen and chosen absolutes because they are the values which attract us into the act of love; they ultimately define the core of that act as self-centered or other-centered. Further, they are the source of love's poverty or richness. To discover them is to know what one's basic love is, how it may grow or deteriorate, and what it contributes to humanity and the universe.

But now our attention must shift in order to find out who or what we as human beings are since we want to discover whether or not we are capable of other-centered love. Just as we discovered a common provisional meaning or definition for the absolute by comparing and contrasting three diverse 'worlds', so, by a like procedure, we now take up three diverse understandings of who the human is and, by contrasting them, come to a common work-ing definition of humankind. These three understandings are the human as totally free and independent, the human as totally un-free and dependent, and the human as partially free-independent and partially determined-dependent. By working with human nature defined by a common provisional understanding which em-bodies Sartrean, Spencerian, and moderate humanist principles, we can discover whether and how other-centered love is possible or impossible. But if the possibility and the fact of other-centered love should be established and explained, then one could move on to investigate the very act of other-centered love for its characteristics. These characteristics, in turn, could reveal the presence of an unchosen absolute operative at the core of other-centered love. This would be the secular transcendent, the unchosen absolute in and yet beyond the world, God himself. Let us therefore move towards a common provisional definition of who the human being is in order to discover whether other-centered love is even possible for the human being.

B. Two Extreme Definitions of the Human

In a godless universe the human is definable solely in terms of self and environment. At one extreme of the full spectrum of godless philosophies, the human dominates the environment. Thus the human defines his or her self as an absolute interior freedom which, in using the environment for self, is limited only exteriorly by the array of environmental options. At the other extreme of this spectrum, the environment totally dominates the human and defines the person as simply the sum of its converging influences in him or her. Jean-Paul Sartre in *Being and Nothingness* takes the first position of absolute interior freedom; while Herbert Spencer in *Synthetic Evolution* takes the second position of total relativity. Joining Sartre on the side of the absolutely free person would be such strange allies as Ayn Rand, Rousseau and Nietzsche.[11] Linked with Herbert Spencer on the side of the totally relativized person would be the Leninist-Marxists and also the Behaviorists such as B. F. Skinner and William McDougall. In the first group, the human is absolutized and divinized in his or her freedom. In the second group, world process becomes divine and the human is subordinated to it in a rigid determinism. In both groups, the universe is held to be totally self-explanatory in terms of its own dynamism so that God, even if he should exist, would be irrelevant to the developing life of the universe.

The Human Being as Absolute Interior Freedom: The Psychological Person

Let us first explore the psychological person of Sartre, the human of absolute interior freedom who owes nothing of his or her inner self to anybody.[12] It is to Sartre's credit that, with piercing honesty, he has shown that the absolutely free person must so dominate others that he or she cannot love them, and they cannot love him or her.[13] Further, in Sartre's eyes the absolutely free person cannot accept the existence of God since a freely provident God could only interfere with the person's absolute freedom by attempting to turn the human into a puppet. Therefore, there is no need for God, no role for him to play in humankind's universe.

B. Two Extreme Definitions of the Human

Study of the inner workings of the psychological human's absolute freedom paradoxically reveals how inevitable is enslavement in a Sartrean godless universe. First, the Sartrean person must have total inner control of his or her own existence out of which the person's decisions flow.[14] This, of course, does not mean that, like Descartes's capriciously omnipotent God, he or she is exteriorly free of all other people and things. It does indicate, however, that the individual human being alone initiates the use of these extrinsic people and things, and that they clearly limit what his or her inner control can accomplish exteriorly through them.[15] But they are only negative exterior limiting conditions which have no positive intrinsic effect on the individual's interior freedom itself. Thus the inner control responds only to the absolutely free existence of the individual person. It is impossible for another person or thing to influence directly and positively this inner control without the permission of the individual.[16] Otherwise the absolute interior freedom of the Sartrean man would be compromised.

Now if the Sartrean person's inner control is totally self-contained so that it receives nothing outside itself, then this inner control must precontain all human adaptive operations on the psychological level—something that Sartre would be loath to admit through it is a hidden presupposition of his thought.[17] Consequently, the Sartrean lover has no hope of ever changing or enriching, by means of his or her love, the inner life and existence of the beloved; and vice versa. The reciprocal gifting of self, so essential to love, cannot occur. But then the omnipotence of inner control, though limited within the individual person's range of environmental opportunites, nevertheless becomes the omnipotence of manipulation. For if love's basic dynamic is to develop the intrinsic goodness within the lover and the beloved, and if such intrinsic gifting to the lover and to the beloved is impossible, then the sole remaining alternative is to deal with the lover or the beloved extrinsically. But this is to manipulate the other person through strategic maneuvering. Lovemaking then becomes political, technological, instrumental; and the lover becomes an imperial ego. These are not the only implications of the Sartrean person's absolute interior freedom—implications which Sartre himself would want to deplore theoretically and which he would abhor in his own personal life.[18]

In addition, sin and error are impossible within the Sartrean universe. For absolute interior freedom implies that the Sartrean person's decisions are somehow precontained in his or her being. They cannot be influenced by a non-existent God, nor by other existent humans, lest the absoluteness of the Sartrean person's interior freedom be lost; nor by the environment which can only extrinsically limit the human decision through the range of situational resources offered to absolute interior freedom for manipulation. In some way, the interior thrust of the Sartrean person's every decision, past-present-future, must always be within him or her from the first embryonic moment and be triggered into activity as the environmental conditions allow. The spontaneity and surprise of love may well be swallowed up in one's interior omnipotence. Sin and error, the negative signs of creative inventiveness, have no place in the Sartrean universe, if the Sartrean person owes nothing of his or her interior freedom to the environment except extrinsic limitation. Thus, too, there are no occasions for forgiveness and amends wherein one learns the depths of love in the other and finds one's own love enkindled. What is left is the polite slavery of political manipulation by which one learns to win friends and influence people. Though Sartre and his very life history would deny these implications of his systematic thought, nevertheless they lie hidden like land-mines just under the surface of his thought.

For these reasons, Sartre's universe is not just godless, it is also loveless. As a consequence, Sartre's psychological person is truly ungodly. It is no wonder, then, that Sartrean existentialism is hypnotized by love and by its rejection of God—so hypnotized that it denies even the possibility of other-centered love. Such a denial makes eminent sense—if our universe is Sartrean—since any subordination of the self to the beloved is loss of one's interior freedom, one's identity, one's humanity. But then is the human person to be defined as an interior absolute freedom who cannot give other-centered love? Is this what we have experienced in our lives, namely that subordinating the self to the good of the beloved leads inevitably to enslavement? Or has our occasional experience been that such subordination actually gives liberty and a sense of humaneness beyond the ordinary?

The Human Being as Total Relativity: The Sociological Person

Just as Sartre's *Being and Nothingness* offers with stark honesty terrible insight into the implicit dynamism driving the absolutely free person; so, too, Herbert Spencer's *Synthetic Evolution* provides a less honest disclosure of the horrors hidden in the totally relativized person.[19] First of all, the Spencerian person is necessarily godless insofar as he or she is simply the focal point of constantly changing environmental influences. For if one's immediate environment totally constitutes the self and keeps it in being solely by reciprocal causality, then there is no need for God's action within oneself. In fact, there is no place for God in this universe. Even if God were to live alongside the universe, he would be for the Spencerian person unknowable (as Spencer admits) and quite irrelevant (as Spencer refuses to admit).[20] God could not enter into this person's experience; nor would this person have any reason to allow God to influence his or her behavior.[21]

This totally relativized human being is not merely godless but also unfree. For the Spencerian person has no inner counteractivity of his or her own by which to resist the environment, or better, by which he or she could reorchestrate the environmental influences to his or her own purposes.[22] Rather, the totally relativized person's very response to the environment is simply a reaction to a previous environmental influence—something like a tennis ball ricocheting from one wall to another, though the person's ricocheting is more complex.[23] In this pure behaviorism, freedom is an illusion, an expensive illusion that the Spencerian person cannot afford if he or she is to concentrate energies on rational survival amid the overwhelming complexities of modern civilization.[24]

Of its very nature, then, the totally relativized person is incapable of interpersonal relations. With every action impelled by outside forces and with no freedom to resist these forces, the Spencerian person cannot love freely, cannot think inventively, cannot feel spontaneously. Hence there are two reasons why the totally relativized person would be incapable of freely giving self in love. First, the environment would dictate that so-called gift and thus render it a necessary reaction like the involuntary knee jerk or eye blink. Secondly, the Spencerian person has no self to give, no perduring identity to offer to the beloved, insofar as the self is only the constantly changing sum of the environmental realities whose convergent influence constitutes it. Indeed, without perduring identity, the totally relativized person lacks that self-awareness or self-possession which enables one to reflectively give the self to the beloved.

Further, the Spencerian person is incapable of that inventive thought and initiative which reorchestrate the environment with a radical novelty never previously present in the universe. If a person is merely the focus of environmental forces, there is no way for him or her to surpass the environment with an original gift. In fact, the distinction between the self and the environment is not real; the person *is* the environment if the self cannot in any way dominate it. Of course, the routinizing of the totally relativized person makes any spontaneity of feeling quite impossible. This person is truly the mechanical man whose complexity, like some mammoth computer, serves to hide basic unoriginality, radical rigidity.[25] Under the superficial changes of flickering lights and electronic humming, there is the dreadful routinized circuitry running its inevitable patterns.

Spencer's sociological person is not merely godless; he or she is also programmed for a loveless and basically mindless existence. In such a universe, other-centered love is not only impossible because there is no freely responsive center in the human, but even unthinkable because the sociological person cannot sacrifice a self of which he or she is unaware. Again, we ask ourselves: Is this the self I experience from day to day—a person incapable of subordinating self to the good of the beloved, incapable of giving self with a sense of freedom and human expansion? Is this the universe I experience—one which so totally possesses me that I am simply its puppet dancing on strings of forces?

It now becomes clear why the theoretical proposal of a godless universe theoretically turns human love into a total dependency incapable of heroism. If the supposedly godless universe were the real universe and not just a theoretical construct, community would be impossible for us. Frustrated lovers would enter into Sartre's hell of manipulated groping and grouping or into Nietzsche's land of promethean despair or into Thrasymachus's cynical republic of brute force. In theoretically denying the existence of the divine absolute, these philosophers theoretically take the divine out of love-making and condemn the human to being less than human, though their intention was the direct opposite of this. Fortunately, the godless worlds of these philosophers are projected worlds, not necessarily the world of our experience, though the dark shadows of their purely theoretical worlds do bring out by contrast many positive aspects of our everyday world.

C. A Moderate Definition of the Human Being

Absolute and Relative

For diametrically opposed reasons, the Sartrean and Spencerian definitions of person present a human being which of its very nature is incapable of interpersonal relations that are free and non-manipulative. The totally absolute interior of the Sartrean person and the totally relativized interior of the Spencerian person are both incapable of other-centered love. In direct contradiction of the experience of not a few women and men, the two philosophers must deny the very possibility of other-centered love. Yet Sartre has touched upon a real factor in the human being's makeup: the deep independence of its interior freedom. And Spencer has put his finger on the reality of the human being's profound dependence upon its environment.

The human person is remarkably independent. For instance, he or she does rearrange the environment to build a mighty technological civilization, does feel free to reject another's love and to resist threatened enslavement from the community; does, against fearsome odds, inventively create and build meaningful worlds of love in the present and for the future; does at times even reject and exile God from these worlds.

The human person is also remarkably dependent. No offspring is as bereft of protective instincts and as dependent on its parents for such a long period as is the human infant. No world is so complex that it demands twelve to twenty years' education—except the human world of high technology and science. In fact, it can be said that atomic weaponry, twentieth-century economics of employment and of goods-exchange, worldwide pollution of the air-water cycle, and propagandized communication are rapidly deepening the human person's dependence.

Indeed, it would seem that the very tension between these two factors of independence and dependence best defines the human person and at the same time offers a solid basis for other-centered love.[26] In seizing one of these polarities and forgetting the other, Sartre and Spencer have made us aware of both polarities and of the creative tension between them. We recognize the penalty of denying one in order to emphasize the other. Do we accept the reward of simultaneously affirming both? Let us consider some reasons for taking this last alternative.

First, if person is basically characterized according to dependent independence and independent dependence, there are only three possible definitions of the human being if the principle of contradiction is to be trusted. For the human is either totally independent and free within its interior being (according to Sartre) or not thus totally independent and free. If the human is not totally independent and free within its interior then this is because it is either totally relative and determined in its interior being by the environment (according to Herbert Spencer) or not thus totally relative and determined (according to moderate realism). Another way to state this last of the three sole alternatives is that the human is only partially relative (and therefore partially absolute or independent) and only partially determined by the environment (and therefore partially free). This third alternative for defining the human being is the middle ground between the extremes of Sartre and Spencer. It is characteristic of Whitehead, Aquinas, Bergson, or Kant, all of whom define the human as a living and growing tension between the absolute and the relative: the human being envisaged by a moderate realism.

Thus, if one wants to preserve the mystery of human love, one must affirm human independence against Spencer's totally relativistic and rationalistic definition of the human person as merely the resultant of the parallelogram of environmental forces which dictate his existence. Or if one wants to preserve the problem of love, one must affirm human interior dependence against Sartre's definition of the absolutely free and independent person. For this latter definition declares the problem of love to be simply a favorite human delusion inasmuch as the human being is constitutionally incapable of other-centered love.

Further, if one finds that the loveless loneliness of Sartre's totally independent person is simply unreal, if one feels deeply that Spencer's totally relative person is smothered by a loveless environment, and if one recognizes clearly that both these types of person can only destroy community and never build it, then one will experience more explicitly the everyday reality of the actual human being, the person who is both dependent and independent in a tension that demands constant integration and growth.

Human independence is precisely a person's liberty and his or her strength for exercising that liberty. Yet this moderate person is deeply dependent because of the essential reciprocity of love and of other environmental influences.

Thus the human's simultaneous dependence and independence makes him or her capable of other-centered love. For the independence of strong liberty enables the person, freely and without self-depreciation, to subordinate the self to the good of the beloved; while this person's reciprocal dependence on the strengthening responsive love and trust from the beloved helps this lover to desire the good of the beloved beyond all else. In this way some men and women have *de facto* given up their lives for the beloved in magnificent independence from the world and from their own powerful instinctual fears of death—and they did this gladly. These historical facts make suspect any definition of the human person which denies their possibility.

The Human Being as Tension between Absolute and Relative

But what is this tension which defines the human being? In the first place, it is the human ability to possess the environment without being possessed by it. Though the moderate person's sensitivity, intelligence, and love enable this person to receive into the self and to cherish much more environmental influence than any other being, these same powers also are the person's ability to freely and inventively reorchestrate these influences to her or his own development. Even though moderate person is heavily conditioned by an interiorly stored past history of experiences, he or she can also reorganize these for a higher integration of new growth. This person can take on a new life-style or a second career at forty-two years of age. Within the moderate person is the mysterious power to stand up against the whole exterior world and even against his or her own whole interior world of personality and to reintegrate both worlds simultaneously. The moderate person has the power to convert the self from within. A secular saint is not simply born that way but is fashioned gradually out of a costly series of heroic decisions.

The strangest anomaly is that this independence is achieved in and through human dependence. For example, in the reciprocity of

50

C. A Moderate Definition of the Human Being

a perduring love, the loving older brother depends greatly on the beloved younger sister's trust in him. For this trust empowers the lover; his desire to be worthy of such trust makes him willing (with supreme independence) to lose the whole world in death rather than to betray his sister's trust. Family life gives another example of a person achieving independence through dependence. By marrying and having children, a woman expresses her dependence on other people; in fact, her dependence grows insofar as her love for husband and children absorbs more and more of her time and energy in the endless routines of daily family life. Yet out of all these dependencies can rise a full womanhood, a deep independent serenity of assured love from others and of confidence in her own competence to handle most family tragedies and successes with intelligence and a warm heart. For her family she is willing to rip up roots by moving to another city where her husband's new job is; willing to tell a favorite son to go live somewhere else because he deeply troubles the family; willing to start a second career after the family is raised in order not to burden the children; willing to suffer even divorce if her husband's behavior seriously hurts the family. Yet all the while, insofar as she asserts this independence, this mother grows more deeply aware of her familial dependence both through the strength it gives to her independence and through the simultaneously exhausting demands it continually makes upon her physical and psychological energy.

Thus the very struggle between independence and dependence reveals their seemingly contradictory cooperation within the human person and dramatizes the process of integrated human growth. Within each decision which shapes the human personality, the principles of dependence and independence both impel the moderate person to define the self by integrating them wholesomely. Thus the moderate person, in his or her dependence, continually receives from the environment food and pain, ideas and errors, trust and betrayal. Out of these this person forms reactive decisions wherein, by means of independence, he or she tries to reorganize his or her own interior life by reforming the exterior situation towards greater good (or, at times, towards greater evil). This assertion of the self in the situation is an expression of independence through dependence; a person cannot live without a situation nor without rearranging it. The more uniquely—the more inventively and heroically—the moderate person acts in the situation on which he or she depends, the more independence is recognizable to self and to others. Ironically, the more the moderate person experiences this dependence, the more aware he or she becomes that this independence is either potential, if one suffers from cowardice and ennui, or actual, if one faithfully struggles for integrity of body, mind, and heart.

The moderate person's independence, far from removing dependence, deepens it. The more loves a person has, the more he or she is vulnerable. Yet it is just as true that the larger the network of loves a person enjoys, the stronger can be his or her independent confidence in self and community. From another angle, the deeper a decision is meant to penetrate a situation and to refashion it, the more one needs physical stamina, accurate information from others, and strong backing from them. Still the depth of the decision is a mark of the daring independence of the decision-maker. Thus the human being is truly a living paradox.

Human Being as Tension between Absolute and Relative— Possible?

Is this independence, which is found compenetrating the moderate person's dependence, the absolute in him or her? And is the dependence what we mean by the relative? Are they both interior to the moderate person? How is this possible? Let us respond to these questions in the order asked.

Human independence displays itself at four distinct levels in a person: the biological, the psychological, the moral, and the metaphysical. At the biological level, one's health is the continuous ability of one's organism to survive and to grow in the midst of constant environmental challenge. Without the independence of health, the other levels of a person's life struggle against heavy odds for a sometimes meager independence. At the psychological level, one's independence is in proportion to the clarity of one's chosen absolute or life-aim. The aimless person may exercise independence fitfully, violently, and shortly like a spoiled child. But perduring, patient, adult independence is always energized by a single dominating life-aim whose growing clarity increases the stability, ingenuity, and stamina of a person.

C. A Moderate Definition of the Human Being

At the moral level, an unrelenting willingness to suffer for this incarnate ideal of the chosen absolute or life-aim—even to death—is the final basis for a person's independence. Because this life-aim is ultimate with no other value rivalling it, no exceptions are made (except under extreme stress and perhaps not even then) to the driving ambition for the chosen absolute or life-aim. This is why it is called an absolute. At the metaphysical level, the very uniqueness and unity of the developing personality indicates continuity and stability in the individual's life. For this unique unity cannot occur unless the person continually surmounts the situation at the physical, psychological, and moral levels to establish freely and inventively one's individuality. On the other hand, the totally routinized person has been machined by the situation into unfree uniformity and the fragmented distraught personality has lost its unity in mulitple, mutually distracting endeavors. This is not to say that the uniquely unified person has despotic control over the self and the situation. One is continually surprised by error and sin both in oneself and in others; one integrates oneself and the situation only through the process of trial and error. But the difference is that one learns from error and sin and uses this experience to build more inventively and freely both the situation and the self.

Such independence surely has many characteristics of the absolute as provisionally defined earlier. The central life-aim or chosen absolute for which the independent person is willing to suffer even to death acts as a center of meaning and a spring for action in his or her decisions. Its vigorous pursuit, based on good health, gives immanent stability and continuity so that the person can cooperate with and direct others in the building of community. Such independence operates although the person is unaware of despotic control over self and others—especially when the community achieves puzzling complexity. It seems, therefore, that a person's independence is an absolute in action since it involves all four levels of one's being in the unified and unifying activity of decisions. Furthermore, the deeper these decisions flow and the more widely they embrace, the greater suffering they demand for the good of a particular person or community. For this reason, love calls upon all four levels of the human being, and includes the chosen absolute as the central thrust of its dynamism—indeed as the basis for its continuous independence. Thus attaining Broadway stardom, the perfectly muscled body, full family life, the presidency of the United States, inner serenity of prayer, or any other ultimate goal or value could be the personally chosen absolute upon which a person builds independence.

If the moderate person's independence is seen as flowing out of the chosen absolute, then what is the relative in this person? It is everything which operates under the dominance of the chosen absolute and which contributes to the latter's maintenance and growth. It is one's eating and exercise, one's information and ideas, one's hopes and ideals, the emotional support received from others, one's potential not yet achieved but achievable through a cooperating community. The relative, then, is whatever is subordinated as means to the end of the chosen absolute (one's concrete independence).

Consequently, the relative is constantly shifting in meaning, use, and importance according to the direction of the chosen absolute. Thus the relative derives part of its meaning, use, and importance from the chosen absolute and the other part from its own structure or being. The relative is, therefore, the dependent in a person's makeup. As means to the chosen absolute or life aim, the relative enables the absolute to exist in the moderate person and to become incarnate in the self and in the situation. For this reason, through his or her dependence the moderate person becomes aware of, develops, and achieves independence. Both are dynamically immanent to the person. Factually, then, the human being is a dynamic tension between the absolute and the relative immanent to the self.

But how is this fact possible? How can the person be both independent and dependent, absolute and relative? This is the question which Sartre solved by stressing the absolute to the loss of the relative and which Spencer answered by asserting the relative to the disappearance of the absolute. This is the question which led Descartes into the dualism of unintegrable body and soul and which shocks B. F. Skinner into calling human freedom a too expensive delusion. Is this fact of the human being's dependent independence meant to drive us to the despairing declaration that the human being is, of its very nature, absurd or self-contradictory? Does this fact simultaneously offer the basis for other-

C. A Moderate Definition of the Human Being

centered love and then shroud this basis in a cloud of contradicting confusion? Does any further explanation of this dynamic tension between the absolute and the relative within a person inevitably fall into the conflicting dualism of Descartes and the vitalists or into the despairing monism of Sartrean absolutism and of Spencerian relativism? The second step of this approach is taken in the hope that an alternative explanation is viable.

SECOND STEP

Person as Both Absolute and Relative in Being and Loving

independence and the relative (the degrees of which constitute the biologically, psychologically, morally and physically divide their being and loving. Persons crave a totality that ... but such tension is possible only if an interior ... situates all points beyond all chosen absolutes suppose ... ... as I ... yet, for the denial of such an absolute ... many drives us back to either a partition or a Spencer ... ... which are impossible because both of ... for opposed reasons, falsely imply ... of ... humankind.

Phenomenologically, this unchosen absolute is ... ... a person's act of other-centered love that ... ... cludes a continuously developing self-tran ... ... sovereign demand, a creative unity, a resp ... ... tral world meaning, and a freedom for ... total liberation).

Demonstrative analysis then shows that ... ... ties enable a person to act absolutely even though his or her existence is not absolute, and therefore, that this ... ... absolute qualities in an absolute monument to the human being an absolute beyond, yet within, all chosen absolutes ... The unchosen absolute, the secular transcendent ... and

In turn, these qualities reveal that this unchosen absolute is a personal and compassionate former of communit ... ... initiator of all loves, the center of all persons ... ... guarantee of the ... the demand ... ... toward total ... a ... human love, the basis of ... ... of ... ...

How is it possible for a person to be both absolute and relative, both independent and dependent, in his or her very being? The response to this question will occupy us throughout this second step. To do it justice, one must look at the human person again, but now in more detail according to the four levels of his or her being: the biological, the psychological, the moral, and the metaphysical. Only at this last mentioned metaphysical or substantial level will we reach the being of a person in such a way as to understand how one can be both absolute and relative. But we can reach this fourth ontological or substantial level only through the other three operational levels. Further, we must first explore each level according to a person's dependence or relativity so that we can later recognize the independence or absoluteness within the dependence. Then it will be possible to understand the fact of the person's basic interior tension, that is, his or her relative absoluteness or dependent independence, without thinking that these expressions are either contradictions or cute paradoxes. Such an understanding will enable us to discover whether the person's absoluteness or independence is totally self-explanatory or whether it is supported by something other than itself, namely, the absolute which is beyond, yet supports from within, all chosen absolutes. In making these discoveries, we can learn whether other-centered love is possible, and, if possible, what its dynamic structure is. This structure may then reveal the secular transcendent or God.

A. Human Dependency or Relativity in Being

Human dependency is dramatically evident when a person absorbs at all levels of being the elements for growth found in his or her situation. Then the person is seen to be a dependent part of the kingdom of life, of the human community, and even of the universe of beings. The persons's whole being takes its beginning, its developing, and its achieving of mature wholesomeness from dynamic relationships with other beings. Let us see this more concretely in the four levels of the human being.

Human Biological or Physical Dependence

Many centuries before the science of genetics came to birth, people were conscious that offspring owed not only their existence but also some of their characteristics to their forebearers. They kept pedigree charts for both humans and animals. But the science of genetics opened up this truth so that its full breathtaking perspective could be appreciated. For genetics tells us that each human being is not merely the convergence of gifts from his immediate parents but also the sum of all human couples in the continuous line of parentage stretching back to the first pair or pairs of human beings existent as far back as a million years ago. Indeed, if one accepts that the evolution of life is continuous from first primitive plant to humankind, then each human carries within himself or herself the sum of a parentage which goes back beyond humankind to the anthropoids and, through the plant kingdom, to that first primitive plant from which all life branched out. In this way, each person sums up millions of years of evolving life. One's dependence stretches horizontally like a great chain from the beginning of all life till now. The unbroken horizontal line is seen as historical and cumulative.

Unbelievably, this vast horizontal dependence of each person upon the evolving accumulation of millions of years is matched by one's vertical dependence upon the present ecological moment, that is, upon a cross-cut of momentary convergent influences. There never was a time when the human was not affected—though with the most distant indirectness—by all the beings contemporaneous with him or her on this earth and in this universe at a particular moment. Weather conditions, the migrations of fowl, fish and beast, the ravagings of marauding tribes, and earthquakes would be only some of the world-girdling effects rippling out to every living being of an era. But nowadays, because of burgeoning world population, because of worldwide transport, because of universal science applied to farming, fishing and weather control, because of world-englobing communication systems, and because of world-circling satellites and rocket weaponry—to mention just a few factors—the world has shrunk and no contemporary rippling effect is too far distant to leave us untouched. Nowadays one can feel and see what was once a seemingly abstract philosophic dictum: no single being reacts to change without changing, no matter how slightly, all other beings in the universe. Since the human being is the most sensitive of animals to change, human biology is under constant and powerful influences. Since human reaction to change is so powerful, it deeply influences all other beings in the world in their physical existence.

What in the human being enables us to receive all the past cumulative history of the human race, of the animal kingdom and of plant life at one moment of conception and then at the next moment absorb all the contemporaneous physical influences of the universe? There must be in us a principle of remarkably receptive passivity by which we are capable of receiving all these vast environmental riches. Otherwise, we could not take in and assimilate food, could not receive sense impressions interiorly, and what is more, could not accumulate this food to build physical structure, and could not integrate sense impressions to form a single unified imagination. These environmental factors would not really affect us humans intrinsically unless something within us received them in such a way that they remained and then accumulated as structure in us. Nor would these received affects be received just as they are—according to their proper structure, in complete fidelity to what they are—unless this principle of passive receptivity, biologically and sensately, were of itself *totally* passive. Thus this principle in the human being is much like Aristotle's prime matter.

Yet this accepting of environmental influences into the living body is very strange. It is not simply the totally passive receiving of soft wax stamped by a signet ring. It is an active receiving, a receiving which is an appropriation of what is received. For example, the digestive process is not simply the transfer of food from the mouth to the stomach and intestines, not simply the receiving of nutritional chemistry into the bloodstream and thence into the cell. It is also the appropriation or active reception of food: the food is broken down chemically for transport to the cells and then transformed within the cells to the special chemical needs of the total organism.

A second example of this would be the sense impression of seeing. The eye of the unconscious person passively receives a visual impression of the object before it, but there is no active appropriation of the image, no active reception of it, until the person becomes conscious. Such active reception implies that the human must possess, besides the principle of total passivity which assures the person of accurate or true reception, a second principle to account for the activeness of this biological, sensitive receiving which is characteristic of the living body. This second principle would be something like the Aristotelian form.

Together these two principles would constitute the principle of active passivity in humans. They are our structure, our principle of limit, whereby we are members of the species of man and not of the species of zebra or rhododendron. This structure or limiting principle of active passivity would, then, be the human essence. For a particular person's horizontal dependence on the great genetic chain of parent couples finally issues in this person's being a particular zygote with this unique human genetic structure at this definite moment in time. In the next moment, by reason of this person's vertical dependence on the contemporaneous environmental influences, he or she is receiving these contemporary influences according to a prior, specifically human, genetic structure. But again the vertical contemporary influences are received actively; they are assimilated into the person by this prior human genetic structure. In other words, he or she is also a principle of active receiving or appropriation: a living human body, not a merely passive corpse.

By the principle of total passivity, then, I am passively related to all my past genetic history and to the contemporary environmental influences; but by the principle of active reception or appropriation, I become dynamically related to my past and present. Such appropriation implies cumulative development. Not only do the environmental influences remain true by means of the principle of total passivity, but also their appropriation or active receiving implies that they are integrated into the living body of a human, that is, that they are accumulated and transformed into the human being. Thus the embryo accumulates its structure in an organized way as its cells begin to form tissues, as the tissues shape into organs, and as the latter begin to systematize throughout the organism—always in direct proportion to the environmental influences received, always according to the specific genetic structure of the human being, and always according to the previous unique historical accumulation of events within the organism.

As a result, every part of a person's living body is in continual and cumulative dynamic relation with its past, with its contemporaneous environment, and with the other parts of the body. Here, again, one meets with the philosophic understanding of homeostasis. It is the process not merely of the inner relatings between systems within the human but also of the latter's outer relatings with all the influences of the environment, not merely of momentary and passing relatings but of enduring and cumulative ones. The human being is seen, then, as wholly relational by way of the accumulating structure of his or her living body.

In this sense, the human being is totally relative; and for this reason, if only human dependence on environmental influences is considered, then Spencer's totally relativistic person is the truth of the case. But this is only one side of the human being and is only the more exterior aspect of the self. Nevertheless, this more exterior aspect, with its compenetrating principles of total passivity and of active appropriation, acts as a single reality when it operates to digest food or to sense things. This single reality demonstrates that it is not a Cartesian person composed of two beings, but one being, bodily person, totally related to environment by constant cumulative operations.

Human Psychological Dependence

The more interior or psychic aspect of the person contrasts with the more exterior or bodily aspect of this same person. Yet this contrast does not remove the parallels between the two aspects. The psychic aspect of the human being also has its horizontal and vertical dimensions of dependence. Not only genetically but also psychically, the human being stretches back to the beginning of life—and even beyond that to the beginning of time. This is to say that psychically the human person is historical, time bound, and cumulative.

Through the sciences of paleontology, archeology, and history, the human person can become consciously aware of his or her uncivilized and civilized past in great detail and can appropriate it to the inner self of mind and imagination just as unconsciously, through his or her genetic given, the person recapitulates all personal past genetic history within the zygote. Thus education is seen as a person's attempt to discover and to assimilate like food all human past experience, literature, science, technology, art, religion, and history so that the person becomes related consciously to as many peoples and physical epochs as time and intelligence allow. All of the human past, then, contributes to the individual's developing personality; because the individual actively receives this contribution, the person appropriates it in a unique life synthesis and individuality. Thus a person's past becomes identified psychically with part of his or her very being; in this way, a person becomes ontologically related to all past civilizations and cultures. Only in the last century with the rapid and full development of science, libraries, universities, and museums has a person been so capable of appropriating the human past and all physical epochs to the self.

Besides this horizontal historical influence and appropriation, there is a contemporaneous vertical assimilation. For the surrounding present culture also influences the individual person. A person is not only historical, but also communitarian. Because of the marvelous new systems of communication—from television to computer networks, from magazines to encyclopedias—it is possible to share worldwide information and concerns almost instantly, to form international businesses as well as scientific organizations, to send help in times of national catastrophes, and to rejoice about common successes over great distances. Civilizations and cultures are no longer hermetically sealed off from each other by vast oceans and towering mountain ranges; customs diffuse among nations and social classes and begin to blend. Urban culture throughout the world is rapidly homogenizing. One becomes ontologically related in one's deepest interior not only to past history but also to one's present contemporaneous worldwide culture.

Because the individual has the opportunity to be more historical and communitarian than ever, he or she can be more deeply influenced in his or her psychic interior. The human being is not living sealed inside a Leibnizean monad with no portholes or snorkel tube, and only with the radio signals of pre-established harmony. Rather, the human being risks being overwhelmed by the vast riches of psychic influence inundating human consciousness from the past and present. A person's more interior self shows the principle of total passivity when one's education requires the memory of so many facts for simple survival. But this more interior aspect of the self shows how active one's reception is when it appropriates much of this material by understanding multiple facts through one powerful insight and by thus integrating them to the individual's personality. For example, Einstein's central insight enabled his theory of relativity to organize most of the facts of physics. At a less rarified level, each person's deepest insight into life becomes the life-aim around which he or she organizes more or less the multitudinous details of his or her life. The more one does this, the more deeply related an individual becomes to the environment, and the more dependent upon it, precisely through one's thinking and imagining, and, consequently, through one's willing and feeling. No thought, no imagination, no feeling, no willing of a person escapes being related to the cultural world outside the person. If all these factors are integrated within the individual, each factor is related to all the other ideas, images, feelings, willings within the particular person. Again, at this psychic level, one appears to be totally relational and dependent—and nothing more, if one looks at only this aspect of mankind.

Human Moral Dependence

Out of this psychological dependence issues human moral dependence: the person's receiving of traditional and contemporary values from the community through its educational process. Unless the child accepts the values of its people without question, it cannot grow strong or even survive physically. Unless the adolescent at least temporarily accepts the deepening of these same values, he or she cannot prepare psychically to cope with the surrounding civilization; no one will hire the adolescent for labor or attempt to teach him or her techniques for survival. In other words, no adolescent can create his or her own world and get others to cooperate physically and psychically in building it. The adolescent has to allow the community's traditions to possess him or her utterly so that the good of the community becomes identified thoroughly with the adolescent's own personal good. This compenetration is not a fifty-fifty proposition. The community's good dominates the adolescent and this domination is part of patriotism or community loyalty. The adolescent accepts the community good actively; that is, he or she works at appropriating these values received from the family as the community tradition. Insofar as the adolescent accepts the whole communal value system and is thereby integrated into the community, so far does he or she attain a certain liberty, that is, the freedom to cooperate with the community in its work systems, its rituals, its family life, and its sports and recreations. But the adolescent does this on the community's terms and therefore with a received or passive freedom. This is the adolescent's moral dependence.

This horizontal historical dimension of absorbing the community's past tradition is complemented, of course, by the vertical cross-sectional dimension of contemporary community influence. The traditional values are always interpreted by the contemporary community experience of them. Thus, the adolescent is somewhat less passive than the child that acts mainly out of rote memory and mechanical living of the values. There is room for interpretation and thus for active receiving or appropriation of these values. Thus, the plain receiving of these values emphasizes humble acceptance: it also implies the pragmatic worthwhileness of accepting a traditional folk-wisdom distilled from much suffering and experimentation. But the active reception of the values stresses a sense of gratitude to the community and implies that these values have viability in everyday life.

The humility and gratitude, in turn, are expressions of the adolescent's openness to structure and hope in the community. This has not only a healing effect upon communal wounds but also a wholing effect in the individual. For openness and hope are the conditions for communal and personal integration. Finally, as the adolescent subordinates personal good to the larger good of the community, through a process of identifying with the latter, he or she becomes open to an adulthood of sacrifice and becomes able to dedicate the self to something much larger than self. This process not only expands the heart and mind but fills them with new strength, new intelligence, new hope, and new love from the community. Here moral dependence becomes fulfillment of the person.

But, inasmuch as the largest part of the meaning and value of the adolescent's life comes from communal indoctrination, he or she is deeply dependent, is totally relational, and shares only those loves and hopes offered by the community. The young person is, from this side, only the sum of the community's influences upon him or her. This adolescent is certainly not the Sartrean person of absolute interior freedom; he or she is more the Spencerian person who acts as the mere focus of environmental forces. Even if the adolescent should try to fight against a particular set of community values, he or she would have to use other received community values to attack the prior set.

Human Metaphysical Dependence

The biological, psychological, and moral levels of dependence reveal the metaphysical level to us. For these first three levels are operational levels of being. Their source, cause of recurrence, and radical meaning is the perduring operator and their structure mirrors the operator insofar as effect reveals cause. Thus the operator level of person, the metaphysical level, has thus far been revealed as totally relational, totally dependent on the environment of things and of people, by the three operational levels of the biological, psychic and moral. The human being is an active receiver; but he or she is first of all a receiver.

If the person is taken as the end result of biological genetics, cultural history, and community tradition, then he or she receives biologically, psychologically, and morally from the environment all the conditions or preparations necessary for existing. At the first moment of a person's existence, there is a totally passive reception and in the second moment an active reception just as the zygote is at first a total gift and then a moment later becomes an appropriating receiver. Taken vertically as the focus for contemporaneous environmental and communal influence, one is being continually held in existence by receiving at all three levels. Failure to receive means stunted growth and inevitable disintegration. Evidently the human being is not a deist's perpetual-motion machine which, once set in motion by God, never stops operating. A person is literally held in continued existence by what he or she constantly receives from both the past and the present. The human being would seem to be, then, the point of tension or center of convergence for horizontal traditional forces and for vertical contemporaneous influences.

Thus the person is discovered to be a relational substance. One does appropriate or receive actively all these influences and one does perdure to establish continuity of life. That is, one accumulates growth biologically, psychologically, and morally. Therefore one is a substance, if by this we mean a perduring presence which is productively directing and integratively accumulating all of a person's appropriative operations into a developing structure. The human being is thus a substance whose beginning and development is relational or dependent at every moment of its existence and in every operation it performs. Of one's very being or essence, the person is related intrinsically, and not just extrinsically, to every being of the past and of the present and is so related biologically, psychologically, and morally. These past and present beings are the reasons why the person exists now and has not disintegrated in the past. They are the reasons, too, why the person is this individual and not that one as this person receives from them a particular genetic, cultural, and moral structure and uniquely appropriates all their gifts to personal needs. The human being is a receiver of existence from others, but according to unique biologic, psychic, and moral structure. Though an active receiver, the human being yet is limited to what he or she receives.

Human Relational Dependence Is Loving

Because the human person is an active receiver at all the four levels of being, the biological, psychological, moral, and metaphysical, the human is capable of a total receiving in the act of love. In other words, one is capable of being the beloved at the deepest roots of one's being. Because the four levels of the human being form a single reality, therefore, all human love, no matter how elevated in sentiment and noble in ideal, has a bodily element to it. In this large sense, all love is sexual, that is, all love is according to the male or female structure of the body and will therefore carry appropriate emotional resonances. Through bodily dependence or relativity, then, the human being is apt for the act of loving which is essentially relational because it is essentially reciprocal. It is the beloved's acceptance or active reception of the lover's bodily presence which enables the lover to express love. Though passivity is required of the beloved if the lover is to make a gift of his or her bodily presence, still this passivity must be an active receiving if the lover is to know the gift has been appropriated and is acceptable. This is shown by the smile, the pat on the back, the embrace, the handshake, the wink, the relaxed laugh, the vibrancy of expectation, and a thousand other bodily expressions.

Human relational dependence shown by the beloved in bodily acceptance of the lover, is also displayed at the psychological level. Unless the bodily acceptance of the lover by the beloved is matched and directed by psychological acceptance, the beloved is either torn by inner dissension or exhausted by the attempt to pretend acceptance on both levels. Psychological acceptance is as necessary to the beloved's wholesomeness as it is to the lover's initiative if their love is not to be a mutually frustrating sham. So, the beloved, through the imagination and body, accepts a knowing of the lover into the mind and a hoping for the lover into the heart. There these knowings and hopings integrate and accumulate to form the personal love-relationship between beloved and lover. This is the psychological acceptance or active receiving within their sharing. It is the contribution of the beloved to the lover; it is the beloved's response taken passively. Here the beloved's dependence attracts the lover's independence into the act of love. Yet ironically, the lover's independent act is dependent upon the demonstrated psychological and physical dependence of the beloved's response.

This irony holds true also at the moral level of their being. For this act of love requires that the lover's own person (the highest good) be offered as gift to the beloved. Somehow, in order to retain independence, the lover must simultaneously retain selfhood and yet give it away by identifying this self with the life good of the beloved. Somehow, in sheer dependency, the beloved must accept the lover's self into the beloved's independent good or self. The passivity here is the beloved's subordination of personal independent good to the good of the lover. But it is an active receiving insofar as it is done out of gratitude for the lover's trusting advance. Here is a terrible gambling of the future if the acceptance is deep because the compenetrated good or selves of lover and beloved must now pursue growth together in the closest cooperation of mutual dependence. The compenetrating spirituality of the two persons renders them more relational and dependent than ever before in proportion to the depth of their union.

Though such a union would seem to exclude other love relationships of comparable depth, it has an opposite effect. As this mutual love grows in them and as they consequently become more human, each becomes more loveable not only to each other but also to others outside the union. Indeed, the knowledge and skill developed by their mutual love makes each more capable of eliciting and giving love to others. One sees this phenomenon in the mother happy with her large family, in the doctor dedicated to his patients, in the priest or minister married to his parish. A prime love relationship is contagious and the spreading of a network of loves out of this contagion renders the lover ever more dependent, ever more vulnerable, ever more human. At the moral level, then, insofar as loves make the person more relational and dependent, the person becomes more human and loveable.

If one considers only this side of the person, it look as though the human were not a totally relational substance but rather simply a sum of relationships and nothing more. For there is nothing in a human that is not related to some thing or someone in the environment. In fact, there is no level or element of a human that is unrelated to other levels and elements within the self. Because of this totality of relationships, a human is essentially a receiver. In fact one becomes more capable of receiving from others, the more relationships one enjoys, the more richly dependent one becomes.

Furthermore, the very richness of these successful relationships makes one more capable of an active receiving since one develops a skill for receiving the gifts of others graciously. Thus a benevolent cycle of developing dependence spreads, the more widely and deeply the beloved accepts a community of lovers for a fuller life. This would seem to turn the beloved into the Spencerian human of total relativity. But as a matter of fact the very opposite occurs. The more deeply rooted one becomes in a community of loves, the more independent one can become. The very need of others paradoxically becomes independence. The beloved's dependent acceptance of the lover becomes the base for the beloved's independent giving of self to the lover in return. The compenetration of their lives in body, mind, heart, and destiny makes each more independent instead of less so.[27] To understand these paradoxical statements, it is necessary to see how independent the dependent human is. This is the purpose of the next section where we study the absoluteness within human relativity, the independence within one's dependence.

B. Humankind's Independence or Absoluteness In Being

Earlier we stressed that the human being is a receptive part of the life kingdom, of the human community and of the universe of beings. Now we must note that the human is a dominant part. One is not merely an active receiver, an appropriator. One is also an inventive, even heroic, giver. The human being is not the passive creature of events but their molder. Within the limits of gifts received from the historical past and from the contemporaneous present, one creates freely one's own future. But how is this possible if the previous description of human relational dependency has been accurate?

It is possible and occurs precisely at the vertical dependence in the four levels of the human being. The horizontal dependence of one's biological genesis, psychological indoctrination, childlike acceptance of moral values, and metaphysical reception of existence, suffers interpretation at this vertical dependence. Here one blends one's genetic past with the contemporary environment, adjusts the community's traditional meanings and values to contemporary changes, and, with one's perduring presence, serially integrates one's cumulative, personal relationships. In a person's dependency, this vertical dimension is not so rigidly deterministic as is the horizontal because the vertical is the interpreter or adjuster of the horizontal. This intrusion of interpretation, therefore, makes room here for independence.

Let us see what this means in each level of one's being. For if, within human relational dependence, one can find a compentrating absolute independence, then one knows much better who the human being is and how he or she exists. Next, if one can calibrate this human independence, one can observe how it may be the basis for other-centered love and how it may need the support of the absolute beyond all absolutes to account for the remarkable characteristics of other-centered love.

Human Biological-physical Independence

Even in plants and animals, but much more in the human being, biological independence shows itself through adaptation to the environment and through radically novel developments. Adaptation is characteristic of horizontal independence presently issuing out of past cumulative development; while novel growth indicates vertical independence now issuing out of present horizontal independence and moving into the future.

In first considering horizontal biological independence, one must recognize that its basic characteristic, adaptation, is not just a truce with the environment. Instead, adaptation is domination of the situation. The species of plant or animal or human organism survives because this species has such a rich genetic pool that, by natural selection, it can meet the new environmental demands in such a way that it is improved. Thus, as a region grows drier, a plant species may respond by developing a deeper root system and a thicker cuticle on the leaves. Even environmental threats to a plant species can be converted into its richer growth. Indeed it should be noted that organisms do not lie supinely under environmental influences. Trees change their own soil; they put down roots into it, drop leaves upon it, and thus enrich it for their own betterment. Certainly grazing animals change their surroundings as they closely crop herbs, drop manure on them, and break the soil with sharp hooves, so that the herbs improve and thus better nourish the grazing animals.

Such dominance of its environment and of its past produces the healthy individual within the infrahuman species. Then survival of the fittest is more than survival because it assures not only continuous existence for the species but also its perfective growth. This is exemplified in the common housefly, which has successfully resisted the pesticide DDT by developing a perfected immunizing system. The living being has then made its past history serve its present needs in a new way. This is adaptation, the characteristic of biological independence.

Such independence is even more striking in the human species. The remarkable correlation between the greater sophistication of tools and the growing size of the human brain (as well as the increasing strength and versatility of the human thumb) leads physical anthropologists to surmise that the more successful way of life produced by better tools has acted reciprocally to evolve a better brain. Nevertheless, for a million years human biological and technological progress was slow—until the last forty thousand years. Then primitive forms of the human species disappeared; while anatomically modern man and woman arose to dominate the world theater by producing a technological revolution with entirely new complex tools, invention of boats, introduction of fish into diet, migration to the Arctic and to the Americas, and development of new arts and dress ornamentation.

This acceleration of control over environment (actually a speed-up of adaptation affecting the human species physically) continued as humans learned to work metals, to make long voyages, to tap new energy sources of wind and water power. In addition, humans domesticated the wild grains, fruits and animals around them. This development of agriculture and animal husbandry not only furnished sufficient food for enlarged populations but also established a protein rich diet for better health. Human adaptation had changed the environment and improved human physical being. Thus, out of a relational dependence on the new adaptations in diet, travel, work tools, power sources of wind and water, and experiences of immigration, art, and dress, came human horizontal biological independence. In a reciprocal paradox, the growing population of the world made possible by these discoveries is greatly dependent not only on their continuing but on their becoming more successful. The so-called green revolution dare not slow down or pause. It would seem that human horizontal biological independence is asserted only insofar as humans enter more deeply into relational biological dependence.

Consider how the novelty of vertical independence further illustrates this paradox. Such novelty is particularly striking in the phenomenon of speciation, the branching of widely diverse species out of a single or a few original species. There are presently about two million species existent in our life world, each of them once a novelty. What is more astounding: 99.9% of all species that have ever lived are now extinct. This means that about two billion species have appeared on this earth during the past 600 million years—a rather remarkable display of novelty and of living into the future. Thus the vertical dimension of biological independence occurs when, in establishing the ongoing continuity of the present out of the past, a particular species is building a new future called a subspecies which will later evolve into a distinct species. This is no routine reproduction of the past in an eternal round of sameness.

Novelty, something never before existent and never again to be replicated in some future novelty, has gradually broken into the universe as subspecies turn into species.

Thus each species declares its independence of the historical past precisely because each species carries along in its genetic pool many of the riches and poverties of the past in continuity with its progenitors. Without such novelty amid continuity, our textbooks could not feature the burgeoning 'tree of life' to illustrate general biological evolution. A glance at Gaylord Simpson's charting of the genesis of the modern horse out of a tiny waist-high animal or a glance at a map of the bird evolving out of the reptile astonishes us with the novelty of this development: unpredictable yet reasonable after the fact—even though it took thousands of years for this novelty to manifest itself fully.

Vertical biological independence is intensified incredibly in man. Not only can humankind improve the human species's health through medical technology and through controlled diet made possible by animal husbandry, the green revolution, and pharmaceuticals; humankind can also change the environment dramatically so that it contributes to human physical betterment. For example, the human person can dam rampaging rivers destructive of life, and use the dams to furnish the electrical power for running the hospitals, research clinics, food-producing factories, sources of sun warmth and sport facilities which can improve human physical development. Furthermore, the human person, as the species dominant by reason of reflective intelligence, can protect and improve all other species of plants and animals so that the biological basis for better community living is provided. The human has put intellectual evolution to the service of biological evolution so that the biological can serve better the higher levels of human development. Consequently, the human person looks ahead to control not only human evolution but also that of all other species.

Human beings can assert their vertical biological independence, however, only through a growing number of dependencies on the situation. Again, the paradox. For human adaptation (horizontal independence) reorchestrates all the environmental influences which make and keep humans dependent. For example, the environmental challenge of providing food impelled humans to produce finer strategies for capturing animals and better tools for planting and gathering grains, vegetables, and fruits. This challenge simultaneously stimulated them to develop their imagination and intelligence, to say nothing of methodic self-discipline of the body. In as much as humans exult, as it were, in such environmental dependence, by accepting and integrating into themselves all these environmental and communal influences, they also assert their independence by adaptively refashioning these influences for their own novel growth and that of all other species.

In this way, humans demonstrate independence of the whole world at the exact moment when, through observation, controlled experimentation, and manipulation of environment, they immerse their energies more deeply and widely in relational dependence upon all the species of the world. Thus, through intelligent bodily activity and through physical dependence on all other living beings, the human person dominates them independently. This domination is a creation of unique human novelty through adaptive physical growth which thus betters the biological existence of the human being and of all other species. But this growth of independence is in direct proportion to humankind's cultivated dependence on the environment.

This holds true especially for the vertical independence of speciation which makes radical evolution possible. For a species must perdure over many thousands of years before it can produce a subspecies and, much later, out of that subspecies, a totally distinct species; it must make thousands of minute adaptations to issue as a novel species. But neither infrahuman nor human independence can so adapt for novelty except through a total relational dependence among all beings of the universe. For at the infrahuman levels, the new subspecies occurs and perdures only when environmental pressures are such as to favor its emergence and persistence. The everchanging environment selects out the hardy organisms which in turn survive by dominating this environment through adaptation and novel development. At the human level, persons must know, work laboriously with, and finally integrate all the environmental influences which give and mold their existence so that they, in response, can adapt these influences to their own novel growth. This shows how much horizontal and vertical biological independence are immersed in their horizontal and vertical biological dependence, namely, the human relationship to all other living beings of the world.

Second Step

Humankind's Psychological Independence

Actually, human biological independence is grounding itself more and more upon human psychological independence, that is, upon inventive intelligence and disciplined freedom. For the human race's recent scientific discoveries in biochemistry, biology, and ecology and its present willingness to sacrifice in the scientific pursuit and in the technological exploitation of these discoveries are now the dominating influences in human biological development and may well enable it to determine the destiny of all other species.

This intimate relationship between human biological and psychological independence is seen in the fact that horizontal psychological independence is based on personal adaptation. This latter is the human ability to build a self freely and inventively balanced between the dialectical extremes of past history presently received from community experiences. Examples of these extremes would be conservative-liberal, democratic-authoritarian, sensual-spiritual, technological-humanistic, and so on. On the other hand, vertical psychological independence would be the human being's ability to grow beyond both the individual's and the community's past and present influences from these extremes. This growth would be a novel personal synthesis of the extremes for a balanced living into the future. Some instances of this synthesis would be the attempts to set up national economic systems which would preclude economic depressions, such as the United States's Social Security System, or the attempt to establish a worldwide governing body, such as the United Nations, to protect peace, to promote world health, and to share technological education, and thereby wealth, among the have and the have-not nations.

Of course, all this vertical psychological independence arises out of horizontal independence. The latter consists principally in the human ability to multiply the opportunities for building a more balanced personality through widened and enriched experiences of literature, art, science, technology, religion, leisure moments—sports, museums, libraries, concerts, parks, zoos—philosophy, theology, and ascetic virtue (the willingness to suffer for and to enjoy worthwhile values). Only a rich variety of experiences can broaden the human mind and heart and only the organization of these experiences into knowledges and virtues will enable the human being freely to use these opportunities and to create new ones. In this vast project, each person is aided by family life whose intimate traditions instill self-respect and discipline, by church life whose spiritual traditions awaken a person to the great values of life, by civic life whose national traditions alert a person to the duties of preserving and protecting the community, and by education whose mind-stimulating traditions link the individual with all other humans in the great enterprise of making the world more humane.

This self-building begins when the individual person, having received the community's historical tradition by way of indoctrination and having undergone its contemporary lived interpretation of this tradition, starts to achieve his or her own insights and to reconsider values within this tradition and its contemporary interpretation. Because the situation of these insights and reconsidered values is constantly evolving, each person must eventually work out his or her own interpretation of how communal tradition is to be used in these insights and reconsiderations of communal values. Rote knowledge and a rigidly lived value system, no matter how true, will not keep one abreast of the changing situation but will only serve as mummy wrappings for the routinized person. To stay alive as a person, the individual must receive as many elements as possible from the communal tradition (this is the horizontal dependency) but must adapt them inventively (this is the horizontal independency) so that they meet well the demands of the newly evolving situation.

When the person thus responsibly reorganizes the community tradition within himself or herself according to inventive insights and reconsidered values, then this person is building her or his personality. This is a balanced personality if the person manages to keep between the dialectical extremes operating in both the communal tradition and the contemporaneous situation. Thus the individual person, insofar as he or she constantly reassesses the self and the situation, is in a steady conversion process which leads towards a healthy wisdom.

This person is a quiet revolutionary insofar as he or she gradually introduces novelty into the self and hence into the situation and insofar as he or she slowly thus becomes more and more uniquely individual. Consequently, a person's horizontal psychological independence of his or her own past (both the community tradition and the person's own previous personality development) involves a vertical psychological independence. for this orchestrative conversion of the self and its situation must be done without yielding too much to the political, economic, familial, ecclesial, and psychological pressures which are the very matters to be orchestrated.

As a result, the quiet revolutionary may sometimes have to stand alone to confront the whole community in defense of his or her quietly revolutionary insight or reconsidered values. In other words, vertical psychological independence requires that one grow beyond one's own and the community's past history in an insightful, freshly evaluated decision which is new to the community. This is the novelty of human development. Only in this way can the community advance, through the unique initiatives of revolutionary individuals, to new levels of cultural growth (consider the effect of Homer's and Dante's epics), to new orientation for its destiny (consider the impact of Jesus Christ, Mohammed, Buddha), to a revolutionary idea of the world (consider Galileo's and Newton's 'new science'), and to a sense of life's tragedies and hopes (consider the power of Catherine of Siena, Kant, Marx, Freud, Darwin, Pope Paul VI). Thus the inventively free and balanced personalities of individuals combine to constitute the vertical psychological independence of the community which then reciprocally promotes this same independence in each and all of its members. Here is community novelty. Through imagination, mind, and will, the dominative person achieves new existence for himself in giving new existence to the community.

But the more the individual proceeds along this path of independence, the more deeply aware he or she becomes of psychological dependence. The balanced decision which founds the balanced personality requires more and more information, insight, and cooperation of others, as the world evolves into more complexity. Without community tradition and encouragement, the individual gets tired and courts defeat. Besides, from the negative side, the quiet revolutionary's independence demands that he or she risk loss of friends, job, family, future growth-opportunities, and even life. This comes at the very moment when the revolutionary is most sensitive to what all these factors mean and most aware of how dependent he or she is on them for physical sustenance, psychological knowledge, and moral support.

Thus one's independence is expressed through one's ever multiplying and deepening dependencies—or it is not expressed at all. The height of the contemporary quiet revolutionary's leadership is measurable by the depth of his or her dependence; no longer in this complex world is there much room for the one-man show or for the caper of the solitary genius. Yet the more dependencies a person has, the more he or she can play them against each other for independent decisions. Hitler's deeply felt dependence upon his generals and admirals goaded him to make startingly inventive military decisions which were at first successful but later disastrous. Albert Schweitzer's uniquely successful hospital work at Lambaréné in Africa, was dependent on his European organ-concert audiences for financial support, on his patients' families for physical and psychological support, on the perdurance of his philosophical and theological reputation for the inspiration which would draw followers to continue his experiment. What distinguishes the human being, then, is the profound ability to build horizontal and vertical psychological independence precisely out of human dependencies with vast adaptation and amazing novelty.

Human Moral Independence

But such building, if it is to produce the balanced person and the healthy community, must be based on goodness. If one cannot sift out the disvaluable (the evil) from the valuable (the good) in the received cultural tradition and in one's inventive decisions for the community, how can one avoid destroying as fast as one builds? It is not enough for a person to blindly accept the values of tradition and the interpretations of these values by the contemporary community, although it is evidently necessary to accept these values by and large if one would identify one's good with that of the community and if one is to cooperate fruitfully with its members. A person must also assert moral independence which is the ability to accept or to reject communal values critically and creatively. One does this for the sake of friends with whom one lives out these values. In other words, one must complement the moral dependence (passive liberty) received from the community with the moral independence (active liberty) of one's own unique contribution to the values and good of the total community. These statements require some explanation.

By means of one's psychological independence, one learns to pick out the good present in one's tradition and community. But to integrate the good inventively and freely within one's own person requires a second costly process: the horizontal dimension of moral independence. It is not enough to know the good. One must identify with it, that is, invest suffering in promoting it within one's life decisions. For example, a young lawyer has completed his law studies and been admitted to the bar. He has specialized lately in property laws, especially those concerned with mortgages. This gives him moral dependence (passive liberty), the skill and the devotedness to begin the practice of specialized law. In this particular area, horizontal moral independence (active liberty) develops when he begins to identify his own good as a lawyer with the good of the people who practice and live under property laws, especially mortgage laws—people such as the judges, lawyers, civil administrators, and property owners. At the same time he becomes aware of the evil practices protected by poor laws and by incompetent or unjust officials. Under the guidance of an experienced senior law partner, he begins to offer original suggestions to legislators for strengthening these laws and to administrators for ridding the government of incompetent officials. At this point, a group of lawyers who have been manipulating the laws and the law courts in order to reap profits from slum property offer the young lawyer a cut of their profits if he will desist.

Here the young lawyer will move from horizontal moral independence, namely his personal and inventive identification and integration with the property law community, into the vertical moral independence where, in taking a stand for good against evil in this community, he begins to contribute long-term practical good to it. First of all, at the risk of his health, he spends long hours preparing and delivering court briefs, visiting legislators, and investigating cases of mortgage injustice. Secondly, at the risk of losing friends and, perhaps, even his place as junior law partner, he continues his pursuit of better laws and fairer court practice. Finally, even his life may be put in jeopardy. But gradually amid all the tension, he sees the laws improved and the judges delivering fairer verdicts. Because of his exercise of moral independence, the young lawyer has himself grown in active liberty and induced more freedom into the practice of property law within the community. The horizontal dimension of his moral independence is more his own personal liberty gratefully identifying with the good of the law community. The vertical dimension is this same liberty insofar as it uniquely develops the good of the law community and of the larger community served by property lawyers.

The young lawyer has dominated the situation inventively and freely by increasing the good within it and decreasing its evil. He has given it a new existence or radical novelty. But in reality he is helpless without the tradition of law he received and without the encouraging and intelligent cooperation of fellow lawyers, politicians, and property owners. His moral independence arises within this deep, complex moral dependence and cannot live without it.[28] The young lawyer's active liberty and his contribution to the community are admittedly his own and no one else's. But the community has made this possible not only by helping him build a greater justice into property laws but also by furnishing him with his existence as a lawyer. This is his passive liberty. He responds in gratitude by exerting his active liberty and risking everything to introduce novel good into the law community and its client communities. This is vertical moral independence issuing out of horizontal moral independence.

Human Metaphysical Independence

If there is one element common to the biological, psychological, and moral levels of human independence, it is self-possession. We are so independently successful in our biological adaptation, in our psychological revolutionary conversion, and in our moral assertion of liberty for ourselves and for the community because we possess our own existence dominatively. Through intelligent reflection upon and disciplined sacrifice for the good of the community, we achieve an assertive sense of our own uniqueness and personal liberty. This is our existence asserting itself through the three levels of our operations. The assertion is, of course, by way of our dependent limiting structure (essence), yet it expands this structure. Let us observe this in more detail.

Second Step

First of all, when does the horizontal dimension of human metaphysical independence occur? It occurs when I as a human being simultaneously acknowledge with gratitude my debt to the biological, psychological, and moral tradition which gave me essential being, and then assert my independence in this tradition by adapting it to a changing environment. This is a free and creative movement out of the past into the present. At the biological level, I establish my personal independence by intelligently adapting my genetic gifts so that physically I and my performance become uniquely developed whether in the sport stadium or the stock exchange or the art studio or the tunnel construction or the high-fashion salon. The very adaptability of my physical development proves my independence or self-possession and manifests my assertion of personal existence. At the psychological level, the balance of personality achieved by me as I draw upon a complex and seemingly contradictory culture, shows my inventive personal conversion. To be a quiet revolutionary, I must know deeply and assert confidently my existence as it powers my personality. At the moral level, if I choose freely and live adaptively the traditional cultural values, I inevitably make painful sacrifices since I must be critical of these values if I am to make decisions independently of cultural pressures. This is to say that, in loving my fellow workers, family, friends, and nation according to my adaptively developed genetic gifts and my unique personality, I must be willing to sacrifice the affection of these people in order to live life-values which challenge their values. This happens when I dare to speak and act against easy divorces, chosen abortions, national nuclear policy, and so on. This is my self-possession, my assertion of existence, seen in the horizontal independence of my being and life.

But the full appreciation of human dominative existence comes only with the vertical dimension of human independence. There the human assumes obligations for the community's present existence and future destiny and at the same time uniquely asserts personal independence within service of this community. At the biological level, humankind establishes its independence by attempting to inventively direct not only its own evolution but also that of other species. By assertion of its own existence as dominative, humankind intends to modify the existence of all other existents in a novel way, even to give or withhold existence in some instances. At the psychological level, when the individual person achieves some liberty, he or she becomes able to support others in their pursuit of liberty, in their conversion or quiet personal revolution, so that the community can build a new future which can be ever expanding with goodness rather than ever narrowing from restrictive selfishness. The union organizer, often tempted to walk away from the frightened textile workers in a North Carolina town, discovers that his willingness to risk his life to better their community is a contagious freedom which strengthens them to unite and to fight for their rights. This last event, in turn, encourages the organizer to more strenuous efforts. Thus the individual person's own existence expands in a novel way through costly decisions. For these decisions embody the community's cultural past as well as its present inventive novelty as this person fights to provide better wages and working conditions or better urban government or an educational system better meeting the needs of its students. This would be the metaphysical meaning of psychological leadership.

Meanwhile, at the moral level of human independence, a person finds the self strong enough to risk losing personal existence in order to promote a better future for community. Because of dedication to the community, this person is willing to risk his or her life and the community's respect if he or she can attain a communal good worth this risk. This ultimate independence is an active liberty demanding full self-possession, an extensive dominative control of one's existence. Indeed, this metaphysical liberation of the self is the novel expansion of one's existence beyond one's past essential-traditional structure. It is done through heroic decisions and through the cumulative personal relationships enhanced by such decisions. Here, at the community level, we recognize the pride of a neighborhood or the *esprit* of a nation as the expression of this dominative existence.

For these reasons, the human being is not simply a relational substance, a perduring presence constituted of mere relationships—as our analysis of human dependence could leave us believing. No, the human is also a substantial relation, a perduring presence who causes relationships to be. For a person's activities reveal remarkable independence at the center of his or her being—an independence that is dominative, inventive, free, unique.

Moreover, it is an independence that grows by accumulating communal riches and by introducing radically new elements into their synthesis. This novel cumulative growth marks the substantial. This is the assertive existence working within the essential but never satisfied with the latter and always improving it through expansive operations at the biological, psychological, and moral levels of the human being.

One's assertive existence does not deny one's essential structure. In fact, one principle cannot be without the other since together in their compenetration they form the single being called the human being.[29] For human independence is asserted only through human dependence, namely a person's past development and the community's cooperation. On the other hand, this dependence can survive but a short time without human independence—how long can one live if one's body does not adapt to environment, if one's psyche does not achieve new insight and make free decisions, if one's will does not offer or accept any sacrificial love?

There is, then, within the human being a basic reciprocity between the dependent and the independent, between the limiting-restrictive essential and the expansive existential. This reciprocity of really distinct, though never separate, principles constitutes the human person. Existence in the latter is more substantial (less relational), more independent, more unique and novel, more future-oriented, more liberating, more responsive, more giving than essence. Essence in the human is more relational (less substantial), more dependent, more universal and routinized, more past-oriented, more restrictive, more passive, more receptive than existence.[30] But only comparatives may be used since the distinct human existence and the distinct human essence form a single indivisible being called the human being so that as a result all these qualities compenetrate in each of a person's activities to form each indivisible operation.

Now this reciprocity interior to one's very substantial being is the source of the reciprocity more exterior to one in one's operations as they issue out of that being. The existence of Jim London asserts itself operationally in his trusting advance of love to Marjorie Chicago. With gratitude, her essence allows her to accept operationally his advance (and thus to encourage subsequent advances). But her own existence demands that she assert operationally her own uniqueness by offering, in turn, her person to him. Because he has enhanced her with his trusting advance, she wants, out of her very existence, to enhance him with an assertive response which goes beyond mere acceptance of him in order to affirm his goodness and to identify with it by her assertive self-donation. And so, Jim London, in his turn, accepts her assertion in his essence and thus encourages her. In this way, the interior reciprocity of essence and existence within each of the two lovers produces, in the operational act of love between them, that more exterior reciprocity which is the very structure of love's dynamism. Without this interior and then more exterior reciprocity of assertion and acceptance in both Jim London and Marjorie Chicago, their love cannot occur.

This act of love, being reciprocal, naturally produces in lover and beloved a mutual intrinsic modification which is the relativity of their essences, that is, Jim and Marjorie each accepts the other's assertive advance of trust into his and her essence. The absolute of their love, on the other hand, is the assertive advance of each arising from the act of existence of each. Thus the relativity of the trusting dependence found in man and woman issues from the essence of each; while the absoluteness of the assertive independence arises from the existence of each. Because of the reciprocity of essence and existence in constituting one's very being or substance, a person's relativity is never without a compenetrating absoluteness and vice versa. Because the substantial reciprocity of a person's being causes the operational reciprocity of his or her subsequent act of love, the person's being produces the absoluteness of this love act within the relativity of the same love-act. The independence of the love act can be displayed only within its compenetrating dependence. For this reason, it is not a cute oxymoron but the statement of a hard fact to say that a human being is a relative absolute or a dependent independence. For this reason, too, it is easy to lose sight of human absoluteness within its relativity. Therefore, it would be good for us to survey this absoluteness in human loving.

Absolute Independence of the Person in Loving

How does human independence show itself within dependence in the act of loving? At the biological level, human absolute independence appears in the physical novelty with which a person's love adaptively reorchestrates life's bodily routines. As soon as two people discover that, amid the necessary fundamental routines of life, nothing new is happening in their friendship—no show of any deepening affection, no novelty of physical expression, no new sensitivity in gesture and smile, no eagerness for face-to-face exchange about life's little excitements, no desire to be near one another, no sense of a growing, day-to-day familiarity with each other's physical needs and joys—they know that this love no longer expresses their independence but only their dependence on mutual convenience. In other words, one's willingness to risk some painful bodily discomfort in order to protect or to increase the physical life of the beloved through adaptive novelty becomes the paradoxical assertion of the lover's existence. For it seems to demand physical self-diminishment for the sake of the beloved's good.

At the psychological level, independence reveals itself in the lover's total giving of mind, heart, and imagination in order to better the existence or life of the beloved. This total giving is, first, a full attention of the mind in which the lover affirms the full truth of the beloved, all the latter's defective wholesomeness. This realistic focus on the beloved does not divinize by projecting good qualities actually absent from the beloved. Rather, it includes the unchangeable evils present in the beloved and yet seldom overlooks the handsomeness of the beloved in body and personality. This total giving is, secondly, a full blending of the lover's heart with the beloved's good as the lover seeks out the best for the beloved whether this best hurts or gives joy. The lover does not confuse kindness, the desire to please and not to hurt, with love which reluctantly but steadfastly approves the hurtful for the beloved so long as the latter is benefitted. This attention of the heart, therefore, carries compassion for the defects of the beloved and hope for the latter's growth.

Further, this attention of mind and heart opens wide to embrace the beloved's total situation—friends, family, job, obligations. The beloved is not loved ideally but concretely in all the communal facets of life with the lover. Such a total giving must be inventive if it is to perdure—so complex is the evolving personality and situation of the beloved, so demanding of constant adaptation is a deep relationship. This total giving must also be continuous and very patient if it would last with perduring fidelity and with cumulative growth through bad and good times. When all this happens, tough independence surfaces in the midst of love's most tender dependencies.

By sharp comparison, note how lacking in independence is distracted or unfocused love. Superficial love avoids permanent commitment to the beloved, hedges the giving of self with self-protecting conditions, resents any new obligations shouldered by the beloved, and is impatient when the beloved is sick or mentally disturbed. It either avoids facing the beloved's faults or dwells on them neurotically, either places false hopes in the beloved or underestimates the latter's strengths. Halfhearted or half-attentive love is consequently erratic and fitful, abruptly terminated by the appearance of a new beloved, not patient enough to discover its own unique identity, highly selective in its attention to the beloved, overly desirous to please, and easily satisfied with routine expression of love. These are the marks of dependency characteristic of a child's attempt to love another person. Independence is barely perceptible.

At the moral level of the human, one finds independence when the lover can simultaneously give full support to the beloved's balanced growth in personality and yet leave the beloved totally free to develop in his or her own unique way. Here love is bestowed without conditions being laid down for the giving or without demands being made for acceptance; it is a supreme trusting of the other's goodness for response. Here, too, the lover subordinates the self independently (that is, freely, knowingly, trustingly, hopefully, prudently, gladly) to the beloved's good—without fear of being tyrannized or debased. Paradoxically, the lover's independence makes the subordination possible and free. It is a love willing to go beyond physical and psychological exhaustion to death itself if this would fulfill a great need of the beloved since no higher human value can be sought or lost than the existence of the beloved.

Strangely, this love so concentrated on the beloved nevertheless is not jealous, proprietory, or totally exclusive of others. The lover's independence rejoices that the attention given by others makes the beloved grow in wholesomeness of personality. The lover does not see the beloved isolated from, but rather situated within, that community whose interests and destiny are also the object of his love. For unless the whole community grows in wholesomeness, neither the lover nor the beloved can grow well in personal liberty, namely, in the human personality's growth towards wisdom. The loving father of a family wants good relations with the neighbors for his beloved family; he wants playgrounds, police protection, decent schooling, and a healthy neighborhood atmosphere. Thus the lover's affirmation of the beloved contains implicitly an affirmation of the beloved's larger community. The dependency of both lover and beloved on the community is accepted at the same time as the independence of both increases. The lover's independence grows because the lover leaves the beloved and the latter's community free to reject himself or herself; the beloved's independence increases because the beloved is receiving new confirmation of personal value and loveableness.

If the independence of human love is revealed biologically in the inventive uniqueness of this love, psychologically in the undivided attention of mind and heart on the beloved, and morally in the cherishing of the beloved's liberty, then metaphysically it appears when the lover on all three of the above levels offers the totality of self, the lover's very own existence, to the beloved and to the latter's community at the risk of losing this existence.

Ironically, this total gift is best recognized in a resounding no. For example, the wife may have to call her cherished but career-mad husband back to sanity by refusing to move the family to another city and another job for the third time in five years even though her no risks breakup of the marriage. Or a prophet, like Jeremiah, may have to say no to the nation's foreign policy and to her way of life at the risk that the anger of his beloved Jewish people will crush out his life. Or another man may feel that he has to say no to what he thinks is God's call to service of his church because he feels that his unworthiness will hurt the people of God; indeed he may risk his beloved God's displeasure at that time in order later to say yes to the same vocation out of freedom and not out of compulsive fear. But in all three cases, the no is given in order that the naysayer can achieve integrity and in order to protect the community from disintegration. Even in the no there is the

B. Humankind's Independence or Absoluteness in Being

positive drive to bring a more wholesome existence to the community even if it should mean loss or diminishment for the naysayer.

Only a lover with full self-possession can so exercise dominative control over personal existence that the beloved's existence and the community's existence become more important than the lover's existence.[31] Other-centered love which demands such a revolutionary conversion of the lover is the fullest expression of man or woman as assertive existence. It is a disciplined, patient heroism quietly hidden in everyday dependencies but slowly accumulating strength out of good decisions made for the sake of the beloved and the community. As a result, when the great sacrifice is needed, the strength is there to make it. This is a person's absoluteness or independence immersed in the relativity or dependence within human love. It can be seen graphically in the bachelor fireman's support of his widowed sister and her three children through twenty years. It can be appreciated in the psychiatric nurse's doggedly competent devotion to her ward patients through thirty years of seemingly small triumphs and large defeats.

C. THE SOURCE OF HUMAN INDEPENDENCE

It has taken us quite some time to define what we mean by the absolute and the relative, the independent and the dependent, in the human being and its activities, especially in love. The compenetration of these dual qualities in human activity and the reciprocity of their two originating principles in the human being (namely the limiting-restrictive essential structure and the expansive-assertive existence) make analysis of basic human reality so difficult that much time and energy had to be spent in finding and defining gradually the absolute and relative within the human being. But now we are ready to tackle a deeper problem: is human independence totally accounted for simply by the human act of existence or does this independence require an additional source to explain it satisfactorily? Would this additional source be simply the human environment or would it be another source deep within yet other than the human person, namely, the absolute beyond all chosen absolutes, the secular transcendent?

Human Independence Is More than the Human Act of Existence

There are several reasons for asserting that the human act of existence cannot adequately account for the absoluteness present in human activity, especially in other-centered loving. The first reason is this: if the human act of existence should totally cause the absoluteness or independence present in human activity, then the human person is Sartre's unloved and unloving being. For a person cannot perform absolute activity alone without setting up himself or herself as the absolute beyond all chosen absolutes. In so considering himself or herself, the lover is compelled to dominate the beloved all the way to enslavement since the lover cannot subordinate personal good to the beloved's good lest the lover lose personal ultimate absoluteness or independence. For unlike an infinite or already completely achieved God who does not need to enslave the other to achieve full selfhood, the finite person, if he or she is to be the ultimate or supreme absolute, must grow and must grow precisely by reciprocity of love. But within that reciprocity this person must constantly assert absolute domination, never allowing the self to receive anything from the beloved lest the latter dominate the self (if only for a moment) and thus destroy its supreme absoluteness, its very act of existence.

Because in Sartre's eyes the lover's very existing requires domination of the beloved, three results occur, each of which would make other-centered love impossible. First, the Sartrean lover can adapt to the beloved only insofar as the adaptation lures the beloved into subordinating self totally to the lover in every act of love with never even a suspicion of genuine assertion. Secondly, because of such clever manipulation, much of the Sartrean lover's attention of mind and heart must be placed on the self rather than on the beloved. Thirdly, in this way, the beloved's good is constantly kept subordinated to the good of the lover. Thus the Sartrean person's so-called love is always and only self-centered insofar as the latter's act of existence is the absolute beyond all chosen absolutes. The Sartrean lover consequently can never subordinate his or her existence to the good of the beloved in any act of love. Therefore, the Sartrean lover inevitably attempts to enslave the beloved for the lover's own self-centered expansion.[32]

It is also inevitable that the Sartrean lover cannot be dependently receptive of the beloved's independently free return of love. Thus the lover cannot encourage the beloved to give totally so that the beloved can discover in herself or himself depths of generosity and realms of richness hitherto hidden through disuse. Nor can the Sartrean lover experience his or her own trusting dependency in giving self to the beloved since this lover must demand inexorable returns from the investment of love. Otherwise, under the cover of this dependency, the lover's absoluteness is shamefully not recognized. The Sartrean lover dare not merely hope for return of love, leaving the beloved free to refuse; the lover must require commensurate return lest the lover's assertive existence or humanity be denied. Therefore if the Sartrean lover experiences a sovereign demand to subordinate the self dependently (with total trust) to the good of the beloved, this lover must interpret the demand as an urge demonstrating mankind's basic absurdity and then must resist the urge with the iron will of absolute existence. Consequently, in the Sartrean world of dominative love, there are only lovers, no beloveds. Reciprocal other-centered love has become impossible, absurd.

Second Step

This conclusion points to the second reason why a person's independence must include something more than his or her own act of existence; in human other-centered loving, the person discovers a willingness to lose the self, one's very existence, if the beloved should need this. Within this willingness the lover does not normally find enslavement but rather an exhilarating freedom and a sense of deep worthwhileness despite the suffering and tensions involved. This is the experience of heroism of everyday considerateness or heroism of extraordinary sacrifice for the beloved. But how is this possible? The contradiction of one's own existence should produce confusion, self-hate, emptiness, a sense of doomed future. For it seemingly involves

1. a denial of the basic instinct for survival in the sacrificing of one's life for the sake of the beloved,
2. a neglect of one's own personhood in the affirmation of the beloved's personhood, and
3. contradictory separation from the beloved in a supposedly unifying act of love.

To account for human readiness to lose the self and the beloved, something more than the human must support a person in this act and assure the latter that it is worthwhile. Otherwise, the normal reaction of joy in an other-centered love directed to self-sacrifice must be considered an abnormal reaction produced by delusion. But, then, how can the average familial or civic or religious life long perdure without its basis of strong joy in other-centered love? It is this readiness to sacrifice that is the basic life-giving energy of any vibrant civilization. The first symptom of cultural collapse is the spread of the disease of comfortable self-centeredness unwilling to serve the needs of others. Consequently, the preservation of civilizations and cultures requires that the lover act beyond his or her individual existence in time, that the lover be willing to sacrifice his or her own life for the beloved community's survival and enrichment.

A third reason for asserting that one's own existence cannot be the source of independence and absoluteness is this: within the seeming self-diminishment for the sake of the beloved, the lover experiences a sovereign demand for this heroism. The demand is neither a compulsion nor an unreasoning fear; it can be refused—at times, quickly and decisively. But it cannot be suppressed or

94

easily forgotten. Whatever name we give it—categorical imperative, expression of fidelity, hope beyond hope—this sovereign demand assures the person of deep loss if he or she habitually fails to honor it, and of personal growth amid apparent loss and of perduring worthwhileness if he or she does honor it.[33]

Cowardice—a Negative Analysis for the Sovereign Demand

There are those whose modesty would never allow them to admit to an heroic decision in their lives. Consequently a slight phenomenology of the cowardly decision may help them appreciate what this sovereign demand is in the heroic decision. Why? Because the same sovereign demand is present in both types of decisions albeit with a difference. In the heroic decision, it encourages; in the cowardly decision, it shames.

Most of us have had the experience at some time of backing down before the schoolyard bully, or of freezing in rigid fear at the poolside while a friend goes under, or of failing to speak out against a majority opinion at a crucial meeting, or of telling a lie under the threat of large financial loss. Each has experienced the sweaty palms, the accelerated heartbeat, the racing mind; then the sinking feeling as one capitulates; finally the unending seeking for excuses often furnished in abundance by sympathetic friends and the frequent imaginative replaying of the scene with, of course, a happy ending. The memory of the cowardly act is the hardest to change, to dull, to bury. It rises suddenly to haunt a man in the midst of his deepest joy—occasioned by a face or song or striking event.

But why the persistence of this memory? Why does the delicately balanced pyramid of excuses suddenly collapse? Why the sweaty palms, the sinking feeling, in the cowardly decision? Why the humiliating sense of being "less a man" or "less a woman" even before one makes the cowardly decision—and even more so after the decision? Could it be that at the moment of decision I had experienced in me the mysterious strength and serenity of that sovereign demand urging me on to the heroic decision? Could it be that I had acted directly against this assurance which called me to a fuller manhood or womanhood? What else could be the source of that forever-haunting shame in view of the fact that the heroic decision always demands that the hero go beyond the rational evidence for success, beyond the present situation into the future, beyond his own personal good to the larger good of the community? What could make such harrowing demands upon the ordinary individual unless it be such an assurance?

Anyone who has faced one's own cowardice will admit that the shame of this cowardly decision is not merely negative; it is rather the dark side of something very bright and beautiful which is challenging one to deeper loyalties and to fuller sensitivity to others' needs. It is so bright and beautiful in its demands for suffering and even for death that it can never quite be forgotten as it echoes and reechoes later in decision after decision. If after a cowardly decision one later succeeds in making an heroic decision, one will quickly recognize the haunting assurance of the previous cowardly decision now rising to encourage one towards the heroic decision. It is unmistakable. This assurance or sovereign demand may well be that factor of experience which is the last to be submerged in forgetfulness, ennui, or despair because it is the strongest and deepest call to greatness within the person. Its misuse, then, is self-betrayal as well as community betrayal, self-diminishment as well as community impoverishment, a denial of one's own capacity for greatness as well as connivance in the defeat of the community. The 'something more' that the coward could meet in the future, the 'something more' that he or she could be, are both refused—at least for the time being.

Here one meets mystery—something which reason can touch without being able to comprehend, something which calls and reassures the atheist in the act of other-centered love even as she or he denies the existence of all absolutes. Yet this sovereign demand would be slavery if it came from the beloved alone. On the other hand, it would be a manipulative domination of the beloved if it came from the lover alone (I'll die for you so that you are forced to love me.) This sovereign demand would also be assertive domination if it came solely from the lover since, to avoid delusion, it would require immediately supportive, unfree reciprocation from the beloved lest the love die of starvation. After all, reciprocity is the very nature of love.

Human Independence is More than Environmental Support

If a cause other than the human act of existence is needed to account for human independence, could one say that perhaps this other cause is the human environment? The argument would go as follows: if it is a true paradox that man's independence arises within his interior dependencies, why should not the surrounding world on which he exteriorly depends be the second and definitive source of his independence? Again, there are three reasons to deny the adequacy of this argument. First, if the surrounding world is said to be the second and definitive source of human independence, in addition to one's act of existence, and if this explanation is considered to be adequate and thus excludes need of any other third source, then the world is made the absolute. For if the world outside the person is the completing cause for human independence, then this world is the absolute beyond all chosen absolutes since without its influence one could never be independent in any way. Human reactions to the environment would be simply borrowed operations of the world since the human being, defined as the convergence of environmental pressures, would have no responsive actions other than those already received from the environment, the ultimate source of human independence.

However, is this not the world of Herbert Spencer where the human is seen as loveless and unloving since one is totally constituted by the sum of the environmental influences impinging upon the self? Would not so-called human independence be a delusion? There is no question that the environment contributes to human independence—one's freedom grows when the diet is adequate, when friends support one's ideas and endeavors, when education is informative and attractive, when events foster a career rather than disrupt it. But if the environment is made the ultimate or finally completing cause of human independence, then the world is that absolute beyond all absolutes which totally supports the chosen absolutes present in a person's life. Once the world outside the human being is declared the absolute beyond all absolutes, then a person is subordinated to that world unconditionally. One is its slave no matter how one squirms, no matter what neat explanation one gives for one's plight. For example, the Spencerian lover is not free to sacrifice the world for the beloved. Instead, the latter must be offered up for the sake of the world's progress.

Nor can the Spencerian lover allow complete freedom when the beloved is about to respond to the offer of love. For the most powerful environmental cause of the lover's independence is precisely this response of the beloved. Without the beloved's response, the lover's independence decreases. The Spencerian lover cannot risk the beloved's not responding. Contrarily, then, the lover's independence becomes dependence on the beloved. Thus the beloved becomes concretely the central factor in the absolute beyond all absolutes which is the world. At this point the lover's independence is not merely jeopardized but lost. For even if the Spencerian lover were to multiply the beloveds in simultaneous love-activity, this multiplication would not make this lover any less dependent on general response from all the beloveds, only less dependent on the particular response of one or other of them. Thus, one cannot set up the world as the completing cause of human independence without indirectly making this independence impossible. At this point the Spencerian lover becomes unloving because not free, and is unloved because the beloved is not allowed to be free to love or not to love. Without such liberty, the beloved's love becomes a loveless mechanical response.

A second reason why the world cannot be the ultimate cause of human independence is this: occasionally other-centered love · leads to the sacrifice of the whole world, life itself, for the beloved. This implies that within every other-centered love such a drive to sacrifice one's life may dwell, although it need not always be activated. Yet such a drive would be absurd, if the world is the absolute beyond all absolutes. How could a lover give up life or the world for the sake of a beloved who is a tiny part of the world? In giving up the world for the beloved, this love act would destroy, for the lover, the absolute beyond all absolutes (the world) in the name of that absolute. Is the human being constitutionally absurd, then, so that as a result one's highest act of love must be self-contradictory, self-erasing? Or, from our experience of living wholesomely, is the other alternative more likely, namely, that the drive to self-sacrifice for the beloved is not absurd but healthy and, therefore, there is an absolute beyond all absolutes which is other than the world and other than human existence and which guarantees the worthwhileness of such love?

The third reason for being dissatisfied with accepting the world as the absolute beyond all chosen absolutes is simply that within other-centered love a sovereign demand is found which is not under the control of either the lover and beloved or their world. If human existence is the ultimate source of this sovereign demand to subordinate one's good to that of the beloved, then the demand is suicidal. For, clearly, the lover's existence is calling for its own death or for, at least, its own diminishment of exercise. This it does without the slightest chance of recouping the loss. Even if death does not occur as a result of the lover's action, still the impairment of physical health or psychic energy, although temporary, is never recovered. A year is simply lost; opportunities never again reappear in the same way. This is the constant worldly lament so piercingly expressed in the poems of A. E. Houseman, the novels of Willa Cather, and the odes of Horace.

On the other hand, if the world outside the human being is the ultimate source of this sovereign demand, then how does a person escape its necessitating forces? Again, whether or not a person escapes, what guarantee of future worthwhileness can this world give him or her for this heroism? The heroic act is heroic precisely because the world in itself offers the hero or heroine such low probability of success. Is the hero or heroine not asked to mortgage or destroy his or her own future with little or no hope of enjoying the world that is lost? It would seem that neither the human act of existence nor the world's influence can guarantee the future result of its demand. Would this not say that neither human existence nor the world control this sovereign demand and that there must be a third factor behind the world and human existence? Would this third factor not be the absolute beyond all chosen absolutes?

For all these reasons, then, the absolute beyond all absolutes must be something more than the human act of existence and more than the world surrounding man. Yet if this absolute is to work through the world of chosen absolutes and if it is to cooperate within human existence and activity, then it must be immanent to the world and to the human person. If the lover's activity carries within it an independence capable of rejecting the world, and even God, out of love for the beloved, and if this activity can be absolute enough to risk losing even the beloved for the sake of the beloved's good, then the supportive absolute beyond all chosen absolutes must be present within the lover's act of existence out of which this activity issues. So needed is this support that, as Freud has noted, man will attempt to substitute for it his own projection or fictive goal. The Freudian psychologist, F. Sierksma, indeed, believes that the absolute beyond all absolutes is a human fiction.[34] But this is truly the counsel of despair. For if this absolute is simply a fiction, then it cannot support the person truly but can only lure him or her with its emptiness to attempt the impossible. This would leave a person without the possibility of loving the beloved, of building community, and of attaining personal wholesomeness in his or her decisions since only through the presence of the absolute beyond all chosen absolutes can the human being escape the alternatives of either lovelessly dominating the beloved or lovelessly being enslaved to the latter.[35] In other words, only conflict is possible since there is no final basis for unity among people. There is nothing real to lure them together finally and to strengthen their resolve to suffer for greater union with each other.

Consequently there must be an absolute beyond, yet supportive of, all chosen absolutes—an absolute present within the human act of existence yet other than it and other than the environment. But if this be the case, then the operations of this absolute within man's activity must be recognizable in that same activity. For though human activity arises from the human act of existence, it nevertheless rises through the support of this absolute within human existence. What characteristics within human activity, particularly within other-centered love, would reveal this supporting presence? If one cannot discern these characteristics, does this not lead us into delusion or into the state of being unable to distinguish delusions from genuine support of the absolute? It is hoped that these questions will be the beginning of a response when we take the following third step in order to approach, through our experiences of other-centered love, the unchosen absolute beyond all chosen absolutes, the secular transcendent.

THIRD STEP

How the Unchosen Absolute Is Present in the Human Act of Other-centered Love

B efore a person attempts to discover phenomenologically, within human experience, the absolute that lies beyond and yet within all chosen absolutes, one would do well to map the area where discovery could occur, namely, the area of other-centered love. A previous working definition in the introduction described this love as a trustful centering of the lover's life on the ultimate good of the beloved despite the lover's risk of self-diminishment. Actually this trustful centering is a subordination of the lover's life to the good of the beloved. It was also stated earlier that this love could be familial, friendly, romantic, sisterly, brotherly, parental, and so on.

But now, with the new insights of the second step, a more precise definition can be formulated out of the dialectic between the Sartrean and Spencerian person, and out of the analysis of the four levels of dependence and independence recently discovered in human being and experience. For the self-centered loves of Sartre and Spencer negatively highlight the reciprocity of dependent trust and of independent affirmation of liberty found in other-centered love. This mysterious reciprocity or inter-personalism not only unmistakably defines other-centered love but also starkly clarifies the need for an unconditioned (or unchosen and totally independent) absolute to initiate, support, and guarantee this inter-personalism.

A. Towards a More Precise Definition of Other-centered Love

The Reciprocity (Interpersonalism) of Dependent Trust

Because the Sartrean person can never allow personal interior liberty to be dependent on the other, he or she is incapable of the dependency called trust. For Sartre interior dependency is theoretically always a subhuman condition worthy only of animal pets and potted flowers. As a result the Sartrean person can offer the beloved only a substitute for love, namely, genial slavery or self-centered love. The latter is a state of continuing polite manipulation whose aim is domination of the other. It involves a careful violence since the lover must lure and trap the beloved first into an unreciprocated trust and secondly into a surrender of liberty. The lover has thus captured the personhood of the beloved so that the beloved is always and everywhere subservient to the lover's well-being without any return of dependent trust or freedom surrendered by the lover. This is the reciprocity of tamer and tamed, not interpersonalism. It is not what Sartre envisioned for his philosophic system; but it is what he implicitly derives from it; it does not describe the way Sartre lived, but it is what he describes in *Being and Nothingness*.

The experience of other-centered love is quite different. It contains the trusting dependence of both beloved and lover.[36] The beloved, in receiving the assertive devotion of the lover, adapts to the latter's understanding and loving intent. The very adaptation is a trusting dependence. On the other hand, the assertive lover also acts with trusting dependence upon the beloved's acceptance of the self-gift. For the lover's act of love is not some faceless or structureless universal function. It is an act rendered individual and rich in content not merely by the lover's dynamic personality focused upon the beloved but also by the lover's self-adaptation to the unique receiving personality of the beloved.

Thus, not only do the husband's childhood experience of parental affection, his later adolescent puppy loves, and his still later adult relations with women form and color his experience of loving his wife; but also her personality structure of motherhood, wifeliness, past sorrowful love-rejections, and present loneliness indicates to him how he can adapt his love to her present state. In fact, the subjective aspect of the husband's assertive act of love, as it issues from the center of his being, cannot even exist without this correlative aspect of his wife's changing personality. Thus his very adapting to her needs is an act of trusting dependence within his assertive advance since he extends himself to her according to her wishes in the hope of her accepting his adaptive advance. Her refusal would leave his act of love empty and his trust crumpled.

For this reason, trusting dependence on the part of both the giving lover and the receiving beloved is essential to the act of other-centered love. Such simultaneous and adaptive mutual trust not only enables other-centered love to exist but also distinguishes it totally from self-centered or domineering love. As we shall later see, this trust is, in both lover and beloved, a surrender of freedom which paradoxically results in the liberation of both.

The Reciprocity (Interpersonalism) of Independently Affirmed Liberty

If Sartre's loveless person negatively demonstrates the essential need for trusting dependency in other-centered love, Spencer's unloving person shows a second basic need: the independent supporting of the beloved's liberty by the lover's liberty. For example, if the lover husband offers himself to his beloved wife out of some unfree compulsion, such as his coercive fear of losing a neat housekeeper, firm custodian of children, and clever entertainer of business friends, then his lack of independent liberty diminishes his love and thus makes her free response to him more difficult. For she directly experiences his manipulative depreciation of her very being. Indeed, in this ever more vicious strife of daily family bargaining for position and influence, the loving mother's failing liberty allows an oppressively demanding environment to smother her love; that environment more and more dictates what will be the final content of the act once called love.

In a Pavlovian, stimulus-response atmosphere, the husband's failure to act with independent liberty not only degrades him with hypocrisy but is an attempt to manipulate his beloved wife like an unfree thing. Ideally, the husband should find that he grows in independent liberty as he helps his wife to expand her liberty. But actually he and his wife are locked in a wrestling hold, each trying to strangle the other's liberty through petty bickering over each other's respective rights—the mark of self-centered love.

On the other hand, the beloved wife must assert independence in the receiving of love since it is an active receiving and not simply a passive impression. Thus the beloved must have at least the ability, if not the intent, to refuse her lover's self-offering. Without this liberty, the beloved's reception is involuntary and fails to affirm the worth of the love and the lover, because only a freely chosen value is truly esteemed for itself. It is a common experience that each of us resists strenuously any attempt to coerce affection from us or to dictate who our friends will be. Indeed, the beloved who plays hard to get becomes more attractive because the pursuer feels so free in the pursuit.

But, in addition, the beloved's active receiving reveals further independence in its degree of adaptive inventiveness. For the beloved's receiving must be equally as adaptive as the lover's giving if the receiving of the love is not to become a stale routine. Both the lover and the beloved bring new experiences, hopes, fears, and risks to the latest moment of love exchange; they are different from yesterday. Therefore, it is only right that each should freshly adapt to the other's new face and not pretend that the other is unchanged and deserves merely the usual response. Alertness to each other's growth urges each to selectively invent a fresh response to the other.[37] If, instead of free inventiveness, the response of the beloved is marked by routine instinctual reaction to an environmental change such as a perfunctory kiss, a highly ritualized dinner, a begrudged visit, then the beloved displays little independent liberty in receiving the lover. The environment, not the beloved's liberty, clearly dictates the beloved's response.

This lack of independent liberty in the beloved makes the act of love less attractive to the lover and this lessens the latter's liberty. For just as the lover's liberty, in risking an advance towards the beloved, affirms the beloved's independent worth and calls forth depending trust from the beloved; likewise, the beloved's independent ability to refuse the love or to inventively adapt in the reception of love affirms the lover's independent worth and strengthens the latter's dependent trusting of the beloved. As a result, the lover's very liberty is enhanced. Here one notes the positive beauty of other-centered love in both lover and beloved.

This remarkable reciprocity of independent liberties in lover and beloved is ironically illustrated by its very absence when one observes the proverbial domineering husband with his clinging-vine wife or the obsequious, henpecked husband with his imperious wife. The failure to respect and to promote liberty in the other or in oneself gradually enslaves the less independent spouse and reduces the loveableness in both spouses. For the very act of love itself is slowly transformed into hate as its insistent demands narrow personal liberty in the overly dependent person and expand the domineering power in the other. The enslaved spouse bartered away liberty for a little peace and quiet; the domineering spouse has sold off the other's self-respect and trust in order to buy other things of less importance. The result is mutual degradation and contempt. In self-centered love a type of commercial reciprocity is substituted for the liberty-building reciprocity of other-centered love. Clearly than, the latter type of love demands simultaneous and reciprocal affirmation of a growing independent liberty between the lover and the beloved.

Amical Reciprocity or Interpersonalism

The instant and proportionate mutuality of dependent trust and of independent liberty in other-centered love shows that this act of love is essentially reciprocal.[38] This means two things:

1. in their loving, lover and beloved modify each other intrinsically; one of them cannot change without simultaneously and commensurately changing the other deep within;
2. consequently, such intimate cooperation is a single act, not two acts; not only can neither exist as lover or beloved without the other, but it is impossible for the act of other-centered love to occur between them unless each is simultaneously giving dependent trust to the other and simultaneously affirming the liberty of the other with independent freedom.

This rich reciprocity of other-centered love is the truth underlying the lover's declaration: I cannot exist without you.

Moreover, the reciprocity of dependent trust and that of independent affirmation of liberty do not occur at two different moments within the act of other-centered love but compenetrate and modify each other at the same moment. Thus, the trusting dependence of the beloved not only calls forth from the lover a matching dependence of trust but also builds the lover's sense of self-worth which is radically the latter's independent liberty. On the other hand, the independent liberty of the lover, expressed in freely choosing the beloved to be the world center, not only affirms and builds the beloved's sense of self-worth or independent liberty but also strengthens the latter's depending trust in the lover.

In stark contrast to this, the self-centered love of the psychological Sartrean man is filled with a distrustful fear of being utterly dominated (not liberated) by the beloved and is animated by a profound contempt (not respect) for the beloved's liberty in the desire to control the other through careful manipulation. This can elicit only distrust and contempt from the beloved in such a way that the beloved, like the lover, must scheme to cripple the other's liberty in order to keep self-respect. Likewise, at the opposite extreme, the Spencerian sociological lover cannot recognize liberty in the self, cannot assert it for self, cannot recognize and build it in the other, the beloved. Thus there is no ground for respect or trust of either self or the other. At best the sociological person is condemned to complete, irremediable self-centeredness.

Clearly, other-centered love is characterized negatively as non-dominative. Positively, it is a single indivisible cooperative act in which mutually trusting dependence and mutually respected and affirmed independent liberty evoke and build each other in lover and beloved. The fact that this love is other-centered excludes any self-centered moment and yet assures indirectly that the self grow strong, balanced, and deeply self-aware. This interpersonalism we can observe in more detail as we further develop our definition of other-centered love by using the previous study of the four levels of human development in which the absolute (the independent) and the relative (the dependent) compenetrate to produce the single indivisible act of other-centered love.

Other-centered Reciprocity in the Beloved's Dependence

The literature of interpersonalism constantly stresses other-centeredness—and rightfully so, because other-centeredness is at the heart of interpersonal intimacy. However, if one is to avoid merely mouthing redundant terms, one must describe other-centeredness in concrete detail and thus define other-centered love more completely. Let us then proceed to reconsider dependent trust and independent affirmation of liberty, using our previous analysis of the physical, psychological, moral, and metaphysical levels of human existence.

Within other-centered love, the other-centeredness of dependent trust is radically the beloved's total acceptance of the lover. This total acceptance is not solely the fact that the beloved's response includes all four levels of his or her operational being. It is also the fact that this response is perduringly faithful, intelligent, expansive, liberating, wholesome, and self-sacrificing. Each of these six characteristics should therefore be explored since they define other-centered love in contrast to self-centered or dominative love. (Later, too, they will turn out to be the phenomena useful for possibly discovering that absolute beyond all chosen absolutes, namely, the unchosen absolute.)

But for the moment let us note that the beloved's total acceptance of the lover is possible only if the beloved totally accepts the fact that he or she is being held in existence physically, psychologically, and morally by the traditional community of the past and by the contemporaneous community of the present moment. In other words, the beloved is tempted to say: All that I am I have received from others. To put it metaphysically, I am a relational substance; I live and grow within the restrictive limits of my received essence. To put it metaphorically, "no man is an island." For each person is at least the integral sum of a unique genetic heritage, a unique historico-psychological genesis, and a unique moral tradition of values received through the family community.

As a consequence, insofar as the beloved is integrated deeply within the community, he or she will be filled with a deep gratitude. For the beloved's bodily health arises out of the community's genetic past and contemporary ecology; the beloved's confident soundness of mind and of heart in the face of contemporary problems is due to an ample education in the community's tradition; and the beloved's wholesome value system is derived from rich community living, insofar as the latter is found relevant to the contemporary scene and to the community's future destiny. Gratefulness for these mutually enriching gifts of life enables the beloved to trust deeply the members of his or her community.

A. Towards a More Precise Definition of Other-centered Love

Thus the beloved is readied to accept the lover's advance wholeheartedly, and to subordinate life and being to the lover trustingly. For the latter uniquely represents and focuses upon the beloved all this goodness of the community. The beloved's gratefulness to the community is now centered on the lover—with new warmth and knowledge.

A quick warning should be interpolated here: throughout this book for the sake of clarity, we always sketch a fully achieved other-centered love. Obviously only the rare human is capable of constantly other-centered love. For most of us it is an uphill and downhill progress with spells of self-centered love intervening. Indeed, even when a person's love is other-centered, it has varying degrees of quality, intensity, and endurance since one's degree of health, clarity of insight, balance of emotions, and felt pressures of external circumstances fluctuate. But to get a clear picture, one must take other-centered love at its purest intensity, highest quality, and greatest endurability during a person's life-experience. In doing this, we now observe, one by one, the six characteristic phenomena of other-centered love which were mentioned earlier. This will now enable us to define other-centered love more precisely and more concretely. Then later we can test this love and its six phenomena for the supportive presence of the absolute beyond all other absolutes. We begin by observing how these six characteristics are found in the beloved's *dependent* acceptance of the lover's advance. Later we will observe these same characteristics in the lover's *independent* total self-gift.

1. Perduring Faithfulness

The beloved's total acceptance of the lover, amid gratefulness to the community for physical, psychological, moral and metaphysical existence, is characterized by perduring faithfulness. For in contrast to self-centered love, the beloved's acceptance is not directed to some outside event nor bent on some personal acquisition from the lover. Instead it is focused on the lover's self-gift, which may or may not be symbolized in some event like a family picnic or in a personal acquisition like an expensive anniversary gift.

Now, the person of the lover is the most perduring, as well as the most mysteriously rich, of all realities. Because this person can grow indefinitely in understanding, imagination, love, and sensitivity, the beloved discovers a 'forever' quality in the love relationship together with a cumulative quality. Healthy friendship is always promising a fuller future of indefinite length with ever growing intimacy, joy, and satisfaction, no matter what future events may bring—even though fulfillment of this promise often leaves something more to be desired.

Thus faithfulness forever is based on hope—a hope rendered solid by all the past loyalties between lover and beloved and by the way each uniquely embodies within the self all that is traditionally beautiful, true, and good in their community. Such could be the relationship between grandfather and granddaughter, between mother and daughter, and between long-time friends from high school days.

2. Trustful Intelligence

The beloved's grateful and trusting acceptance of the lover is based on a deep appreciation of how the latter embodies the community's genetic-ecological providence, its education for contemporary living, and its presently relevant value tradition. As a result, the beloved's total acceptance should be highly intelligent in its trustfulness. Otherwise the beloved would never be able to appropriate these rich gifts of the community into his or her personality with proper gratefulness. This trusting intelligence shows itself within the total acceptance when the beloved's reception of the lover is not routinely stale but inventively fresh with pleasing surprise and unexpectedly fitting response. The beloved child who experiences in its parents' affection the richly intelligent tradition of Bavarian or Japanese family life, to name only two, becomes the adult who confidently receives the lover with supple warmth and inventiveness.

3. Expansiveness

When the total acceptance of the beloved is intelligently trustful and perduringly cumulative, it tends to become expansive toward others than the lover. A person who has been loved deeply and has responded commensurately to this love over a length of time develops the ability not merely to receive love well but also to attract the love of others. Such a person has an assurance, a trusting warmth, an alertness, an understanding receptivity for the need of others to love. Every hospital has a nurse whom patients admire and love more for her willingness to accept their affection than for her thoughtful service to them. This receptivity invites love without promising anything in return except the beloved's unselfcentered attention and trustful respect for the lover. The irresistibility of such attraction multiplies loves seemingly without effort; yet, as we shall see, such generosity implies deep sacrifice in the beloved.

Nor does the multiplication of loves diminish the original love in which the beloved first learned to receive love trustingly and graciously. Rather, it enhances this root love. The young grandmother who returns home very tired from six-hours' work at an inner city day-care center for children nevertheless has new youth in her affectionate, trusting response to her husband and a fresh expansiveness of embrace in receiving the affection of her daughter's four children.

4. Liberation

This expansive total acceptance within the beloved's other-centered love has a liberating effect on both the lover and the beloved. The beloved's grateful receiving of affection gives confidence to the lover's self-estimate of personal loveableness and affectivity. No doubt one strong reason for the engaged man's ecstatic life is that he has discovered his manliness in the new-found confidence that he can love deeply, perseveringly, and totally. He owes this conviction to the beloved fiancée's reception of his love. Such confidence releases new energy for his architectural work, for giving economic advice to a naive secretary, for being more patient with his dyspeptic father, and for listening to his younger sister's piano practice. He is more free to grasp opportunities for helping others, to give affection and attention without making demands for return. He has been rendered generous by the beloved's total trusting acceptance of his love. Her dependence strengthened his independence.

But this liberation also occurs within the beloved. For the lover's free decision trustingly to risk the total self-gift upon the beloved is the most breathtaking compliment to the beloved's person. It is a centering of all the lover's being and powers upon the beloved in complete self-forgetfulness. Such total gifting lures the beloved into a trustful total acceptance. And suddenly the beloved cannot help but become aware of inner gifts hidden within the self. When the orphaned child, sent from home to the home of distant relatives, finally settles for good within an affectionate and serenely trusting family, she discovers within herself unsuspected gifts: she can laugh and make others laugh; she becomes eager to achieve in school, wants to mother kittens, listens eagerly to her foster mother describe her Alaskan childhood, trusts in the friendship of two sixth-grade classmates, and soulfully adores her older foster-brother, the hunter and the star fullback who nevertheless occasionally plays checkers with her. The lover family has liberated the beloved child's inner powers so that she can receive life's opportunities gratefully and totally. They have enabled her to grow into the liberty of full womanhood.

5. Wholesome Healing

From this it is evident that such liberation heals and expands the person of both lover and beloved. This is the wholesome process: the building of the whole person by the whole community forming around such a person. The orphaned child, maimed by inattention, is healed and then expanded to mature wholesomeness by a family's other-centered love for her. Later, when at twenty-one years of age she accepts the love of a neighbor boy, the wholesomeness of her total acceptance elicits from him a wholesome love so that they form a wholesome family. This last remark is meant more realistically than may be suspected since wholesome or total acceptance includes the bad as well as the good. Her acceptance, then, includes the facts that the neighbor boy is not ambitious, that his father is miserly, that her future husband works the night shift in an automobile assembly plant noted for wildcat strikes, that her desire for a college education is matched only by his craving for TV entertainment, that her Anglican faith somewhat conflicts with his Pentecostal interest.

But her total acceptance also includes the positive aspects of her lover which are valued realistically insofar as they are contrasted and partially explained by the previously listed bad points. For some of his lack of ambition is due to his prizing friendship so highly; and his father's miserliness has challenged the young man to generosity with friends. His working the night shift enables him to spend time coaching basketball at the local elementary school; and his deep attachment to Pentecostal faith experience has made him more sensitive to the inner life of the spirit and less interested in cheap entertainment. The beloved's total acceptance, then, includes a wholesomely balanced view of the self, of the lover, of the family situation, and hence of life itself.

6. Self-sacrifice

Such realism takes for granted that sacrifice is necessary if the love experience is going to heal the participants into whole selves and to form a wholesome family life. Thus the liberating effect of other-centered love, which makes the wholing process possible, is energized by the discipline of continual self-sacrifice, the heart of other-centered reciprocity. For example, in the case above, the young man may have to change to day-shift work and give up basketball coaching if his wife needs more of his companionship. She, in turn, may have to put her college ambitions in cold storage for twenty years as she raises a family. Both will have to respect the other's faith difference and not attempt to coerce the other into a new religious alliance which would be more a hostile truce than a conversion. Here, again, total acceptance is terribly realistic in its wholesomeness and in its other-centeredness. For implicit to this self-sacrifice is the unspoken and ironic agreement that the partner is willing, if necessary, to suffer physical and psychological diminishment and even death for the vital wholesomeness of the other. No more costly or total gift is possible, no greater other-centeredness will ever occur.

At this point it should be clear that the total acceptance of other-centered love requires the gift of the beloved's total being at all four levels. Such a love would be mocked by its own being if it were not perduringly faithful, intelligent, expansive, liberating, wholesome, and ultimately self-sacrificing. Indeed this trusting dependence basic to total acceptance is so gracious in the beloved and so beautiful to the lover that anything less would be tragic for them.

A glance at self-centered or dominative love reemphasizes this conclusion. For self-centered love cannot be perduringly faithful; it must be pragmatic if the beloved is to measure acceptance of the lover by what can be secured from the arrangement. Dominative love must be more cunning than intelligent, if the beloved, holding back a full self-gift, is to maneuver the lover into the full gifting of self. Indeed, self-centered love must narrow such gifting exclusively to the jealous beloved. Further, the maneuvering must be such as to trap the lover playfully into a 'forever' commitment so that the latter is more enthralled than liberated. Once the lover recognizes this genial imprisonment, he or she feels diminished and less whole. The resultant resentment tends to shrivel the love and to isolate the lover from the beloved so that their relationship becomes more divisive than wholesome. Self-sacrifice, then becomes pragmatic, or conditional on the other's equal response. The consequent narrowing of reciprocation tends to induce other-sacrificing instead of self-sacrificing, a complete reversal of what may have begun as an other-centered relationship. Thus, other-centeredness, taken as the beloved's total acceptance of the lover in dependent trust, is directly opposed to self-centered or dominative love.

However, in noting that dependent trust is the basis for the beloved's total acceptance of the lover, one should make it clear that this dependence arises out of the beloved's independent liberty to affirm or not to affirm the supreme worth of the lover's self-gift. The beloved's acceptance must be free if it would liberate the lover, if it would be an intelligent act of self-sacrifice, if it would form a perduringly constant whole of the lover, the beloved, and their relationship. For when the beloved freely chooses to accept the lover totally and when the beloved then freely adapts to the lover's advance, the lover experiences the beloved's full approval of the self-gift. This approving evaluation of the lover's total person gives the lover confidence to love the beloved ever more deeply and to commence to love others. The lover is also educated to new sensitivity by the beloved's fresh adaptation to this self-gift.

None of this, however, can happen unless the beloved has the independent liberty to refuse all acceptance and to adapt freely the acceptance given. For the beloved's response is not appreciative unless free and inventive. This is to say that the depending trust of the beloved is not trust unless it springs out of the beloved's independent liberty to give or not to give trust, to give it this way and not that way. The total acceptance of the beloved, then, is never managed or coerced; it is either freely done or not done at all. In this way, the beloved's trustful dependence on the lover is radically independent and the beloved's independence enables the latter freely to subordinate his or her life to that of the lover. This paradox is matched only by the parallel paradox describing how the lover's independently free self-gift to the beloved is a deeply dependent act of love. This latter paradox is the other-centered reciprocity within the lover's independent liberty. Let us now consider this remarkably mysterious reciprocity within the lover.

Other-centered Reciprocity in the Lover's Independence

The total acceptance of the beloved must be matched by the total giving of the lover if there is to be the other-centered reciprocity of other-centered love. The total acceptance and giving mutually define what other-centeredness is in concrete detail. In their correlativeness they describe interpersonalism. Hence, discussion of the lover's independence (the independent affirmation of the beloved's liberty in a total giving) will again underline the six characteristics of other-centered love but from a different standpoint with new details.

First, the lover can, with independent liberty, make a total self-gift to the beloved only insofar as the lover recognizes his or her own personal dependence, namely, the fact that the lover is held in existence physically, psychologically, morally and metaphysically by the community. Then the lover can assert self-independence knowingly, respectfully, and strongly. For one cannot adapt physically to one's genetic past and ecological present, nor psychologically to one's education in past and contemporary culture, nor morally to the clash of traditional and contemporary values, nor metaphysically to one's own individual and social development until one knows and respects each of these four experiential levels of dependency which constitute the self. This is the case because adaptation, the mark of man's free independence, is a reorganization of these four levels of dependence into a newly integrated totality.

Thus the lover must first realize that he or she is a relational substance, that is, a being constituted by relations to every other being of the universe. With this self-knowledge, the lover can then commence to be a substantial relation, a being able to grow beyond all these constituting relationships by freely fashioning its own self and its own future in a unique manner never before achieved and never again to be duplicated. The lover must know well his or her constituents before reassembling them according to a free inventiveness and then offering this new totality, the whole person, to the beloved for acceptance. Otherwise, the lover's conversion is weak, halting, and ineffectual.

To put this metaphysically, the lover must first see himself or herself as an essence restricted by the genetic-environmental given. Only then can the lover recognize the self gift as also an assertive existence called to expand beyond this given and to advance into the future by risking that future in total self-gift to the beloved. It is the dependent-relational in lover and beloved which makes their love a single reciprocal act; but it is the independent-substantial in them which makes it possible for their love to be perduringly faithful, intelligently inventive, generously liberating, healingly wholesome, and generously self-sacrificing. The relational makes their love operational; the substantial renders it a friendship forever. The dependence of total acceptance arises out of the more relational, restrictive essence; while the independence of total giving issues out of the more substantial, assertive existence.

Nevertheless the lover's existential independence, his or her free adaptation at all four levels of being, arises in union with an essential dependence on the community at these four levels since the lover's essence and existence form a single indivisible person. For this reason, the self-gift offered to the beloved essentially represents the whole community of family or neighborhood or nation. And yet, because the lover has freely and inventively adapted these levels into a unique totality, the self-gift is existentially fresh and non-duplicatable. It is truly personal.

This gift leaves out nothing of one's being. It is really a total gift insofar as the lover has succeeded in developing:

1. the body through inventive diet, exercise, play, and work so that it expresses adequately the inner life of the spirit, i.e., one's intelligence and moral worth;

2. the spirit through education, discipline, and sacrifice so that it expresses well the lover's unique destiny or call;
3. the act of existence through self-possession and self-assertion so that, in practical service of the community, it expresses more or less completely the needs and hopes of the community as well as the lover's devotion to the chosen absolute, the beloved (and perhaps to the unchosen absolute within this chosen absolute).

Thus the lover has a total self-gift to make if, because of free and inventive, physical and psychological development, the lover has been able occasionally to stand alone beyond the community and its tradition in order to assert the community's true destiny by his or her love. Like Moses, the lover must so intelligently and courageously love the community that he or she can suffer the latter's attacks in order to lead this community toward a better life. This generosity characteristic of the lover's total giving is meant to match the gratefulness of the beloved's total acceptance. The totality of the lover's person is given, according to all four levels of being, to be accepted with the matching totality of the beloved's person. This self-gift exhibits the following six characteristics of independence (just as previously the beloved's total acceptance of the self-gift demonstrated these same characteristics—an expected parallel because love is basically reciprocal).

1. Perduring Faithfulness

When one wishes to make a total self-gift, one must be willing to risk all that one is with the beloved. Yet the lover cannot give the self all at once, but only by degrees through time, since many acts of love would be necessary to reveal the riches of person previously bestowed on the lover by the community. In addition, these serial acts of love must be adapted to the developing capacity of the beloved. Further, unless the lover commits physical or psychological suicide, he or she never stops growing and never stops being able to give something new in the self to the beloved.

An accumulation of these giftings occurs because the human being is constantly organizing and reorganizing its experiences so that a unified personality is developing. In the area of love, this accumulation is called friendship; while in other areas it may be called knowledge or virtue or skill or imaginative set. Therefore, the

119

more generous the total giving of the lover, the more indefinitely long is its perdurance through time. This is why lovers speak of their love lasting forever—even beyond the grave. Since all else but the lover and the beloved disappears or changes on either side of the grave, the foreverness of love must be person-centered. Here is the test for the perduring fidelity of other-centered love.

2. Trustful Intelligence

Because of the cumulative quality of friendship, intelligent gifting is required of the lover; else, the giving may be destructive of the beloved. The overindulgent parent can render the child confused and resentful by showing it too much affection or by asking an affection from it beyond its ability. The very richness of the lover's gift demands that this wealth be adapted to the needs of the beloved for growth rather than to the needs of the lover for self-expression. This is the othercenteredness of intelligent love. But this is also trusting since it is convinced that all this intelligent adapting will be appreciated and accepted by the beloved.

Because the lover's self-gift represents all that the self has derived from the community and has inventively developed in itself by service of that community, the lover must reexpress this gift for the beloved's own unique needs. Thus the lover must be inventively adaptive; this requires intelligent assessment of the beloved's needs, hopes and values—an assessment by which the lover will learn more about self and community. For such inventory of the situation implies intelligent reevaluation of all that the lover has received from the community and integrated into self as a gift for the beloved. Then comes the trusting offer of this intelligently presented and valued self-gift. Here is the greatest of all risks.

Thus the total self-gift is not only endlessly instructive for the lover and the beloved; it is also unsparingly other-centered in its intelligent intent precisely because this totalness must be uniquely adapted to the particular needs of the beloved. At the same time, the lover must ask of self the terrible questions: will the beloved be aware of the lover's pains to suit the gift to the beloved's needs and hopes? Will the beloved value these pains in his or her response to the lover? The lover confidently says yes, and this is the lover's trust.

3. Expansiveness

The independent freedom with which the lover endlessly and intelligently gifts the beloved initiates the love relationship. It takes intelligence to recognize if and when the beloved is ready for the gift of the lover; it takes intelligent courage to initiate the gift and to follow through over an indefinite period of time, to make it a 'forever' gift; it takes intelligent trust to gamble beyond previous experience into future acts; it takes intelligent freedom to make the gift truly a gift and not a compulsion. But all this is precisely the expansive quality contained in other-centered love: the intelligent and free willingness to risk future rejection or betrayal in order to form community.

Such bold and generous initiative gives confidence to the beloved so that the latter's total acceptance becomes possible. The resultant total acceptance not only supports the initiative of the lover's independent freedom but also provokes and enriches the lover so that the latter is willing later to initiate other loves for the children, for business associates, for in-laws, and for leisure companions. Because this total giving is an unconditional offering of the self and therefore a non-manipulative action, its quality of communal expansiveness does not rest primarily on shared business interests or on common leisure pursuits or on dependency relationships the instability of which would constantly undermine the expansions of other-centered love. Therefore, so long as the given and received 'selves' exist, the expansion can continue to operate and to offer the basis for additional expansion despite business failures and changed interests. Here deep trust surfaces again in these later relationships stemming out of the original love for the beloved. If nothing succeeds like success, let it also be noted that the knack for making friends is nothing less than previous perduring friendships.

4. Liberation

Now the expansiveness of total giving has a strong liberating effect on the other-centered lover. For liberty, first seen only in its operational effect of freedom (the ability to choose among options), is later discovered to be substantially the well-balanced human personality. Because a person has developed sufficient knowledge to situate the self well, sufficient discipline to suffer long for a desired good, sufficient virtue to be fair-prudent-temperate-courageous, and sufficient vision to love the community dearly, he or she is free enough to consistently make good decisions for self and community. Thus the person's liberty is his or her fully developed person.

For these reasons, the intelligent total giving which requires that the lover inventively assimilate the community's intellectual and cultural riches so that they may be focused on the beloved, is itself a process of building liberty within the lover. This is especially true when this gifting demands a selfless adapting to the beloved's needs over many years and through not a few troubles. The loving parents who are raising a beloved retarded child in difficult cooperation with other such parents understand this well. Consequently, generosity is a distinguishing characteristic of total giving and gratefulness is a distinctive mark of total acceptance. Their abundance reveals why other-centered love is capable of such great expansion. It is as though the lover's self-gift—as when Christ miraculously multiplied the loaves and fishes—not only expands other people's lives but also builds the lover's own personal liberty.

Surprisingly, this liberation also occurs in the beloved whose total acceptance embraces all the communal riches offered by the lover's intent. If the loving father is a musician, the beloved daughter learns to make the beauty of music a part of her person; if he has deep respect for his wife, the daughter breathes this affectionate attitude into her personality; if he works hard to improve the neighborhood, her social consciousness becomes alert and tenacious for building a friendly community. But this liberation will not occur unless the beloved daughter is so dependently trustful of her loving father that her cooperation with him is centered on his person more than on the ephemeral results of their cooperation such as more freedom to date boys or to go to the college of her choice. So, too, his independent total giving to the beloved daughter must be primarily for her sake. It must be other-centered and nonpragmatic; that is, it cannot have conditions on what the lover intends to receive back from the beloved (such as more attention for the father) or from the situation (such as a more dedicated attitude on the part of the daughter toward her collegiate studies).

5. Wholesome Healing

The perduring, intelligent, and expansive liberation in the lover's total giving naturally produces a wholesomeness in lover and beloved. The totalness of the lover's giving according to all four levels of being (physical, psychological, moral, and metaphysical) guarantees a total or wholesome development of the lover. Insofar as the lover must integrate all the cumulative riches of his or her personality in order to focus them on the beloved, a new wholesomeness occurs in this lover: a new, vividly aware self-possession.

Every lover has experienced this oneness with the whole world and with the self which issues out of total giving. The missionary who gives up her American citizenship to symbolize her total dedication to the beloved Indian people of the Bihar village where her dispensary is situated, now sees the riches and poverty of both American and Indian culture with a fresh poignancy. Although she is married to this particular village, she has become a citizen of the world. Though she will always be living with her inborn American bias towards family neatness and efficiency, she nevertheless is more sharply aware of the more personal Indian family values. Her love for the village people leads her to go deeper than physical healing to the repair of mind and heart, to the strengthening of marriages, and to the building of the local political peace— but always through the holistic focus of her medical skill lest she become more meddler than healer. In this way her own growing wholesomeness causes communal wholesomeness all around her; while the more wholesome community, in turn, contributes to her wholesome independent liberty with its newly found powers of friendly communication and cooperation with the foreigner in its midst.

6. Self-sacrifice

However, the missionary has risked no little by her total giving to the beloved villagers. After cutting the roots of her American heritage, she may find it difficult to send down roots into the Indian village; or a sudden gust of anti-Americanism may rip up the tender roots. Indeed, her attempts to build strong marriage ties or to improve local government may be interpreted as foreign meddling. Ironically, her dispensary could be destroyed by an act attempting to symbolize liberation from foreign oppression. Perhaps with even sharper irony, the death of her own self is required for the full symbolism of this liberation. If her independent total giving with its full awareness of the consequences is not other-centered, what act is?

This illustrates how dependently trustful must be the independent liberty of the other-centered love. In other words, the missionary lover's independent affirmation that her beloved village enjoy the liberty either to refuse a total acceptance or to make this acceptance in the beloved's own way, requires a deep trust of the beloved. The missionary's total dedication to the beloved Indian village people will be perduringly faithful, intelligent, expansive, liberating, wholesome, and self-sacrificing in proportion as it arises within her dependent trust of these people. Just as the beloved village people's dependently total acceptance arises out of independent freedom; so, too, the lover's independent liberty to give herself totally arises out of her dependent trust in the beloved Indian village people.

Interior and Exterior Reciprocity

Through this analysis of the beloved's total acceptance and of the lover's total giving, one gradually becomes aware that a double reciprocity occurs here.[39] Between lover and beloved there is a more exterior reciprocity; within each of them a more interior reciprocity exists. Not only does the independence of the lover reciprocally evoke the dependence of the beloved and vice versa; but also the independence and dependence inside either the lover or the beloved mutually modify each other. The more exterior reciprocity of the love between the lover and the beloved sets in motion an interior reciprocity of dependent trust and independent liberty within each. In response to the more exterior reciprocity, the interior reciprocity acts out and increases or diminishes the more exterior reciprocity of love. This interaction between interior and exterior reciprocity explains many of the paradoxes of other-centered love:

1. the more daringly independent the lover becomes in a total self-gift, the more deeply dependent the lover is upon trust of the beloved and upon the beloved's total acceptance;

A. Towards a More Precise Definition of Other-centered Love

2. the more the beloved dependently trusts in the lover, the more independently free the beloved becomes in total acceptance of the lover;

3. the lover must retain free independence when giving it away in trust, that is, when identifying his or her future and all his or her powers with the beloved's future;

4. the beloved must declare dependence upon the lover through the independence of freely choosing to accept total dependence upon the lover for existence;

5. the deeper the relationship of friendship between lover and beloved, in sorrow and joy amid failure and success, the more they depend on each other; and yet the security of this friendship is a towering liberty, a solid independence, since both experience a stronger sense of self-worth and greater confidence in the ability to love well;

6. the beloved's dependent total acceptance enables the lover's independent total giving; and yet this dependent trust offered by the beloved is valuable only insofar as it arises out of the beloved's independent freedom; and the lover's independent total giving is valuable only if the lover dependently trusts the beloved enough to allow the latter freedom to refuse or to modify this total giving.

Much of our attention has naturally been given to the more exterior reciprocity of the love act. But at this point, one should note the principles of the more interior reciprocity operative within the person of the lover or the beloved. The restrictive essence of each is the living dependence expressing itself in trusting total acceptance; while the assertive existence of each is the living independence expressing itself in the free and total giving of self. Because essence and existence are distinct, though never separate, constituents of the single indivisible being, a persons's trusting dependence and free independence mutually modify each other within the person's very being and then express themselves simultaneously and mutually in the person's act of love as it issues from his or her being. Therefore, this indivisible act of love can be at once dependent and independent, trustful and free, receiving and giving. For a person's love is at once absolute and relative.

Third Step

In this way does human interior reciprocity between essence and existence, between dependence and independence, cause the more exterior reciprocity of the love act. Consequently, the latter's six basic characteristics of perduring faithfulness amid constant change, of trustful intelligence amid human error, of expansiveness amid continual threat of restriction, of liberation amid opportunities for enslavement, of wholesomeness amid divisive tendencies, and of self-sacrifice amid self-centered domination of others, each reveal the independent structure present not only in the more exterior reciprocity of the love act but also in each person's deepest interior reciprocity. Here in each beloved or in each lover existence is the radical source of independence in dialectic with the dependent essence.

By the same account, the dependent quality of trusting exterior reciprocity in the love act reveals the similar quality of dependent essence in the lover's or the beloved's more interior reciprocity. Somehow, the beauty of this trust—despite man's inconstancy, prejudiced ignorance, smallness of heart, jealousy, fragmentation of person, and manipulation of others—shines through both the exterior reciprocity of the love act and the more interior reciprocity of man's very being. In other words, the exterior reciprocity exposes the interior reciprocity which founds it; and in both, amid all the murk of human weakness, there can shine out the six basic characteristics of other-centered love.[40] In fact, the absolute appears as independent freedom in both lover and beloved even when misused to dominate others; the relative, appearing as dependent trust in both, is observable even when misused to manipulate others. The very ugliness of their perversion calls attention to the beauty of these six characteristics of other-centered love. This affords us hope of discovering the absolute beyond all chosen absolutes, the secular transcendent that may well give existence to these characteristics within man and his love.

B. Towards a Phenomenological Discovery of the Absolute beyond All Absolutes

The detailed definition of other-centered love just now achieved gives us a rather precise map of human love-experience; its particular areas of interest to us are the six defining characteristics of other-centered love. The question we face is this: can one love with other-centered love merely by one's own powers of existence or does one need the assistance of some influence within, yet beyond, the self? To put this same question another way: can one's love bear the heavy burdens of absolute independence or liberty without the support of an absolute present within oneself but distinct in being from oneself? That is, can a person love with perduring fidelity, intelligence, expansiveness, liberation, wholesomeness, and self-sacrifice without the interior assistance of an unchosen absolute beyond all absolutes?[41]

Let us first look at this question from the factual data provided by a phenomenological approach. Such data can later be further inspected when demonstrative analysis is used to show why the data are such as they are.

Suspicion of the Underived Absolute in Our Experience

Already the almost overwhelming aspect of man's relativity, his dependence on the world for breath of life and breadth of vision, makes us think of him as totally encompassed by the world: almost a prisoner. A complete worldling. Yet against this Spencerian interpretation of person, there surges a person's own independence, the Sartrean ability to take control of oneself, one's world, and one's community. In the midst of his total relativity, a person finds himself or herself feeling and doing the absolute in commanding freedom.[42] Yet a person, described as the moderate realist, also feels a basic dependence, wonders whether he or she is deluded, and then sometimes suspects that he or she is being supported in his or her absoluteness by some mysterious reality in the world and self but other than the world and self.

Besides the mysterious interior reciprocity of his dependent independence, a person also notes within the self a compenetration of the relational and the substantial, of the essence restrictively defining the self and of the existence asserting it beyond this definition. But in other-centered love this assertive existential drive in the person is strangely not dominative, but rather serving, of the beloved. Though the person's assertive existence is quite capable of being self-serving, it still finds within the self the desire to sacrifice its being for the beloved's good. It is as though the person's assertive, potentially domineering drive is being modified by something other than the beloved, the world, and the self so that the other-centered love liberates, rather than manipulates, the beloved and the world. It is this mysterious other for whose existence we now search within our experience of other-centered love.

1. Perduring Fidelity and 'Foreverness' in Other-centered Love

Our songs and poetry are never tired of protesting eternal love for the beloved. Nor is this eternity merely a 'certain indefiniteness'. Friendship is not indefinitely immortal; it is hopeful of definite companionship beyond the grave when the lovers will at long last be able to devote all their time to each other. In self-centered love, the lover sets self-protective and self-promotive limits: "till we tire of each other," "till the zip has gone out," "till I want my freedom again." But even the self-centered Lothario or Scarlett O'Hara is loath to say "I'll love you for exactly ten hours or ten days or ten months or ten years." This would be too definite and reveal too clearly the ultimate self-centeredness of the love. No, the self-centered lover would prefer to keep it indefinite if only to escape having to live out the promise of ten hours or ten days. Consequently, in other-centered love where there is no ultimately pragmatic "give or you can't take" disguised with vague indefiniteness, the promise of love comes out clearly as 'forever'.[43]

It is not merely a definite eternity which indicates the presence of other-centered love. The mode of the gifting and the type of gifts offered also reveal the other-centeredness. The constancy of mere duty appears almost contractual, and may at times be the mark of self-centered love since such constancy may look greedily towards return, may even demand a quick return on its investment. Fidelity, however, the desire to keep on giving without demanding return, though hoping for and expectant of the return of love, points to other-centered love. The faithful lover continues to give without setting limits—except the needs of the beloved, the scope of the lover's resources, and the commonweal of the community. Within those three limits the lover promotes liberty—a fuller and more balanced development of the personality—in the beloved. Thus the lover offers whatever contributes to the complete development of the beloved's person: education, companionship, financial support, the discipline of suffering and hard work, affection, hope, challenging anger at the beloved's foolishness, and so on. Within the above three limits, other-centered love is a definite unlimited giving—not an indefinitely vague giving which disguises limiting conditions and temporariness. In other-centered love not only is the gift 'forever' in time; it is also all that will develop the beloved's person and all that the lover can muster.

The drive of the lover to promise the beloved fidelity going far beyond the grave can be measured negatively by the profound hurt felt in the lover who has been cast off or betrayed by the beloved. The betrayed one must literally fight for vital meaning, so empty and useless does life appear. Suicide seems preferable to life without the beloved. Only another love will rescue this person from depression. And it cannot be a mocking substitute for love but must be a comparably deep and true love—one whose 'foreverness' blots out the temporariness of the lost love.

The power of the attraction to promise a 'forever' fidelity can also be calibrated by its fearsomeness, its shrewdness, and its freedom. The proverbial groom, awaiting the wedding service as nervously as a cat stepping on tacks, and the proverbial bride suddenly depressed at the obligations assumed in the previous day's wedding, are examples of how fearsome is this attraction to fidelity. The attraction, discovered in the romance and feared deeply in the moment of truth, is not a projected desire which can be flicked off like dandruff from the shoulder. It is a beautiful and harsh fact of life.

Nor is this attraction in itself a favorite diversion for the unwise. The living of a 'forever' fidelity requires shrewdness much more than foolishness. The shallow person finds the depth of love required for 'forever' fidelity both terrifying and hopelessly complex when it occurs at hospitals, angry confrontations, morning-after breakfasts, grinding bouts with overdrawn checking accounts, and unnecessary misunderstandings with in-laws. The deeper person, who is willing to face these harsher events along with the happier ones of discovering new reasons to love the beloved, finds his or her intelligence taxed far more than at the business office or in the classroom. At the very moment when wondering whether fidelity is worth the trouble, the lover may be learning to appreciate the beloved at a greater depth and then later may be discovering that the attraction of fidelity is stronger than ever—even though its new depth means added burdens and new mystery.

Thus the bored wife may puzzle over her freedom to forget the beloved husband, may even try to forget him with some other attractive person, then may freely turn away from this plaything and back to the one who makes the foreverness of fidelity seem both possible and beautiful. Interruption of the fidelity serves only to heighten its continuity, the temporariness of the distracting love points to the foreverness of the true love, her fickle forgetfulness towards the beloved reminds the bored wife of his unforgettable value, the very freedom of turning from the beloved brings the wife back to him with a sweet compulsiveness—if the love is truly other-centered. The sufferings of fidelity make it no easy self-projection; it is too exasperating and too beautiful a reality for that.

But what is this strange attractiveness towards the beloved? What attracts the loving mother towards her beloved daughter? Certainly, it is the indefinitely growing mystery of the latter's person, the 'more' of the beloved. As the beloved grows in wisdom and grace as well as age, there are new depths to discover which surprise even the beloved daughter herself: the ability to sympathize with the weak, to paint, to become a mother, to find fresh humor in old situations, to cook Polish dishes, to take an interest in stocks and bonds, to relax with fishing, to take on a hundred other newnesses which still do not add up to the beloved's mysterious self. Is the beloved's developing existence enough to account for the loving mother's attraction to 'forever' fidelity?

In answering this crucial question recall that our previous investigation (pp. 17–19) revealed how the chosen absolute, such as career, or supremacy of self, or the idolized beloved, is always present in every person's daily life. There is always a supreme value by which all other values are measured, to which all other values cede and around which life is centrally organized. But it is a value which, because it is freely taken up, can also be freely dropped. Can such a chosen absolute be the ultimate source of the attraction in a 'forever' fidelity? No one would wish to deny that a chosen absolute is powerfully attractive, especially when it is freely chosen after years of search. But the problem is this: does the chosen absolute achieve its attractiveness through the prior and more powerful attractiveness of another being—an absolute being which empowers all chosen absolutes yet which is distinct from them and underived from them?

There are two elements in the experience of absolutes which lead one to affirm the existence of such an underived and unchosen absolute:

1. the felt temporariness of any chosen absolute in contrast with the felt need to give eternal fidelity in other-centered love;
2. the felt freedom to move among candidates for the chosen absolute without choosing any of them, the freedom to wait for the appearance of the envisioned chosen absolute, and the freedom actually to choose one and reject other such absolutes.

Certainly, in these days of second and third careers, of multiple marriages, of cynical patriotism, of professional people rendered obsolete by hurriedly developing sciences and technology, and of instant popularity followed by instant oblivion on stage and in political arena, the absolute chosen by a man or woman is hardly worthy in itself of a 'forever' commitment. For its temporariness seems to grow ever shorter. Besides, the lover feels less and less capable of guaranteeing fidelity for tomorrow, much less for some day ten years ahead. Yet despite man's deepening sense of his own weakness and of the potential decay in any chosen absolute, he still feels the need to promise and to strive with all his strength to give 'forever' fidelity. The more people witness foundering marriages and broken promises, the more precious the pledge of 'forever' is to their ears, and the more desperately each searches for a partner to whom each can say 'forever.'

Yet all the while, in addition to personal experience, psychology and sociology warn the lover how limited and weak are one's endeavors to give eternal commitment, no matter how worthy be the beloved and how mysteriously deep grows the beloved's person. The mysterious 'more' of the beloved is felt to be too temporary and too limited compared with the felt 'forever' of the commitment. Therefore, the 'forever', though far from denying the attraction of the beloved, though even taking its beginning from this attraction, and though always happening through the beloved, nevertheless reaches beyond the beloved to a mysterious 'more' totally worthy of the 'forever', always beckoning the lover on, always being more than the lover can encompass or comprehend, and never failing the lover. In contrast to this, the beloved is destined to corrupt physically, to break down psychologically, to be open for final betrayal, and seemingly to lose existence.

This subtle attraction, operating through, yet beyond, the beloved, becomes more evident when one reflects on the experience of establishing a chosen absolute in one's life. The unfree child has an instinctive absolute, its own immediate pleasure-life. But there comes a time when an alternative chosen absolute looms before the adolescent for free choice: a medical career, an easy sex-life on the local campus, the one-in-a-lifetime boy, traveling the world with insatiable curiosity, or celibate dedication to relieving the poor people's sufferings. At that moment, as the adolescent swings between these chosen absolutes, he or she is held suspended by a mysterious attraction to choose one of the options over the others.

Within this attraction pulses the strange intimation that no one of these absolutes binds the person irretrievably to itself but that nevertheless the absoluteness of each requires a total gift implying a 'forever' commitment. For how can a chosen absolute be the supreme value without demanding that a person's every decision submit to it and that its pursuit be 'forever'? Anything less than 'forever' immediately submits this supposedly supreme value to that value which will eventually take its place—unless there is a value lying beyond every chosen absolute and yet operating through all such absolutes in order to free the person so that he or she not only can move among absolutes to choose one over the others but also even patiently wait for that one to appear. This absolute beyond all other absolutes could demand total giving forever since it is always there to meet all the needs of the lover in all the lover's chosen absolutes.

Among the avid seekers of this unchosen absolute, one meets the perpetual wanderer, the ever-questioning and ever-testing cynic, the grail-questing knight, the untiring social reformer, the always dissatisfied saint, and the atheistic fighter for lost causes. They seem to have a more direct experience of the underived and unchosen absolute supposedly well hidden in the chosen absolutes with which other people seem quite satisfied. So sharp is this experience that these strange ones can never find deep satisfaction in the chosen absolutes. This makes their deeply creative lives appear quite unsuccessful and unworldly to us less gifted people. But, on second thought, what else could demand 'forever' commitment of these men and women and support its life-long attraction in them except an absolute beyond all those chosen absolutes which they find so inadequate to their hunger?

2. Intelligent Self-trust of Other-centered Love

The 'forever' fidelity of other-centered love might rightfully be questionable if it were not accompanied by such intelligent self-trust and self-donation. In other-centered love, it may be recalled, the lover appropriates the riches of the community and integrates them uniquely in order to intelligently offer them in the lover's own person to the beloved. But what if the beloved does not accept this gift or fails to respond with love? What if, through an inculpable misunderstanding, the lover must endure even the hate of the beloved? How can the lover unilaterally offer the self-gift if the act of love is essentially reciprocal and if, when other-centered, it is a simultaneous total giving and total accepting? How can the interior reciprocity of the lover's very being continue to work towards the beloved when the more exterior reciprocity of the lover's actions cannot feed the interior?

Yet as a matter of fact, so-called 'unrequited love' is common. Somehow a deep hope in the beloved's eventual return of love operates within the interior reciprocity of the lover so that it does not die. But, again, what is the source of this strong hope? Is it merely and always a delusive or fond hope without real basis? Certainly, the beloved whose response is presently more destructive than constructive is no solid source for this hope. The beloved may have remarkable capacities of understanding, affection, virtue, intelligence, or what you will, but now they are all turned away from the lover though in some distant future they may be turned towards the lover. Now they are reasons for a lover's despair rather than hope.

Nor can the lover be the source of the hope felt within the lover's deepest being. For it is a hope more thrust upon the lover than carefully seeded and nurtured. Indeed, the lover would prefer to escape the agony of unrequited love in the temporary peace of solitude or in an acceptance by someone who would appreciate the self-gift now. The lover is fearful too. When the beloved does accept the love, will it prove to be too small for the beloved's expectancy which has been rendered great by appreciation of the lover's long patience? The shrewd and balanced lover cannot afford to pump up false deluding hope.

Nor can the world which the lover is ready to sacrifice for the beloved be the source of this hope since that world is less valuable to the lover than the beloved. Indeed, the beloved would be the center of any world and the source of its value. Besides, a hope issuing from simply the community surrounding the beloved would not take into account the beloved's freedom to stand opposed to this community. Such a hope might be coercion rather than liberating support of the beloved.

This strange perseverance of intelligent self-trust amid strong reasons for distrust reveals that the interior reciprocity of other-centered love can be constant despite the failure of almost all exterior reciprocity. The fact that a lover can continue to give other-centered love to a beloved who presently hates the lover, even though neither the beloved, nor the world, nor the lover is the source for this strengthening hope, is an indication of the presence of an absolute beyond all chosen absolutes. For nothing else, certainly no chosen absolute, supports this dynamic hope. Yet the lover's self-trust continues.

This conclusion is confirmed by the experience of the woman who continues to give love to an alcoholic husband though he grows less and less able to return that love; or by the experience of the husband who continues to give full love to a shallow wife though he knows that very likely she will never recognize the extent of the riches lavished on her and therefore can reply to him only with small and fitful giftings of herself. How is it possible for this weak, more exterior reciprocity to feed and support the rich interior reciprocity of the deeply loving partner? Yet the strong lover feels within herself or himself a kind of sovereign call to continue to give this love to the weak one lest the latter die from lack of love. Under these adverse conditions, intelligent self-trust does not diminish but grows.

For the neurotic masochist who is happy only in the role of family martyr, or for the sentimentalist who cannot hurt anyone even to help the latter, or for the individual propelled by fear of what the neighbors will say, this sovereign call is probably a compulsion. But for the intelligent person whose sufferings with the beloved have wiped out sentimentality, who could not care less about the neighbors or about domestic martyrdom, this sovereign call is something else. Besides, this call is not a momentary demand—rather, it sounds continuously through the day-to-day grind of family living towards 'forever'. Further, it generates a self-trust which accumulates responsibilities, for example when the mother must substitute for the alcoholic father in fulfilling the ever more complex needs of growing children. This call summons the lover beyond the constancy expected from a dutiful wife. It leads her toward the special fidelity of a loving spouse. If ever other-centeredness is in love, it is here.

The source of this sovereign call cannot be the beloved; the alcoholic husband, in despair of himself may well have told his wife to forget him. Besides, his loveableness diminishes as his mind reels giddily off course, as his emotions gust in all directions, and as his self-pity flaps loudly with the wind of unending excuses for inexcusable conduct. Yet there is the hard fact that, despite all the fierce tuggings in other directions, this long-suffering wife feels deeply the stabilizing conviction that she should continue to support her beloved with love. Likewise, the husband who lives with a shallow, fickle wife experiences the same hard fact, the same conviction. This is the self-trust of other-centered love.

What is particularly disconcerting about the long-suffering wife is that she dreads giving pity to the beloved and hates herself for any condescension. Pity, the kindness given to the unfortunate who are not intimates, and condescension, the attitude of bestowing attentions upon those whom we consider to be below us, are hardly the characteristics of other-centered love between peers. The loving wife has certainly experienced the drift towards pity and condescension. But a cold and farsighted intelligence combined with a strong and warm heart reveals these dangerous shoals and strengthens her to steer a hard course down the mainstream of love.

There is in this lover, however, a constant wondering about this sovereign call, and about the destination to which it seems to be bringing her. Yet amid the wonder and seemingly against the laws of psychology, she finds self-trust growing within her despite the growing distrust she feels from the beloved. In such intelligence, more than instinct is operative, more than community pressure, more than any past attractiveness of the spouse, more than the children's ever lessening affection for their father. Who or what could give such support and make such demands upon this lover except an absolute which is beyond all other absolutes yet works through them to support the demands for perduring self-trust in a total self-donation?

3. The Steady Expansiveness of Other-centered Love

Within human experience, the mystery of 'forever' fidelity powered by the attraction of self-donation and the further mystery of intelligent self-trust founded in deep hope and sovereign call can both be rediscovered strangely united to the steady expansiveness of other-centered love. This statement takes on meaning as we note the following problems and facts.

If other-centered love is essentially reciprocal, how can it ever come into existence unless both lover and beloved simultaneously give and receive totally? But this is against our experience of the uneven starts, hesitations, exuberances, falterings and slow-downs of love. First, from where does the lover get the courage to begin loving when as yet the beloved is incapable of responding? And yet someone must begin this reciprocal process of love. Secondly, if the lover begins, from where does he or she draw the stamina to continue to love, to persist in this seemingly non-reciprocal relation while awaiting the beloved's response? A mother, for example, may wait fifteen to thirty years before a child has matured sufficiently to offer her a return of other-centered love. A family doctor, or a 'Mr. Chips' professor or a genial senator from Arkansas may wait just as long for a favorite patient or a student or a political assistant to recognize the elder's depth of devotion and to reply with an other-centered love. How can the interior reciprocity of other-centered love begin or, once begun, continue without the stimulation of the more exterior reciprocity of acts of love? Indeed, the latter seemingly cannot happen without a simultaneous response from the beloved.

Yet the strongest desire in man or woman is to elicit the beloved's love, to commence the reciprocity, even though the lover may well know that a response may take years to well up in the beloved. Such eliciting of love is the basic creative act that begins and knits tightly the family, town, and nation. Without the endless patience of this love and without its readiness to accept tragic disaster, lovers' lives become safely robot-like. And yet how can this risky creative act start out and continue without proportionate response from the beloved since other-centered love cannot exist without being reciprocal?

Here we must clarify the nature of this desire to elicit the beloved's response, to teach the beloved the meaning of the act of love. It is not the Pygmalion drive to change the other into one's own image of beauty. Rather, it is the other-centered desire to watch the beloved grow in knowledge, virtue, and emotional resonance so that he or she becomes capable of supporting more and more people with other-centered love. In the lover's eyes, the only pleasure that rivals the reception of the beloved's total self-gift is the delight of seeing the beloved admired and loved by others. This delight arises not merely because others confirm the lover's estimate of the beloved's personal worth, but also because the lover witnesses a splendid flowering of the beloved's worth and a resultant building of community around the lover and the beloved. The birthday party at which friends gather is so much fun because it celebrates and promotes this community's beauty and the splendor of the beloved person at its center.

No one would deny that this desire to elicit the other's love can become slightly rancid when the supposed lover attempts to make the beloved overly dependent, or tries to jealously limit the beloved's freedom to support others with friendship, or decides to decree that the beloved must accept the lover totally. Here the lover's drive to domineer is subtly taking over the relationship only to smother the beloved's creativity and liberty. But this perversion of the desire to lead the beloved towards a mature response serves to emphasize the true dynamics of this desire. The true desire to elicit the beloved's other-centered response gambles unselfcenteredly with the unknown since at the beginning the lover risks misunderstanding, rejection, and cruel manipulation at the hands of an immature beloved. In addition, the long wait for the beloved to mature may be rewarded with only a weak response. Yet the more generous the lover, the more ready he or she is to risk. This readiness is the expansive quality of other-centered love.

But, again, is it not against the very nature of love, against its essential reciprocity, to speak of eliciting the other's love since there is no reciprocity here but simply a one-way flow of giving or, at best, a lopsided reciprocity? Can the interior reciprocity within the lover survive without feeding upon the more exterior reciprocity of acts of love? Here it is necessary to distinguish the fact from its explanation. As a matter of fact, mothers, fathers, teachers, doctors, counselors, social workers, and politicians, to name some, do begin and do patiently teach or elicit other-centered love—not by calling attention to what they are doing but simply by doing it.

Given the hard fact, we must now work towards an explanation of it which will not deny its existence. But first there is a second hard fact to face: other-centered love cannot exist unless it is reciprocal. Reciprocity is the very nature of this love because reciprocity is the very nature of man, the lover. Man is dependent or relational in his essence although he is also independent and substantial in his existence. Love, the most human act, cannot escape its relational dependence any more than it can shrug off its substantial independence.

These two facts make it clear that, unless the lover is achieving reciprocity despite the beloved's failure to respond, no other-centered love can exist. Unless the lover receives a rich reciprocity despite the beloved's poor response, other-centered love could rarely last. Then from where does this anticipatory reciprocity and its anticipatory richness come? If it were merely the projection of the lover's well-founded or ill-founded hopes, it would be a destructive delusion of the lover. For example, how often has not the parents' playing of favorites among the children produced disastrous results? The loving mother or father, judging a particular child to be specially gifted for response, pours out special attention upon the beloved child in the hope of future response. This self-initiated hope of the loving father or mother is more than a delusion about a future which will never be. On their part it is both a pretending that the child has already responded and a consequent giving of total devotion which is supposed to match the pretended response. The immaturity of the child can manipulate this situation only to harm both the child and the parents.

Nor can the anticipatory reciprocity and richness of this yet unrequited love come from the community since the latter would then be an ersatz substitute for the beloved.[44] The return of love from the husband and from the other children cannot be substituted for the particular child's inability or failure to respond to its mother's love. Again, this would be merely the projection of a future dream upon the child with the result that the child could not be seen and valued for itself. It would teach projection, not love. In addition, it would not explain to us how the widow with three children under ten years of age can nevertheless love her children other-centeredly. Somehow this widow is 'teaching' her children to love in an other-centered way seemingly without the possibility of reciprocation from them. Yet reciprocation must go on and must have a certain richness if the widow is to carry through for another twenty years until the children learn to love other-centeredly. Her assurance of the worthwhileness of her life and her perduring courage could only come from a deeply reciprocal relationship other than that of the nonfamilial community and of her children.

The possible chosen absolutes of her life, such as a career as a bank officer by which she supports her family, the desire of finding a partner to help her raise the family, the hope of one day being appreciated by her children, are all basically irrelevant to her actual here-and-now reciprocation with the young children. If her career is a chosen absolute, then her children become subordinated to the career so that other-centered love for them becomes more difficult if not impossible. If the desire to find a partner suitable for raising her children becomes a chosen absolute, then either the partner is self-centeredly envisioned as a convenient shoulder for carrying her responsibilities or he is being loved for himself and then is not connected directly with the reciprocal love for the children. If the distant hope of one day being appreciated by her children is the basis for the reciprocation, it is simply a projection of the possible future upon the children. This is at best a distracting delusion, at worst a cloying demand for recognition of sacrifice which reduces the beloved children's freedom of response and naturally provokes their resentment.

The widow's sense of a strength far beyond the love returned by her children, her conviction of the worthwhileness hidden in so lonely a twenty-year enterprise, her strong refusal to enter a second marriage of mere convenience, her ability to elicit from her children other-centered love seemingly without the experience of other-centered love in her relationship with them—all these experiential phenomena converge to indicate the immanent presence of an absolute beyond all the chosen absolutes. What else could bring about this anticipatory strength and then ask that it be used with the assurance of its present and ultimate worthwhileness?

The presence of this underived and unchosen absolute is also demanded by the experiential phenomena found when other-centered love multiplies itself to form a community. A couple at their golden wedding party may look reflectively at their children and grandchildren and wonder how they ever managed to survive those fifty fruitful years with all their heartaches, their constantly multiplying obligations and tensions, their successes and failures at loving, teaching, and learning.

When first they married, the grandmother and grandfather could not know how many or how few loves would spring out of their own. Yet this original love, being other-centered, felt that it had the strength to support other loves and so allowed children to be born. This original love, insofar as it was intelligent, knew that it had left itself open and vulnerable to all the loves which these children would have in their wives, husbands, children, friends, and in-laws. For other-centered love is not afraid of being expanded to give birth to an indefinite number of other loves. In fact, other-centered love of its very nature sets only these two limits:

1. the original love must not be diminished by neglect,
2. the physical, psychological, and moral powers of the original love must not be unnecessarily damaged—though seeming diminishment of life must be accepted in the total giving of other-centered love if protection of the beloved requires this.

B. Towards a Phenomenological Discovery of the Absolute

But from what source do the lovers receive this assuring strength whereby, within the original love, the lovers anticipate, accept, and carry the multiplication of other-centered loves and their attendant burdens? Here again, one meets the need for an other-centered reciprocation which long precedes the ability of beloveds to reciprocate. And now the anticipated reciprocation is multiple and cumulative. The grandfather and grandmother have found in their love the strength to bear patiently not only the immaturity of their own children but also that of their children's friends and of their children's children. This is the expansive quality of other-centered love which cannot be explained by vague projections into the future nor by substitutional projections. For the strengthening reciprocation must be felt now, not later, and directly from the immature beloveds, not indirectly from someone outside the immediate community. For the burdens are especially heavy now when the beloveds are immature and very demanding; and any attempt to employ substitutions for other-centered love is to prolong and perhaps to preclude the development of other-centered love in the beloveds.

Such unlimited reciprocation needed now, not later, would seem to require an immanent, underived, and unchosen absolute beyond all chosen absolutes whose activity in the lover through the beloveds is the anticipatory reciprocation sustaining the lover. Otherwise one cannot explain the following phenomena of an expansive other-centered love:

1. the strong desire to take the risk of beginning a new love,
2. the courage to support the long years of waiting for the beloved's response,
3. the strength to allow and then to support the indefinitely expanding number of love relationships when a community builds up out of the original love.

Indeed, unless there is a sustaining anticipatory reciprocation from and with the underived and unchosen absolute, one cannot explain a fourth phenomenon: that the quality of the original love is raised rather than lowered by the increased responsibilities of the multiple loves springing from this original love. The grandmother and grandfather surveying their brood on that fiftieth wedding anniversary have not found their radical love depleted by its

141

branchings among the children and grandchildren. For their radical love was expanded and deepened when they were constantly drawing upon it for strength to support the new loves amid suffering, sorrow, and fatigue.

In saying this, one does not deny the evident danger of over-extension: a doctor may become so emotionally involved with his patients that he finds little time for his original family love; a senator may find that her entertaining and friendships with many political allies leave her no longer in need of her husband's affection and attention. But such overexpansion demonstrates the need for intelligent limits to the natural expansiveness of other-centered love, shows the power of this drive, indicates its occupational hazards, and thus does not deny but affirms the existence of this basic quality of other-centered love. All the more remarkable, then, is the steady improvement of the grandparents' original love when it branches into the many loves of their children. This phenomenon of expansive steadiness shows the strength of the anticipatory reciprocation offered by the underived and unchosen absolute; it also points to the previous two characteristic phenomena of other-centered love:

1. the 'forever' fidelity discovered in the steady expansion of other-centered love,
2. the intelligent self-trust needed to risk the incipient love relationship or to gamble with accepting the sovereign call to support the immature beloved (now multiplied in children and grandchildren).

All three characteristic phenomena converge in this mystery of other-centered love.

4. The Discipline of Liberation in Other-centered Love

Perhaps one of the last phenomena recognized in the experience of other-centered love is the discipline of liberation, because it works within and behind the previously discovered characteristic phenomena of foreverness, deep self-trust and hope, sovereign call, strengthening courage, and readiness for steady expansion of loves. This discipline of liberation is experienced as the lure of the 'more'. It is forever promising a future more than the present. It hints at a future love for the beloved more intense than ever and at a future community of loves far more beautiful and deep than is presently possible. Somehow this 'more' will occur within the lover (since love is an essentially reciprocal act) but also outside the lover (since other-centered love is always directed to the other).

This experience of the 'more' is most evident when the lover discovers within the self the willingness to risk the self in total gift to the beloved. The lover wants the beloved to grow in beauty, to be 'more' the goodness which the beloved already is; wants the beloved to be more physically attractive, more intelligent, more joyful, more imaginative, more generous; wants all this even before the beloved is able to accept totally the self-gift. Suddenly, the lover is aware that, although hoping fiercely for a total response from the beloved, the lover will do nothing to require or demand it. For the beloved must be left totally free to grow or not to grow into this response. The lover discovers that his own or her own freedom will be as large as the freedom allowed to the beloved. Insofar as the lover lets the self be free to pour the riches of its life into the beloved's life and insofar as the lover is able to allow the beloved freedom to reject or accept these riches poorly or well, the lover is undergoing the discipline of liberation. This can bring much agony into the lover's life.

Not only is the beloved liberated, the lover is too. Both can experience growth in self-confidence, in knowledge, in temperate control of their drives, in willingness to sacrifice for others, in hope for their community, and in inventive warmth of imagination because each, but especially the lover, lets the other grow uniquely. All of this, when integrated, constitutes the personal liberty of lover and beloved. But this involves the ultimate risk: to let the beloved be free enough to easily reject the lover. How can one sweat through this risk without some sort of assurance? Yet the lover cannot give this assurance to himself or herself, else why the sweaty feeling of terrible risk? Nor, on the other hand, can the beloved give this assurance, for the beloved's freedom happens to be the reason why the lover sweats it out in risk. Nor can the community give this assurance unless it decides to take away the beloved's freedom. From where comes the assurance if not from the 'more' of beloved and lover, that is, from their growing liberty, if not from the 'more' of the community, that is, from its potential, not yet actualized, for new friendships? Is it possible that the 'more' which causes the assurance of the lover must, nevertheless, be beyond all of these chosen absolutes even though operative through them?

The strength of such assurance, in the experience of the 'more', is even better measured when the lover's willingness to risk is stretched to the extreme of accepting the actual loss of the beloved through physical or psychological separation, on the supposition that the separation will let the beloved grow in liberty and thus will let the beloved become the fully developed person first envisioned by the lover. The woman who supports her beloved's entrance into the celibate life of monk or priest knows the excruciating pain of total separation; she also can experience the magnificent assurance of the future 'more'. For her the discipline of liberation is an agony based on a strength as unexpectedly deep as the pain—perhaps deeper. In another instance, a husband who sees his cancer-ridden wife losing the struggle for life knows this assurance as he prays for her quick death out of the love which simultaneously cries out for her continued life. But how can one account for such willingness to let the other be free at the risk of ultimate loss—unless there be a supporting 'more' beyond physical or psychological death, beyond this helpless community of the present moment, and beyond this apparently disintegrating chosen absolute of the beloved? Would this 'more' be experience of support from the unchosen absolute?

5. Imperturbable Serenity: the Wholesomeness of Other-centered Love

The willingness to risk everything for the beloved's liberty or healthy growth as a person is always accompanied by agony—even when the beloved finally responds totally. The suffering is, of course, worse when the beloved uses the freedom granted to separate from the lover for the sake of another person. Such hurt amid the discipline of liberation would seem to deny any healing or wholesomeness to the other-centered love so sacrificed. But as a matter of fact, there sometimes occurs within the lover a mysterious deep-down healing and wholesomeness which is manifested by the phenomenon of imperturbable serenity.

What is this great peace? It would seem to be, first, the lover's recognition that any action other than that of freeing the beloved would have attacked both the beloved's person and the lover's integrity. There would have been less liberty in both even if the lover had succeeded in manipulating the beloved to live out their life together. The manipulation would have set the scene for later domineering behind the curtain of apparently other-centered love—the ultimate hypocrisy.

Secondly, this serenity would seem to be the lover's new awareness of the depth to which other-centered love has permeated the lover's life, a new sense of the liberty to love others graciously as the future unfolds.

Thirdly, it would seem to be a deep assurance that such future loves certainly await this lover. For without such an assurance, the lover might find the future merely empty. If this were the case, then the lover's integrity and new-found ability to love deeply would be a mockery of the lover as the born loser. On such terms, suicide is not unappealing and has been the choice of not a few such losers. But from where could come the assurance of future beloveds, especially to men or women in their sixties?—unless from the 'more' which is luring men and women into the future and promising them a community such as the present community and circumstances could never promise assuredly without appearing to mock human loneliness and weakness. Within the serenity of the losing lover, there is an absolute promise of the 'more' which is more than the present community and more than the present moment of this world.

To see, however, the fuller meaning of this serenity, one must pass on from the dramatic limit case of lost love to the more positive instances of fulfilled other-centered love. Deep within a person is the instinct to live on beyond death in the books one writes, the business concerns one founds, the great historical events one generates, the governments one heads, and the children one begets. To achieve this immortality of living on in the minds and hearts of others, one will sacrifice no little of one's life. Allied with this instinct is a person's desire to exeriorize his or her inner life in dazzling poetry, skirmishing armies, towering skyscrapers, rocketing speedboats, precise ballets, brilliant graduate students, and exuberant sporting life. A person needs to reveal the self to others in order to discover what is deepest within this self. Even God is often accused of fulfilling this desire for himself in his creation of the world.

But working through these two basic drives of a person is a third element in one's experience of other-centered love: the dynamic peace of wholesomeness. So often peace is pictured as unruffled waters; so rarely as roiling waves harmonically and quietly molding chaotic bits into a single living whole. Only great power like that in a huge, humming turbine or in a deeply swelling sea can afford to be imperturbably serene. Such is the person's act of assertive existence wrapped in the limitations of restrictive essence. A person, while exteriorizing his or her inner life so that he or she will live on in the minds of the following generations, also experiences the altruistic desire to make the community's life better through contributions to it. A person wants to pass on all his or her accumulated riches to the beloved and to the community surrounding the latter so that they may live more fully, that is, with more liberty and with a deeper sense of personhood.

With this in mind, the doctor may build and staff a clinic for the poor; a fashion designer may strive to dot the streets, stores, homes with dashing clothes of vibrant colors; an architect may try to fill the city with beautiful buildings; a professor may found a university; a composer may attempt to swell the world's heart with the sound of joyful symphonies; a mother may work to charm the hearts of her children and of her husband into forming a family of intelligent concern for each other. There is, then, within each person's imperturbable serenity, the creative desire and power to pass on to the beloved and to the beloved's community a fullness and a wholesomeness that was not previously there.

Remarkable in the lover's desire to increase communal wholesomeness is a twofold readiness:

1. to contribute to a community which will outlive the lover and whose fullness, therefore, the lover may never enjoy,
2. to cut short one's life in order to make that contribution.

The government official who knowingly works eighteen-hour days despite a weak heart so that her agricultural reforms will save her beloved Third-World nation from famine is not merely building her community but is willingly shortening her life to do it. Her self-depletion is meant to complete her country, to make it more wholesome. Deep within, her care for those whom she may soon leave behind by her death is paradoxically building her wholesome womanliness precisely through her seeming depletion.

But how could she fragment her own life in order to break the bread of life for her beloved people unless the imperturbable serenity, with which she gambles away her life day by day, assures her that her sacrifice will bring more wholesomeness into the nation? The future 'more' of this community must somehow be present right now in her sense of imperturbable serenity as she faces imminent death. But who or what could so make this future 'more' present to her?

Such experience of dynamic peace occurs not only in the person sacrificing the physical world for the community's future wholesomeness but also in the person offering up a psychological world for the beloved's future communal wholeness. Take the instance of a fifty-five year old electrical engineer who has spent thirty-two years laboriously building up a small electronics firms. He has centered his life around it so that almost all his friendships are with his business associates, much of his leisure is given to reflection on new developments within the company, all his future plans for himself (including just partial retirement at seventy years of age) are tied into the firm's future, and even his two sons have woven their careers and families into the company's life. Then suddenly his wife has a nervous breakdown, needs his constant attention, must be taken to an Arizona sanitorium two thousand miles from his business. The engineer must now recenter his psychological world in order to take care of his wife. He must turn his back upon the electronic business world, let it sink out of sight, if he is to heal his wife to wholesomeness.

From where does such a man receive the imperturbable serenity, the dynamic peace of powerful resolve to give his full attention to his wife—without bitterness, without future recriminations, without hope of rebuilding his psychological world of electronic business? A Sartre or a Nietzsche would be tempted to say that such a person creates this peace out of his own selfhood; Spencer or Marx would see this person as inevitably determined to leave his electronic world by a peace totally given to him by communal world events; others would see this serenity as partially from the support of his community and partially from the 'more' beyond

147

self and world. This third group of world interpreters could not see the engineer giving up his psychological existence solely by his own Sartrean decree. For he would be dismantling his own self in forgetting his psychological world—this would be suicidal shattering of peace. Nor can it be said that solely the determinism of world communal events pulls down and then erects a new peace within this engineer. For, if the agony of deciding to leave his business world for his wife's sake means anything, it means that he did not have to take up this option but that he could have freely allowed his wife to try to patch up her own life by herself in some expensive sanitorium—the more expensive, the less guilt to be felt by leaving her alone in her struggle.

However, the realistic picture is that partially the support of his two sons and their families, partially his own love for his wife, and partially an interior strength of imperturbable serenity about the rightness of his decision enabled him to start building a new world around the healing of his wife's mental illness. The loss of any one of these three elements would have meant a different decision; but the most crucial is the third element. To have acted against the imperturbable serenity guiding his decision would have been to experience a loss of his own manliness, to sense a cheapening of his life, to feel personal fragmentation. If he had allowed the wholesomeness of his other-centered married love to be broken by not attempting himself to heal the fragmented person of his wife, his own personal wholesomeness would have shattered.

In his decision, the engineer has discovered that his beloved wife means more to him than his whole psychological world of electronics, that his liberty is greatest in this act of so-called sacrifice, and that his own wholesomeness depends on this healing of his beloved. Further, his serenity comes from something more than himself and herself, for how else could he afford to die to his psychological world and still gather strength to come to new life for the sake of his wife? Must there not be a 'more' luring him on past apparent death to a new and real life—a second life which may well include much suffering during the long period of the wife's convalescence? How account for imperturbable serenity in the further prospect that a second death faces him if his wife's mental health is not restored and that a third life must then be found and fashioned? Certainly no sanatorium would attempt to give him this peace, no psychiatrist would ever promise it, the worry that his business will decline under the direction of his young sons is not the cause of such peace. Who or what could ask him to make this decision for his wife's sake and then give him such imperturbable serenity amid such prospects of death unless it be the absolute beyond all chosen absolutes of wife, of business career, of family, and of death?

6. The Ultimate Sacrifice of Other-centered Love

The full liberty discovered within the imperturbable serenity of other-centered love is not the fullest liberty of this love. One may well ask: how could anyone sacrifice more than did this electrical engineer when he chose to center his life around his sick wife rather than around his vibrant electronics firm with its creative community? But a more ultimate sacrifice could very well be asked of him. Suppose that his wife, after a three-year period of convalescence and therapy, did recover her mental health and did begin to be her old self again—except for one difference: she now feels deeply guilty at having been the cause for her husband's sacrifice of his career. Somehow she cannot accept the fact that he wanted to do this for her and that it indicates the depth of his affection for her. To escape her sense of guilt and the unwarranted feeling that her husband now resents her for the sacrifice which her recovery required of him, she requests a divorce. On the advice of the therapist that this may be only temporary but with the sickening feeling that the divorce may never end, the husband decides to allow the center of his life to divorce him. His hope is that she will return to him fully recovered if he gives her complete freedom.

What could possibly give the engineer such strength? Does he simply recall the previous experience where once before he was promised a 'more' than the psychological world he left behind? Or does he have a new experience in which he is now promised a 'more' than even the beloved for whom he abandoned this treasured world? Somehow in this last decision to free his beloved for further growth he must experience a future 'more' which is more valuable than the world, more loveable than his wife, and more giving of liberty than all these put together. This would be a costly liberty: the ability to stand apart from even the beloved and to attempt to build a new, temporary world when one is close to sixty

149

years of age. It is a terrible liberty because it is the last stripping away of all the chosen absolutes. But it is also a priceless liberty since it reveals starkly the absolute beyond all chosen absolutes. There is really nothing else left to support the engineer's imperturbable serenity; there is no one else to whom he can give 'forever' his other-centered love. This is truly the ultimate sacrifice unto the death of one's present life; but it is also the ultimate other-centered love promising a future life of greater richness. It is Abraham's sacrifice of Isaac once again happening in late twentieth-century dress.

Reassessment of the Phenomenological Search for the Unchosen Absolute

In exploring the experience of other-centered love, we came across six basic characteristic phenomena whose adequate explanation required the supportive presence of an absolute beyond all chosen absolutes—a presence immanent within the acts of other-centered love. Each of these phenomena emerged out of the mystery of other-centered love and then converged beyond all chosen absolutes upon the presence of an underived and unchosen absolute within the same love. Thus the other-centered lover's perennial attraction for promising a 'forever' fidelity to a temporary chosen absolute (the beloved) is adequately explained only by the strengthening presence of the unchosen absolute supporting this chosen absolute.

Secondly, when an intelligent self-trust is generated in other-centered love by a sovereign call to initiate and to continue a faithful self-donation to a beloved who is little able to respond to this gift, this call or hope appears to be a flat contradiction of the very nature of love. For the beloved's inability to return love commensurately makes the essential, more exterior reciprocity non-existent—unless the unchosen absolute beyond all chosen absolutes supplies this reciprocity precisely in the deep hope or sovereign call and by way of the beloved.

Thirdly, unlike the narrowing restrictiveness of self-centered love, the steady expansiveness of other-centered love daringly opens out to other loves in ever growing number and quality because at its center is an anticipatory strength and readiness to suffer the joys of these loves—a ready strength furnishable only by one who, avoiding the destructive delusion of self-projection or of false community-substitution, leads the lover and the beloved beyond the more restrictive present into the more open future. All this is done with the absolute, underived assurance of one already living the future.

Fourthly, this experience of the 'more', which frees the person from the possessiveness of self-centered love, accounts for the lover's ability to give the beloved total freedom in the latter's response. This loving risk-taking is the discipline of liberation which, for its strength amid agony, requires something 'more' than deep respect for the separating beloved, more than the community's helplessness, more than the lover's despairing agony.

Indeed, the imperturbable serenity needed to strengthen the lover's resolve to promote the beloved's wholesomeness even to the loss of the surrounding world is the fifth phenomenon which reveals the presence of the absolute beyond all chosen absolutes. For this dynamic peace strongly resists the fragmentation of lover, beloved, and their mutual love, by being the strength whereby the lover heals the self, the beloved, and their love—even though this lover may actually be leaving the beloved community behind through his or her death caused by self-gift to the community.

This the lover does with the wholesome sacrifice of a career world in order to center his or her total life upon the beloved's growth in liberty or wholesome personhood. Thus eventually, within this other-centered love, the lover is asked to make the ultimate sacrifice of all the chosen absolutes so dearly cherished. Only the immanent presence of an underived absolute beyond all these chosen absolutes could make such a decision possible and, much more, liveable.[45]

C. Conclusion to Third Step

It gradually dawns on anyone attempting to define other-centered love that one is also defining person by the latter's fullest act of being. To deny the possibility or even the existence of other-centered love is to redefine person. For interpersonalism is most transparent in the more exterior reciprocity of dependent trust and independent liberty between lover and beloved. And this mysterious personhood starkly reveals itself either in the lover's generous giving of the total self (representing the best integration of the community's riches) or in the beloved's grateful total acceptance of the lover. This personhood of interior reciprocity thus unfolds before us in a perduring faithfulness and in an intelligent self-trust; both of these are the roots of the magnificent expansiveness and the disciplined liberation of other-centered love which, in turn, issue in the imperturbable serenity and deep satisfaction of ultimate sacrifice for the beloved.

The mystery of personhood, however, may appear to be an absurdity when one's magnificent independence struggles to assert itself within one's humbling dependence on community and world. The human being then looks like the incarnation of the world's deepest contradiction, a being that is riven by restrictive essence and assertive existence. But we have discovered that a person's absolute activity is sustained by another being. The latter operates within the lover as well as through the beloved, the community, and the world and makes sure that other-centered love is worthwhile now and in the future. If other-centered love exists as just defined, then the underived and unchosen absolute exists beyond and yet within all chosen absolutes of our world and our experience. To deny that the unchosen absolute exists in every act of other-centered love is to deny the possibility as well as the existence of other-centered love and, further, to deny the specific definition of human being which avoids the ungodly and disastrous extremes of Sartrean absolutism and Spencerian relativism.

But it is not enough to discover simply the existence of the unchosen absolute beyond all chosen absolutes. Phenomenological analysis is also necessary in order to find out how this absolute exists. The basic six phenomena of other-centered love reveal themselves as dependent upon the immanent presence of this absolute. The so-called divinity of human absolute actions now makes sense; so, too, do a person's embarrassing and discouraging lapses from nobility. Human 'divinity' is borrowed and can be easily lost. It can also be just as easily denied by frustrated people who find the six phenomena of other-centered love more mocking than challenging and whose objections can never be answered until they themselves discover and admit the presence of these phenomena within their own experience. For the unchosen absolute's immanent presence is experientially knowable only through the six phenomena. This is to say that no direct knowledge is had of the unchosen absolute. Yet denial of the phenomena is tantamount to denying the existence of this secular transcendent. For the phenomena exist only because the unchosen absolute gives them existence by being intimately present within them. This is the dynamic immanence of the unchosen absolute in other-centered love.

To establish more fully that the unchosen absolute, though immanent to personal experience, is yet 'beyond' it, we should make a demonstrative analysis of the phenomenological data. This consists mainly in discovering how the unchosen absolute, though immanent to human experience, is distinct from this experience; how the same absolute, though operating through the world's chosen absolutes, is also distinct (yet never separate) from them; and finally, how this absolute is ultimately the cause of the six phenomena which characterize the act of other-centered love. Such demonstrative analysis is offered in the appendix to this third step. There one discovers more clearly why the 'beyond' of the underived absolute is not limited to the present moment but also lives in the future, and, further, why this 'beyond' is not limited to the human universe of chosen absolutes but may simultaneously support other universes.

Thus far in the phenomenological analysis our attention has been focused on person and other-centered love, so that little has been discovered about the unchosen absolute taken for itself. This procedure is necessary because any knowledge of the unchosen absolute will be derived from the six phenomena of other-centered love as they show themselves in the interpersonal reciprocity of this love. For as effects caused by the unchosen absolute, they reveal the latter's being. The better one knows this evidence, the more one can learn about the unchosen absolute from analysis of the evidence. We would be too easily satisfied if we simply took the definition of the chosen absolute (the supreme value to which all other values cede and around which a person achieves the integration and continuity of his or her whole life) and applied this to the unchosen absolute. There is a uniqueness about the latter which must be made explicit. Thus, if we decide to skip over the demonstrative analysis of the third step contained in the following appendix, we would move into the fourth step of this approach to the secular transcendent in order to get some knowledge of the underived and unchosen absolute in itself.

APPENDIX TO THIRD STEP

(FOR THOSE WHO WISH TO DISCOVER WITH FULLER CLARITY AND RIGOR THE DIALOGAL CAUSAL FACTORS UNDERLYING THE SIX CHARACTERISTICS OF OTHER-CENTERED LOVE)

A. Demonstrative Analysis Rediscovers the Unchosen Absolute

Demonstrative analysis aims to discover what makes possible the various experiences of the person. Here it asks why the six characteristics exist at all in other-centered love. In other words, it studies the conditions which make possible the six experiential phenomena constituting other-centered love. Descriptive phenomenological analysis, besides isolating these six phenomena of perduring fidelity, intelligent self-trust, steady expansiveness, disciplined liberation, healing wholesomeness, and ultimate sacrifice, has indicated that beyond the lover, the beloved, the world and any other chosen absolute, lies an absolute which is immanent to each of these yet is not derived from any of them. This is the mysterious 'more' of the future, an unchosen absolute, the secular transcendent. The six phenomena, being expressions of one's absolute activity, have revealed that one's radical independence exercised in living one's chosen absolutes is dependent on this unchosen absolute. This far we reached in our previous phenomenological investigation. Now through demonstrative analysis we must determine how this dependent independence of the human being is brought into existence ultimately by the unchosen absolute.

To begin this investigation, let us ask a simple question: what happens if a person denies the existence of the underived absolute and lives this denial? There are at least four possible unhappy alternatives:

1. the polite enslavement of either the lover or the beloved and the loss of the six phenomena characteristic of other-centered love;
2. a life of at least theoretical absurdity;
3. systematic destruction of the other person morally, psychologically, and physically;
4. the blocking of any attempt to explain the experience of the six phenomena (this is done with the simple assertion that they and other-centered love are absurd).

Though all these four alternatives are expressed negatively, exploration of them reveals the positive structure of other-centered love and enables us to know for certain that there does exist an unchosen absolute. The nature of the latter can then be investigated in the fourth step of this approach to the secular transcendent. But let us now look at these four alternatives of denying the existence of the unchosen absolute.

The Practiced Denial of the Underived Absolute Makes Other-centered Love Impossible

If one denies the existence of an underived absolute underlying all chosen absolutes, then one inevitably finds oneself deciding to make one of the chosen absolutes into this unchosen absolute to which all other absolutes pay tribute. One has to have a star around which to center one's universe and by which to guide one's life. To change the figure, one must have within oneself some ultimate principle of decision around which, as a central pylon, one thatches the decisions of one's life so that they accumulate meaningfully into an integrated personality and simultaneously situate one in a purposeful life, a cooperative community, and a liveable world. Otherwise, a person either oscillates between multiple ultimate values like an erratic pendulum or develops multiple personalities—one for each different world pivoting around a different ultimate value or chosen absolute.

A person must inevitably, that is, with utter necessity, either transform a single chosen absolute into an unchosen absolute or discover the latter pre-existent within the chosen absolute. In no third way can one achieve the permanent continuity needed to build a meaningful life and community through many years. The reason for this is obvious. Because of the reciprocal nature of human relationships, cooperation can occur only if both persons mutually assist each other in a regular fashion so that each knows when, where, and how the other will operate; in this way, their actions can be dovetailed to do together the job which neither can do alone.

However, the reciprocity of cooperation grows only if it is continuous and allows for accumulation of skills, products, and mutual confidence. This is a basic reason for business contracts, pacts of honor, marriage vows, and small everyday promises of fidelity. Thus the more permanent the continuity,the greater the opportunity for growth not only in the common enterprise but also in the cooperators themselves.[46] Consequently, the more absolute the common purpose of the enterprise and of the cooperators, the more permanent the continuity of their cooperation. For these reasons, one must either discover or manufacture for oneself an unchosen absolute. If one does not discover it as unchosen and preexistent to oneself and one's world, then one tries to transmute a chosen absolute into such an unchosen absolute.

The transmutation of a chosen absolute into an unchosen absolute is, unfortunately, doomed to very partial success since no chosen absolute of itself is worthy of a person's total commitment and 'forever' fidelity. In its temporariness, the chosen absolute is bound to disappoint one's 'forever' fidelity and, in its merely partial response to one's needs, is certain to make one bitter at having cheated oneself by one's total self-gift. This tragedy is inevitable because the transmuter must necessarily choose either the self or the other as the chosen absolute to be transmuted into the unchosen absolute. If one chooses to take the self as the unchosen absolute, then one dooms oneself to self-centered love in which one must dominate the beloved in order to make sure that the latter responds with permanent continuity to one's love. In this genteel enslavement of the beloved, one must restrict the latter's expansiveness and liberty. This depreciation renders the beloved fragmented, that is, distrustful of both the self and the lover. In this way other-centered love become impossible.

If the transmuter chooses to try to make the beloved or the world or some projected ideal the unchosen absolute, then the transmuting lover submits the self to this other. In the case of the beloved, the lover becomes the slave rather than the master enslaver. Voluntarily the lover depreciates the self by abdicating its liberty with consequent loss of self-trust and wholesomeness. To achieve permanent continuity, the lover and the beloved dare not switch roles of master and slave lest each become more confused and less integral. This holds true even if the beloved is a community. For the mother enslaved to her family or the ambitious junior executive indentured to his business career is each locked into a role whose change means temporary chaos for each. For such a person other-centered love becomes impossible since the voluntary enslavement is simply the lover's ploy to buy affection from the beloved.

If the transmuter chooses something from the infrapersonal world as the unchosen absolute—such as building a conglomerate, or acquiring the reputation as America's finest personal injury lawyer or being the fashion model most in demand or building a human gene out of biochemicals—then he or she cultivates the ultimate loneliness of submersion in things and risks treating human beings as things. Again, such activity lessens or precludes other-centered love.

Lastly, the transmuter may concoct an ideal as the chosen absolute which he or she then transmutes into the unchosen absolute. This is the young woman for whom marriage becomes impossible because no man can match her *beau ideal*; this is the young man whose ideal of social justice for the worker makes him too impatient to be a labor organizer or union negotiator. In each case the ideal is much more important than the real situation and, what is worse, is divorced from it. This unrealistic attitude moves people towards a radically unbalanced life and, because of its isolating proclivity, makes other-centered love less and less possible. For the transmuted chosen absolute gives its chooser a false sense of total control over life, thus justifying, if not inducing, a manipulative love. This is the occupational hazard of the pure activist. Whereas the unchosen absolute requires the lover to give up the attempt at total control of his or her life and to submit in trust to the other.

Transmutation of any chosen absolute into the unchosen absolute thus renders the possibility of other-centered love more and more remote. Yet this is the only maneuver available to the person denying the existence of an unchosen absolute immanent to, supportive of, and yet independent of the chosen absolute. Therefore, to deny the existence of the unchosen absolute and to live this denial is eventually to deny the possibility and hence the existence of other-centered love as revealed in its six characteristic phenomena. Such denial of basic factual reality can only build delusion and potential tragedy at the center of the human person.

Denying the Unchosen Absolute in Practice Means Drifting into Absurdity

The inevitable bitterness caused by the frustrating attempts at transmutation leads not a few people to take the position that the person's very being is absurd.[47] This is to say that a person's very attraction to perduring fidelity or to steady expansiveness is an interior request of his or her very being to attempt the impossible and thus gradually to stretch oneself to death. Other-centered love is, therefore, the supposedly better half of a schizophrenic reaction. A person basically heals the self, so the opinion goes, by admitting both to the call for other-centered love and to the person's total inability to respond to this call. The only absolute, therefore, is the statement (not the fact, nor the being), that there are no absolutes. Gone is any hope of perduring fidelity or expansive liberation in the human being. For there is no continuity to life, no wholesomeness; only purely accidental breaks of the life history and the incidental fragmentation of the person.

Denial of the Unchosen Absolute in Practice Can Lead to Self-Destruction

The absurdists are not satisfied with proclaiming justly that the chosen absolute is not enough for a person, and that the attempt to manufacture an unchosen absolute out of a chosen absolute is frustrating. They feel the need to deny the existence of the unchosen absolute itself even though this drives a person on to the point of absurdity. Indeed, some even deny human independence or liberty because this reveals the frustrating absolute in the human being. Such absurdity mixed with the bitterness of frustration can lead to a perverse and systematic destruction of the 'other'. This attack on human wholeness occurs on the three levels of the moral, the psychological, and the physical. On the moral level, in taking away liberty from the beloved, the husband reduces the latter to a manipulatable thing; such reduction is a mutilation of the beloved's self-confidence, to say nothing of her talents, hopes, and very being. The reverse is just as true if the lover wife gives up her liberty to the domineering beloved husband; she teaches him how to strip her of her womanhood and simultaneously how to destroy his own self-respect.

At the psychological level, the husband's domination of the beloved wife has humiliated her into a childishness that leaves her defenseless before the world. In turn, he has lost his manly instinct to protect the beloved at all costs; instead, he picks at her. On the other hand, if the husband should idolize his wife like a goddess, his consequent submission lures her into a dominating role hateful to her because her womanly instinct to build wholesome self-confidence in others is shattered. At the physical level, the previous dichotomizing of the psychological and moral self produces anxieties destructive of the nervous system. For the inner life of the person is constantly denied by outer expression. An almost metaphysical hypocrisy results.

At this point the lover has partially destroyed self as well as the beloved. This is the inevitable result of theoretically denying the existence of the unchosen absolute and then of attempting to live out that denial in everyday living and loving. Fortunately many, while denying the existence of the unchosen absolute, nonetheless live it. Despite their theoretical protests to the contrary, they love other-centeredly in practice, so natural and so beautiful is such love to every person. In this way they escape the hell of a self-centered love and life based on absurdity. Clearly, then, the unchosen absolute exists. For other-centered love, the mark of the unchosen absolute, exists in action despite all the theoretical denials; and the denials, when practiced in life, destroy not only other-centered love but also its deniers.

B. The Six Characteristic Phenomena of Other-centered Love Demand an Unchosen Absolute

It is not enough to trace out how the lived denial of the unchosen absolute, in making other-centered love impossible, can partially destroy a man or woman. Nor is it sufficient to indicate how such destruction dramatically points to the existence of this absolute. It should now be noted how the six characteristics of other-centered love positively indicate with certainty the existence of an unchosen absolute.

1. The Attraction of 'Forever' Fidelity: (See pp. 128–33)

We have already noted the phenomenological fact that the lover is strongly attracted to promising the beloved a 'forever' fidelity.

But this promise can be only delusive unless an unchosen absolute is present within the attraction and supports this promise. For no individual by himself or herself alone—or even with the help of the community—can dare to guarantee a future love since one's dependence at all four levels of one's being makes such a certain prediction of one's future strength and desire quite uncertain. The human person is mortal and the uncertain future of his or her power makes the godless promise of future fidelity hardly worth the beloved's total acceptance and response in a 'forever' fidelity. Sartre has brilliantly noted that the correlative needs of the lovers are mutually destructive of them if each of their loves attempts mutual domination, that is, if each love is self-centered. This is true—unless they also experience an absolute which calls each to sacrifice for the other.

Indeed, the transiency of the finest chosen absolute makes the attraction to a 'forever' commitment appear contradictory unless an unchosen absolute other than the lover, the beloved, and their community supports this attraction. For the 'forever' commitment extends beyond time and even embraces all the resources of the lover for now and forever. The lover has gladly mortgaged himself or herself eternally to the beloved.

Moreover, this would not be a free act of true love if an unchosen absolute did not exercise its attraction through the chosen absolute. To be free, the lover has to be capable of refusing attention to the beloved (the chosen absolute) even if the lover at present finds this refusal even inconceivable. To be free the love must have more than one possible object. Again, the lover's freedom and the value of the lover's self-gift are more sharply appreciated when the lover has in mind several chosen absolutes such as a career or the ideal of social justice or still another beloved. But for the lover to have the ability to refuse the beloved attention rather than to give it, this lover must experience the attraction of the unchosen absolute as something independent of the beloved and of any other chosen absolute even though this attraction works through the beloved and through other chosen absolutes. In other words, the ambitious actress must experience a future 'more' whose beauty enables her to resist the present attractiveness of her beloved husband and to remain, if she so decides, with a previous freely chosen absolute of stardom.

When the same lover changes from one chosen absolute to another—she chooses her career over her beloved husband—she still needs the attraction of the unchosen absolute. For her radical freedom is the ability to refuse either of the chosen absolutes, although she can never refuse all chosen absolutes simultaneously since every person must live by one supreme chosen absolute around which one can unify life. To be free simultaneously in regard to both alternatives, she must know that beyond both is a 'more' than both.

Beyond refers to the 'forever' future and to the greater worth of the unchosen absolute. Granted that only through chosen absolutes does the unchosen absolute exercise its attraction, one nevertheless feels that the attracting absolute is somehow beyond the chosen absolutes. For the attraction is felt through every chosen absolute and yet is distinct from them taken either singly or as a whole. For it is present in each yet not reducible to any one of them; nor is it reducible to their collectivity since it is later found in still other chosen absolutes not yet in view and perhaps not yet in existence.

Indeed, even when the actress chooses one or another chosen absolute as her supreme beloved, her freedom to give herself totally and forever to one limited and temporary exemplar of the chosen absolutes is radically energized by the 'forever' attraction from the unchosen absolute which she feels within herself. Even as the actress chooses, she knows that she is always free to leave one chosen absolute for another, that her 'forever' and total commitment may be diverted to another temporary and limited being as her chosen absolute. The many changes do not imply frustration, for through commitment to any chosen absolute, a future 'more' which is worthy of total and 'forever' commitment is being reached in each new total commitment. In each chosen absolute the unchosen absolute is rediscovered in a new way.

Note here that a promise of 'forever love' can be mistaken. It can be a ruse to seduce the beloved; it can have mere fantasy as its basis; it can be simply a proud, unwarranted boast. Further, some true promises of 'forever love' are frustrated by events beyond the control of lover and beloved, such as a disasterous misunderstanding caused by the lies of false friends.

Yet our concern here is not with particular promises, true or mistaken, but with that constant basic desire in man and woman which causes 'forever promises' to be made. This desire pulses beneath every love song, every noble love story, every solemn marriage ceremony, every love symbol of imperishable diamond and gold, and every lasting friendship. The desire to give oneself to another forever is natural to every human as a vital expression of one's very being. If this desire is always to be frustrated, then the person is frustrated in his or her very being and is simply absurd. The very meaning of man and woman is in jeopardy.

Consequently, if this desire is basic to the human person's meaning and being and nevertheless cannot be fulfilled without the support of the unchosen absolute, then the unchosen absolute must pulse within the desire in order to give it warrant; and therefore must be existent within it. Otherwise, the human being is a living contradiction forever condemned to schizophrenic impulses. In other words, these desires to give oneself forever to another are vital expressions of a person's very being and cannot be smothered by repression or by comfortable forgetfulness. They will tear anyone apart with their impossible demands and promises. Life would be a series of frustrating loves—unless there were an unchosen absolute able to warrant these promises of 'forever' love.

2. The Strong Hope of Intelligent Self-trust: (See pp. 133–36)

In unrequited love, the lover experiences a strong hope that 'forever' devotion to the beloved will be worthwhile even if the beloved never returns the love. Such hope enables the reciprocity of other-centered love to begin and even to grow before the beloved has learned to love or to make a return of love somewhat commensurate to the lover's total gift. This hope founds a deep and intelligent self-trust precisely when there are many reasons to distrust self.

What is the source of this powerful hope? The beloved is more cause for despair than for hope. The beloved's attention may be directed away from the lover. Moreover, the greater the talents of the beloved and the more disciplined their development, the harder it is for the lover to draw them from another object of allegiance. The community in which the lover and the beloved live cannot induce this powerful hope in the lover by itself. A guarantee from the community would imply coercion. To freely return love to the lover, the beloved must be able to withstand the community's wishes. Such freedom enables love to be love and not compulsion.

On the other hand, simple intelligence would not allow the lover to pump up a strong but delusive hope; this would truly be to hope against hope. Rather the lover is surprised at the hope felt, knows that it is not self-made or community produced, and trusts it. Hope seems strange as part of an experience which the lover might well prefer to forget. For it is humiliating to love and not be loved in return; it is distressing to have someone other than the beloved offer the type of love desired from the beloved; it is agonizing to watch the life span allotted to this love shrink. Yet against these fears self-trust arises out of this hope.

The lover's hope is a mysterious phenomenon, almost a contradiction to itself and thus a large target for the accusation of self-delusion. Indeed, to keep this hope alive, much more to keep it strong, the inner reciprocity of the lover must be continuously enlivened by a simultaneous and proportionate exterior reciprocity which neither the beloved nor the community can offer. Otherwise, the interior reciprocity of love must die. But then who or what could so accurately respond simultaneously and proportionately to the lover except the unchosen absolute immanent to the lover?

If one rules out response from an unchosen absolute, then this other-centered love must be neurotic. For the lover experiences interior reciprocity of love without exterior reciprocity. This is parallel to seeing nonexistent colored figures or to hearing nonexistent shrilling sirens since hope is being generated in the lover by a despair of ever receiving the beloved's love. Risk is taken on the basis of failure. This is hardly the atmosphere for developing self-trust. On this score, the sovereign call to sacrifice for the beloved who does not love in return or who returns the love only weakly would appear to be a call to the impossible. A mere human is being asked to love the way God loves through his other-centered power of creation. Such an arrogant attempt to ape the divine would surely tear apart the human personality. For this reason, if there is no unchosen absolute to support this attempt, then every unrequited lover, every husband who supports a shallow wife and her weak response, and every wife who tries to live with an alcoholic husband must all certainly become neurotic. In some cases, such people do, but this is clearly not the outcome of every case.

Further, if unrequited love were necessarily neurotic, and if many love relationships begin with a period of unrequited love until the beloved can catch up to the lover's offer, many love relations would become warped with neurotic tendencies. In fact, since most love relationships are not perfect balances of emotional intensity, intelligence, and self-sacrifice, the one-sidedness of a relationship would necessarily engender the neurosis, especially if the imbalance were to occur over a long period of time. Love, on this basis, would be not only a high risk but a luxury that few could afford. Consequently, if one accepts the facts that some unrequited loves remain healthy despite the suffering involved, that imbalanced love relationships can often be borne without neurotic results, but that love, being necessarily reciprocal, cannot exist without exterior reciprocity, then one must also accept the existence of an unchosen absolute which alone makes these facts possible. The existence of strong hope or sovereign call within the experience of the lover requires the supportive presence of the unchosen absolute. Otherwise, the lover's self-trust is unintelligent, delusory, and incipiently neurotic.

3. Readiness to Risk in Steady Expansiveness: (See pp. 136–42)

Once the lover, through 'forever' fidelity and intelligent self-trust, has given and received other-centered love, he or she finds a new phenomenon rising within this experience: a desire to elicit such other-centered love from more people and a readiness to risk much suffering in order to fulfill this desire.[48] A lover loves to love. A marvelous strength accompanies this desire and this readiness to risk suffering. For the lover sets no limit to the number and to the quality of these loves. To prelimit love would appear to the other-centered lover quite arbitrary and opposed to the expansiveness of other-centered love. The lover leaves himself or herself open to the freedom of others and to the spontaneous play of events.

If at first the lover lacks a realistic understanding that multiplication of loves involves the multiplication of heavy obligations to the beloveds, the lover learns this fact very quickly. The young minister of an expanding congregation, the ambitious new social worker, and the young parent of a growing family come to the time when their shoulders sag under the heavy burdens of love. At that moment, the tired lover can decide to play it safe and not to use the strength and readiness for risk which has previously kept him or her expansively open to new loves. The tired lover decides, I must think of myself more, then sets the present moment as the limit for the future. Finally the lover feels the youthful expansiveness of love collapse into senescence as soon as the stretch of love into the future slacks off.

Though it is a marvel that the felt strength has brought the tired lover even to this moment of retrenchment, it is even more marvelous when this strength is used to support this lover's reconsideration to remain open to new loves and obligations. For the lover must often support multiple beloveds who are not yet ready to return love or are weak in response. The dedicated elementary school teacher is a lover sharply aware of her thirty-two immature beloveds. Yet this lover is already feeling the heavy obligations of these loves. Not only is there a continuous cumulation of loves and obligations but also the lover worries over the future exterior reciprocity with them. How can she or he fulfill the expectations of all thirty-two beloveds? All of this requires an anticipatory strength in the lover lest the interior reciprocity which feeds all these loves die and lest the anticipated exterior reciprocity with the immature beloveds become impossible.

An additional marvel is that the original love from which these multiple loves spring need not be diminished by their growth but is quite often qualitatively enhanced by them.[49] Nothing better elicits deeper love than new loves. Though at first the rookie cop may feel that the demands of close camaraderie with his fellow policemen drive him apart from his wife and children, later these tight-knit friendships can make him appreciate more deeply his wife's loyal sacrifices for him, and can bring him and his wife into the warm embrace of his fellow policemen's families.

How does one explain these facts:

1. the lover has a strong desire to risk the eliciting and the later burdensome supporting of multiple cumulative loves with all their attendant obligations;
2. the lover must often begin and foster these loved obligations with little reciprocal support from the beloveds;
3. the lover's central love nevertheless continues to deepen and to grow precisely because these other loves branch out of it?

Evidently, the infrapersonal world cannot furnish the personal support of anticipatory reciprocation. Yet the civic community, insofar as it praises and supports such an attitude of generosity, especially by furnishing numerous examples of this openness, gives direction to the lover's desire for the steady expansion of this love into other lives. But community support cannot be the total cause of this desire; otherwise, the community would be promising a future which it cannot guarantee. To guarantee future loves, the community would have to require love, and thus would remove the freedom of the beloveds lest they refuse return of love. The beloved families served by the loving social worker must be allowed time to quell their suspicions of welfare help before they can begin to respect or love the social worker. Besides, the social worker as lover needs exterior reciprocation right here-and-now to maintain the interior strength to serve the beloveds. Evidently, the beloved families also cannot give this reciprocation here and now; this is the crux of the whole problem of sustaining the social worker as lover. If the neighborhood community then tries to offer a substitute exterior reciprocation on behalf of the delinquent beloveds, the substitute would be at best a distraction from the beloveds because the community response would direct the lover's attention to the community itself rather than to her or his beloved clients.

The substitution of the community would also falsify the very nature of love. For the community's attempt to strengthen the lover's relationship with the multiple beloveds would have to be something additional to the community's own love relations with the lover. If this addition were simply an intensification of existent love relations (for example, the husband, two mature children, the grandparents, and two sisters give new attention and depth of response to a mother struggling to bring up the four youngest children of a family), it would certainly give support to the lover. However, it does not take the place of exterior reciprocation from the beloveds. If this intensification were to be considered a substitute for the latter, then the love towards the beloveds is viciously attacked. First, the consideration would be an unreal projection upon this love for the beloveds. It would be an exchange of the communal reciprocation for that reciprocation which the beloveds cannot yet give and which is therefore nonexistent. It would be an attempt to declare the nonexistent reciprocation existent.

Such a maneuver could only fill the lover and the beloveds with the emptiness of a lie—hardly the basis for lasting love. If this be not attempted, the substitution would at least be used to 'teach' or to elicit love from the beloveds (Daddy loves me; so, you kids should love me; or See how much everybody loves me; why don't you love me like that?). The lover would be attempting to 'teach' love by means of its high rate of absence rather than by its low percentage of presence. This can only mislead the beloveds into either faking a higher response or feeling incompetent to ever love adequately. At this point introverted self-centeredness becomes easier for the beloveds: they feel manipulated, not loved, and learn to dominate, not to love. The same unfortunate results are obtained if the loving mother projects her future hopes of returned love upon the beloveds and lets these projections guide her response to them. For these projections, too, are unreal and are used as substitutes for the actual reciprocation itself from the beloveds.

Naturally such pretenses do not increase the quality of the original love out of which the new loves are springing since false expectations induce frustration and resentment into the whole community of loves. Thus the intensity of communal love can be lowered rather than increased by this experience. This conclusion leads to the realization that, if there is a breakdown of anticipatory reciprocation on a large scale, then perduring communities of love (such as a group of friends, a family, a neighborhood, a religious order) can die out and a loveless universe could result since the expansiveness of other-centered love would gradually collapse in on itself. But the fact is that our universe is not without other-centered love and that it is not on the verge of collapsing. Therefore, anticipatory reciprocation must be strengthening lovers so that multiple cumulative loves are occurring and hence communities of love are growing.

Because this anticipatory reciprocation cannot be caused by the lover, by the beloveds, or by their community, it must be caused by the unchosen absolute since all the chosen absolutes of self, beloved, community, career, power, riches, and infrapersonal world have proved inadequate to the causation. Only the unchosen absolute operates in the future ahead of the present moment (whereas the temporary chosen absolutes can operate only in the present) in order to furnish the strength of anticipatory reciprocation. Only the unchosen absolute can exercise the attraction to 'forever' fidelity and to intelligent self-trust precisely through lovers and their beloveds and thus without substituting for them or distracting from them. For only the unchosen absolute works within and through the chosen absolutes—an experience made evident whenever, as we saw earlier, the lover freely selects one chosen absolute over another. Lastly, only the unchosen absolute, having given such strength, could then make the sovereign call to expansive other-centered love without deluding the lover. For only the unchosen absolute can give warranted assurance of the lover's future fulfillment.[50]

4. Experience of the 'More' in Disciplined Liberation: (See pp. 142-44)

When the lover becomes aware of a powerful, intelligent desire to see to it that the beloved achieve more and more wisdom, virtue, experience, and beauty and when this lover feels willing to sacrifice everything forever to this achievement, then the 'more' of the beloved's liberation or fuller personhood is powerful in the lover's experience as it leads the lover to deeper love-acts. But when later the lover also experiences an agonized willingness to adapt the self-gift completely to the needs of the beloved and even to let the latter reject all the richness desired for the beloved, then this lover has attained the discipline of liberation, a remarkably free other-centeredness.

But such freedom is terribly costly. For if one has centered all one's life around the beloved so that one's world could collapse when the beloved disappears from it, one gambles with much more than the beloved in the discipline of liberation. The lover risks quick suicide or crippling loneliness or the slower psychological death of promiscuity. For the alternative to the foreverness, the self-trust, and the expansive liberation of a seemingly defeated other-centered love is a physical death or suffocating self-pity or the psychological suicide of attempting multiple, temporary, self-distrusting, restrictive loves.

Out of many fragmentary, sometimes frantic, experiences of promiscuous loves, the rejected lover could attempt to gather some self-meaning and to build a world around this self. But here one finds oneself as fragmented as one's loves, as tormented as the beloveds, as kaleidoscopic as the daily world. Because the free reciprocity of love has been lost, the lover is no longer a free person, no longer a liberator. No longer does this lover experience the deep security of a central meaning to life. Such a disastrous outcome impels one to wonder about the source of that security which enables him or her to risk losing the beloved in order to help the latter achieve the 'more' of enlarged liberty, of greater personhood. How can such a lover justify this phenomenon of other-centered lover? What is the meaning of this experience of the 'more'?

It would seem that, in the experience of the 'more', the lover receives an intimation that something 'more' than the beloved is being promised for the future so that the lover can afford this terrible risk of losing the beloved by allowing the latter freedom to reject the lover's self-gift. This something 'more', being even worthier than the beloved, will be the reward of the risk. In loving the beloved so daringly, the lover opens up to an even greater love of an even greater beloved. But what could this 'more' be and who could promise it?

Certainly the lover's world could not be this 'more' since the world is built around the beloved and takes much of its value from the beloved's central presence. This world collapses when the beloved leaves it and must painstakingly be rebuilt around another beloved. Nor can the lover's community give the strength for risk and then request that the lover take the risk of losing the beloved for 'something more' in the future. It has insufficient resources for promising a future 'more' which would be more valuable than the beloved and make up for the latter's loss. Since the community is itself made up of free agents, it cannot coerce others into love-relationships which could constitute the 'more' for the lover—even if the lover were to accept them freely. The day when a friend or a community tries to dictate the number and type of friends one may have marks the date when the original friendship died.

Nor can the beloved be the source of this 'more' in the experience of the lover since the beloved would be simultaneously giving and taking away in the most clever Judas-betrayal of the century. For, in order to gain full freedom from the total self-gift of the lover, the beloved would be promising 'more' to the lover and at the same time would be moving to destroy the whole world of the lover. The beloved's person would require the lover to give far more than the beloved's present intent to respond; it would be a type of genial blackmail. This would make the love relationship a one-sided barter and destroy the loving reciprocity.

It would make even less sense to accuse the lover of creating out of his or her own being this experience of the 'more'. For this would be to gamble one's whole world on a self-promoted hope. If the lover alone had built this world, then to risk it solely on one's own authority with no solid hope for a future 'more' would be to commit psychological suicide. For rarely does a person get the opportunity to build a second such world alone. Unlike Job, the person is normally long left sitting in the ruins of his or her life.

It is also no solution to claim that the combination of world, community, beloved, and lover are the 'more'. For the simple combination of inadequate causes does not of itself necessarily form a single adequate cause; indeed, the four causes, even taken together, cannot guarantee a single future love of a single day's duration, much less a community of loves.

For these reasons, the experience of the 'more' can come only from the absolute beyond all chosen absolutes; otherwise, the experience is a contradiction of human nature itself as found in lover, beloved, and their community. One would be asked to be 'more' than oneself so that one could simultaneously be tempted to destroy the self and the world. If this experience of the 'more' is real, then the unchosen absolute beyond all chosen absolutes is at least as real. But what man or woman at some peak time in his or her life has not experienced the great desire to put all the self's riches into the life of the beloved, to adapt this gift as exactly as possible to the beloved's needs, and to give the beloved total freedom to reject all or part of the gift?

171

5. Imperturbable Serenity in Healing Wholesomeness: (See pp. 144-49)

The person's strongest distinguishing characteristic is the penchant to mold order out of chaotic bits, and then to build order upon order in cumulative fashion. Only the human being is the progressive builder of homes into skyscrapers, rituals into elaborate liturgies, families into nations, bridges into continental throughways, games into big business, hunting techniques into agricultural empires, businesses into conglomerates, machines into machine-building robots, marauding bands into armies, recipe books into sciences, chance events into a tradition. Thus only the human builds civilizations and cultures. The human being wants to enter a situation in order to make it better, more creative, more healthy, more rich, more wholesome. Only the psychopathic person delights in causing destructive disorder.

In a similar way, the healthy person's deepest instinct works at its highest quality and intensity when it tries to build a better community, a better network of friendships arising out of larger liberty in each person. This is the wholesome reality most highly prized and most difficult of accomplishment. It is highly prized because one's identity and worth are felt most deeply in the free response of love from the community. It is most difficult to achieve because it requires of the human person perduring fidelity, daring, intelligent self-trust, constant risk of a steady expansion of loves, painful discipline of liberation, and ultimate self-sacrifice.

The correspondingly ultimate irony is that some persons can do all this with imperturbable serenity: the mark of healing wholesomeness not only in the individual but also in the community. The death of Socrates for the truth of his teaching and of his followers' lives not only was a sign of his personal wholesomeness but also was a healing influence in Athenian society. This sense of wholesomeness occurs in the midst of agony caused by a seemingly ultimate defeat. For the community often can grow after the physical or psychological death of the heroic lover who has caused this improvement; indeed, the shortening of his or her life may well be the price of the bettering. Under this twofold risk, how can the heroic lover possibly experience the imperturbable serenity of a paradoxically healing wholesomeness? The fact is that he or she does.[51] Heroes and heroines are often enough wholesome people unaware of their remarkable power to heal others and to restore sanity to the community. They are the hidden saints whose imperturbable serenity, amid disaster, at once shocks and charms us.

But then what is this serenity? Somehow it must be the presence now of the future 'more', the bettering of the community, because it gives an assurance to the heroic lover that the sacrifice is worthwhile in itself and also worthy of the lover's manhood or womanhood. A present other-centered love gains assurance of future responding loves. Here the lover experiences a healing of the whole person, the imperturbable serenity. The healing of the individual is itself the warranted promise of the future healing which will come to the whole community through perduring friendships of fidelity. The heroic lover possesses a sense of the great community of the great tomorrow as a sure reality. On this account, serenity can exist without bitterness, without recrimination, without any false hope of present recovery from either psychological or physical death.

Once again, the question: under these disturbing conditions, from where does this imperturbable serenity come? It cannot come from the world which the heroic lover is sacrificing. For the losing of the world and the possible shortening of the hero's or heroine's life would then shatter that serenity, not build it. The beloved, who will soon disappear from the lover's life with the world just now lost, cannot cause this serenity. In fact, the danger of losing the beloved, the central meaning of the lover's life, should bring about both psychological and physical breakdown as far-reaching and as deep as the love. For the latter is the deeply rooted value or chosen absolute which gives value to all the realities of the lover's world.

Nor can the serenity be a self-created state of the heroic lover. By itself the decision to shorten one's life for the sake of the beloved is not an expansion but a collapse of the heroic lover's person—unless the lover is supported by the secular transcendent. For only the absolute beyond all chosen absolutes is beyond world, beloved, and lover and alone can give credible assurance that the heroic lover will be received by a great community in a great tomorrow where future loves will render this lover more wholesome a person than ever and where this wholesomeness will bring closer unity to others. Nothing else and no one else dare give this actual assurance of imperturbable serenity to the lover since nothing else and no one else can guarantee a single future love or even a single second of the future to himself or herself or to anyone else.

6. The Absolute Promise within the Ultimate Sacrifice: (See pp. 149–50)

Hidden within the imperturbable serenity of other-centered love which risks everything for the beloved community is an absolute promise. For, as one who decides to leave all things and all loves through a decisive contribution to the communiy, this heroic lover receives an assurance that he or she is moving towards a new existence which is more valuable, more loveable and loving, more liberating than all that is being left behind. But this takes a supreme act of trust in the assurance or rather in the one giving this assurance. Consequently, it is an arduous act, more painful yet more comforting than any previous decision, more excitingly daring yet more peaceful, more lonely yet more companioned, more emptying yet more fulfilling. For this ultimate sacrifice is a sacrifice: all one's loves seem left behind; and it is ultimate: there is no lingering, no turning back. All of a person's chosen absolutes are stripped away; there remains only the assurance within the person that a new and better community is promised by one who is the source of all fidelity, self-trust, expansiveness of heart, disciplined liberty, and imperturbable serenity. All that is left to the heroic lover in this last moment of sacrifice is the 'more' of the absolute beyond all chosen absolutes, the secular transcendent which gives vivacious attractiveness to all chosen absolutes.

The basic characteristic of this ultimate sacrifice in other-centered love is the absence of cynicism and the presence of the 'more'. Cynicism, often masked as austerely honest realism, is more accurately described as a jaundiced view of the world and of the loves forming this world. It contains the yellow bitterness of ultimate defeat, the stinging remembrance of being constantly cheated, the numb feeling of being an outcast suffering alone. Ultimately, the total cynic experiences bitter isolation from the community, feels reduced to a fetus, and frantically embraces the 'less than self' as he or she dies alone.

The total cynic's life and death involve a loss of human feeling; they pitifully contrast with the life and death of the heroic lover.

This contrast demonstrates unforgettably that other-centered love is the most humanizing influence in a person's life, that the heroic lover's acknowledgement of the unchosen absolute's assurance is the dynamism promoting this other-centered love, that the unchosen absolute is operative and therefore knowable within a person's experience, although one must infer this supportive presence in order to acknowledge it. For no sane person can freely and intelligently give away everything seen, felt, and loved unless he or she feels the assurance that something 'more' is in store for him or her. Finally, we arrive at the basic insight: if other-centered love with its drive to ultimate sacrifice is not insane and inhuman, but reasonable and human, then an unchosen absolute exists to make sure that other-centered love is such.[52] We are now ready, therefore, to discover who or what this unchosen absolute, this secular transcendent, is.

FOURTH STEP

What or Who Is this Unchosen Absolute

I n the introduction to this book, a survey of opinions concerning the meaning of 'absolute' furnished a common definition:
that immanent ultimate value which gives continuity to one's
life, community to one's strivings for love, central meaning to
one's intelligence, and solid hope to one's future actions (p. 39).
This absolute was later found to be as necessary and ordinary to
human survival as food, lungs, and brain. Its provisional definition allowed us to begin the search for the unchosen absolute in the
human experience of other-centered love.[53] But now we are in a
position to sift through the data gathered from the first through
the third step so that a more concrete existential definition of the
unchosen absolute can be given.

In supporting the other-centered lover so that the latter can 'do
the absolute', the unchosen absolute reveals certain characteristics
of its own operative being. For, in the act of other-centered love,
the lover goes beyond self, that is, beyond the limited relativity of
his or her essence, so that the very 'going beyond' can be attributed
only to the unchosen absolute. Exploration of this 'beyond', in the
first part of this fourth step, will give us the operative characteristics of the unchosen absolute. Then in the second part, these
characteristics, found ultimately operative in all other-centered
loves forever, will show us the unchosen absolute as the ultimate
total object of man's other-centered love. This discovery leads us,
in the appendix to the fourth step, to investigate the conclusion
that the unchosen absolute must therefore be Existence Itself.

A. Operative Characteristics of the Unchosen Absolute

Relativity totally permeates a person's every action; this makes it very clear that the individual's act of other-centered love could not promise a 'forever' commitment without the supportive presence of the unchosen absolute. Nor would the lover be bold enough to initiate deep love, nor be strong enough to accept a weakly returned love; nor be generous enough to support the multiple loves of family life, nor be free enough to seek the full liberation of the beloved even to the ultimate sacrifice of beloved, world, and self. This is the 'beyond human' which is structuring every act of other-centered love; it is the rather direct evidence not only of the unchosen absolute's presence but also of its nature and being. In this first part of the fourth step, we will consider the eight operative characteristics of the unchosen absolute—those characteristics found in the unchosen absolute's cooperation with the lover's act of other-centered love. They reveal that the unchosen absolute is immanent to the lovers, unites them, faithfully creates them, sovereignly calls them to personal sacrifice, totally communicates to them, liberates them, renders their love eternal, and offers them personal love. Let us spend a little time with each of these operative characteristics in order to better understand the nature of the unchosen absolute.

1. The Unchosen Absolute as Continuously and Deeply Immanent (See pp. 222–23)

We have already seen that the six basic phenomena constituting other-centered love would not exist without the unchosen absolute's causative support. Evidently, the unchosen absolute operates within this love act. One's sense of the worthwhileness of other-centered love, one's feeling of strength to bear its burdens, one's hearing and heeding of its sovereign call to ultimate sacrifice, are each the indubitable sign of the unchosen absolute's support within this act of love.

An objection could be raised at this point: does not such support imply that the act of other-centered love is appropriated by the unchosen absolute as its own? The act, then, would seem to be no longer under the control of the individual lover, no longer human.

In response to this, it should be noted that the other-centered act of love is free; it issues from man's independence. Consequently, the individual person decides whether or not there will be an act, whether or not it will be self-centered or other-centered, whether or not the underived absolute's support will be used for a more or less full, other-centered act of love. For example, a woman's sense of shame at her betrayal or manipulation of her beloved will burn deeply within her. For she is well aware that she had the strength and independence to love the beloved other-centeredly, but freely refused to use the strength or to use it fully. In other words, this lover freely controls the extent of her trust in and generosity toward the beloved.

Note also that the six phenomena which structure the other-centered act of love and serve as indubitable signs that the unchosen absolute supports this act are not foreign divine elements intruded into the human act. They are so evidently the very structure of the act that they are taken for granted by the human lover. As a result this book had to be written to call people's attention to the fact that these six phenomena are present only because of the unchosen absolute's support. Often they are thought to be simply the creation of the human person alone with no debt to a higher being.

The six signs, then, are not the unchosen absolute but rather are the constitutive effects of its supporting presence in the human act of other-centered love. They are as truly distinct from the unchosen absolute and as thoroughly human as a person's seeing or thinking. Yet they are just as dependent on the unchosen absolute's support as human seeing is dependent on colored objects and human thinking is dependent on objects of thought.

The fact that the six phenomena of other-centered love are merely signal effects of the unchosen absolute's support in human operations and constitute the human act itself, does not mean that the unchosen absolute is separated at a distance from the lover. Instead, the absolute is present, by way of the phenomena signs, to the act of love and hence to the lover out of whom the act is whelming. For, first, the act of love is an operation continually being modulated by the changing lover for the changing beloved in accord with their always changing situation; consequently, the support given by the unchosen absolute must be constantly adapting to the changing act of love according to these six phenomena which are the dynamic structure of the act. Therefore, these signs or effects, these characteristics, of other-centered love and of the unchosen absolute's supportive presence must be as supple and subtle as the act of love which they constitute.

Such sensitive modulation requires the constant and immediate presence of the unchosen absolute. For the latter cooperates so closely and thoroughly with the lover in the adaptive act of love that the six 'beyond human' phenomena characterize and indeed constitute this act. The fact that the unchosen absolute is not the lover, not the beloved, and not their act of love, does not demand that the absolute be separated from them. The unchosen absolute and the lover or the beloved could compenetrate without losing their distinct identities or being. Their compenetration is discovered in the fact that the six phenomena are constantly being adapted to the lover, the beloved, and their situation by the un- chosen absolute. Such split-second and exquisitely delicate modulation demands the immediate presence of the unchosen ab- solute; while the fact that the unchosen absolute immediately causes the constituent characteristics of the other-centered act of love requires the unchosen absolute to compenetrate not only the act of love but also the lover and the beloved who are coproducing this act with the unchosen absolute.

On the other hand, the distinctness of the unchosen absolute from the lover is evident, first in the latter's conviction that the love goes beyond the merely human and is not a totally human creation; secondly, in the lover's experience of guilt when he or she deliberately refuses to use the unchosen absolute's support for an act of love; and thirdly, in the lover's sense of being loved by the unchosen absolute and of wanting to return this love. Such dis- tinctness between human lover and unchosen absolute, far from demanding their separation, requires rather their compenetrating cooperation, their dynamic immanence to each other.

Moreover, this cooperative support from the unchosen absolute must be as continuous as the other-centered love between lover and beloved; else the love is broken. For this reason, the im- manence of the unchosen absolute in the lover is not fitful but per- during. For not only must the individual acts of other-centered love receive the cooperative influence of the unchosen absolute;

but also the resultant habitual love, namely friendship or marriage or brotherhood, out of which these individual acts serially rise, must be continuously supported so that such habitual love can lend its constant strength to further acts of other-centered love.

Besides being continuously intimate to the other-centered love act, the unchosen absolute can be as deeply immanent to the lover as the latter allows. The heavier the burdens carried by an other-centered love, and the more people embraced by it, the more this love needs the support of the unchosen absolute. The faithful cooperation of the unchosen absolute must match the depth and breadth of assistance needed by the courageous lover. This absolute is present, then, for every act of other-centered love, present as fully and deeply as the lover's act requires, and most present when a person in fullest manhood or womanhood is making the ultimate sacrifice for the beloved. This is why it can be said that the unchosen absolute is deeply devoted to a person's fullest development at the deepest level of his or her being, especially during the most critical moments of life. This is the unchosen absolute's immanence, its immediate compenetrative presence with the other-centered love and being of an individual.

2. The Unchosen Absolute as Unitive and Companionate (See pp. 223-25)

The immanence of the unchosen absolute is not expressed solely in its union with the individual lover; such intimacy also occurs in its union with the beloved. The very reciprocity of the act of love requires that the unchosen absolute be simultaneously present within both lover and beloved if the love is to be other-centered from both sides. For the love is a single act in its essential reciprocity. Thus the unchosen absolute is the deepest reality which lover and beloved hold in common. Indeed, their unity of heart, mind, and body is founded on the operative common presence of the unchosen absolute. The latter, in other words, is the mediator forming every friendship, family, and community insofar as each is based on other-centered love.

Within the human act of love, as lover and beloved adapt to each other and to their situation, the unitive quality of the unchosen absolute's immanent activity can be called companionate, even compassionate. For a remarkable orchestration occurs as the unchosen absolute adapts to the mutual adaptation of lover and beloved in order to support the unique growth of each in this single reciprocal act of love. Since the act of love draws upon the deepest reaches of the heart and stirs the feelings of man and woman beyond all else, the support of the unchosen absolute accompanies the heart's lift in joy and its sudden plunge in sorrow; it is present to expand the heart wide as it sails high in generosity, and to heal the crushed heart when it crashes against the reefs of harsh events.

3. The Unchosen Absolute as Faithfully Creative of Other-centered Love (See pp. 225–27)

Not only does the unchosen absolute support the love-act once begun; the unchosen absolute initiates love and sustains languishing love. In their essential reciprocity, the offer of love and the response to the offer must be simultaneous and somewhat matching in other-centered intent. How, except by chance, could love ever get started or ever recover from decline unless a mediating absolute blends its supportive influence with the act of love between lover and beloved? Such blending would require not merely immanence within both lover and beloved but a balance of timing and of intent so that the slowness or the weakness of one would not mock the quickness or strength of the other.

Only the unchosen absolute could furnish such anticipatory reciprocation to the lover both directly through its presence within the lover and indirectly through its simultaneous presence in the beloved. For it strengthens both lover and beloved according to the need of each so that the act of other-centered love can perdure. The one who carries the heavier burden of loving more and being loved less receives more strength. Yet this strength, which is open to rejection, supports rather than diminishes the freedom of love; when recognized, its very gratuity as being 'beyond the human' removes condescension from the lover's attitude towards the beloved who loves less. Further, this strength, being 'beyond the human', renders the lover realistic about the beloved who loves less. For this support does not substitute for the beloved's failure in love but simply helps the lover accept the failure with compassionate strength. Meanwhile the beloved may also be aware of receiving strength in love 'beyond the human' and, therefore, may realistically assess the failure to love. This strengthening in lover and beloved is not meant simply to arouse guilt and remind the lovers of failure. For it promises to support future growth and calls for this growth. Thus this strengthening tends to enlarge liberty, to deepen communication, and to heighten compassion as the bases for future loving.

For these reasons, we say that the unchosen absolute promotes other-centered love. This absolute furnishes both lover and beloved with the strength of anticipatory reciprocation so that love can begin and then continue despite the uneven response between lover and beloved. In this way, the unchosen absolute enables the essential reciprocity of other-centered love to achieve continuous growth despite human fickleness and weakness. It encourages the child to break out of the narrow circle of self-centeredness, the wife to live on courageously with the self-hating alcoholic husband, the husband to give affection generously to the shallow-living wife. Thus the unchosen absolute is forever loving love into existence. For what is this anticipatory strengthening from the unchosen absolute if it is not a type of love? Does it not complete inadequate human love so that it can freely become more adequate in the future?

4. The Unchosen Absolute as Creative of Persons (See pp. 227–31)

Such strengthening of the lover is a sovereign call to continual sacrifice for the beloved. This involves hazard. For as long as the beloved is free enough to reject the lover, the lover must gamble on the beloved's faithfulness as warranted by the unchosen absolute's support. Nonetheless, the lover also trusts the self more deeply when accepting the interior experience of this support. The lover also becomes less self-centered by entrusting the self to the beloved without demanding a return of love even though, out of respect for the beloved's goodness, the lover desires and hopes for return. In thus acting, the lover transcends the self, that is, goes beyond previous trust and freedom by acting upon the unchosen absolute's assurance found operative in the self and in the beloved. At the same time, as the lover creates new growth in the self, he or she also offers the beloved a fresh opportunity for vital expansiveness.

Yet all this while, both beloved and lover feel free in this creative moment. In fact, because the sovereign call can be rejected, and yet keeps vital options open if the lovers decide to take them (such as how and when and whom they will love), it increases rather than diminishes their freedom to choose. When the choices are good, the sovereign caller becomes coresponsible for the increased liberty of the lover and the beloved, that is, for the fuller and better-balanced development of their personalities.

Such free creativity enables an elder son to sacrifice college education to send his younger sister through high school and college. It helps a daughter to give up plans for marriage in order to keep house for her elderly mother and to allow her married brothers and sisters to be more free to raise their families. This beautiful creativity, hidden in drab, day-to-day sacrifice, builds other individuals into fuller personhood and at the same time fosters deeper family living.

The sovereignty of this call, then, is not a totalitarian crushing of a person's freedom. It is a lordly support of the lover's trust in his or her own capacity for deep and faithful love and in the capacity of others for like response. But the long-term suffering involved whenever the lover creatively tries to help another grow in personhood or liberty requires that this sovereignty of the unchosen absolute be felt as a constant companion. It is here that the lover experiences the compassion which makes his or her creativity possible. Here too the lover recognizes that the unchosen absolute has concern for the lover's and the beloved's growth in free personhood. This is the fourth operative characteristic of the unchosen absolute: creative of persons through sacrifical other-centered love.

5. The Unchosen Absolute as Totally Communicative. (See pp. 231–235)

The unchosen absolute's remarkable ability to adapt creatively to the lovers' changing needs implies an intelligence of high order guiding this strengthening of their other-centered love. For a mark of such love is its bright inventiveness and growing wholesomeness, whereas a characteristic of self-centered love is its drab routines and spasmodic divisiveness. Other-centered love, because it focuses on the everchanging needs of the beloved rather than on the lover's past needs and accomplishments, is frequently fresh, spontaneous and oriented to the future. Its adaptiveness promotes growth in the beloved and thus in the lover so that they remain young in mind and heart. Self-centered love, however, is self-satisfied and therefore busies itself with protecting its past gains. As a result it does not look for new ways to please the beloved; this costs too much time and effort. Instead, it keeps to past actions which soon harden into routines shackling any growth. Active intelligence grows sluggish in such a love, while the shrewd and cunning strategies for self-aggrandizement thrive. It is love growing cold and old from hardening of the intellectual arteries.

For this reason, the inventive uniqueness of each love act, as the lovers swiftly adapt to each other's unique needs in their evolving situation, requires a notably adaptive intelligence of the unchosen absolute as the latter adaptively supports lover and beloved. In other words, the complex event of the act of this particular lover has never before happened in this way; yet it arises out of the love acts of these lovers and simultaneously adapts itself to a fresh situation. If the unchosen absolute would cooperate helpfully in this act, it must be intelligently aware of the total state of lover, beloved, and the situation. Unless the unchosen absolute is thus totally communicative with them in knowledge and love, its sovereign call would be unrealistic and destructive of them. For this call would either demand too much of the lovers or weakly allow them to sink back unchallenged into past performances.

The intelligent cooperation of the unchosen absolute does not stop with the inventiveness of other-centered love. The inventive act of other-centered love both integrates the lover's past more closely with the present situation and builds the lover's and the beloved's common future more solidly into the community's future. Concretely, this means that the lover affirms the total truth of his beloved and the situation of their love. The total truth includes both the bad and the good of the beloved's health, job, home, ambition, relatives, friends, hobbies, and hopes.

This affirmation is, first of all, a knowledgeful acceptance of things as they are; but secondly it is an intelligent desire to increase the future good and decrease the present evil in the beloved and in the latter's living conditions no matter the cost. In order to help the beloved towards more wholesome personhood and community, the lover's disciplined intelligence must share responsibility for the other's intricate growth through many years. This is not the instant intimacy of the sensitivity session or of seating arrangements in a Boeing 747 or of a passionate affair. It is the cumulative intelligence rising out of a perduring marriage or friendship; not the more spasmodic shrewdness issuing out of divergent experiences with shifting love-partners. It is the holistic intelligence of growing confidence in a continuing friendship rather than the divisive cunning of growing cynicism coming from multiple fractured love relationships.

If such intelligence is necessary for lover and beloved so that their love can grow, it is all the more necessary for the unchosen absolute because the latter must adapt to both lover and beloved not merely for the present moment but also for their future which the absolute is forever guaranteeing by his supportive presence. In other words, to assure ever growing communication in love and knowledge between the lovers, the unchosen absolute must communicate itself to them in ever growing totality since it is the immanent mediator for their mutual trust, freedom, companionship, compassion, and personal creativity in sacrifice. As the wholeness of the lover, of the beloved, and of their community grows, the totality of the unchosen absolute's intelligent self-giving must increase in order to anticipate the lovers' wholesome growth with the proper strengthening. Here the only limit to the intelligent giving is the ability of lover and beloved to receive. The unchosen absolute can offer no fuller, more intelligent self-communication than this.

6. The Unchosen Absolute as Expanding Human Liberty (See pp. 235–41)

In proportion as the unchosen absolute communicates itself to the lovers, they find that they can give themselves to a wider and wider spectrum of different people and live more deeply with them. This surprises them; for they know that many of their contemporaries are narrowing their interests to smaller, cozier circles of friends and losing their ability to accept and act upon new ideas, to exploit new opportunities, to make new friends, and yet to live with serenity. The sight of diminished freedom in their contemporaries sharpens the sense of freedom growing in themselves. Yet they also know that this new liberty is not just the daring of their own intelligences but is also the strengthening assurance of the unchosen absolute. The unchosen absolute enables them to go 'beyond the human' and not to succumb to cynical tiredness. The more this assurance grows, that is, the more totally the unchosen absolute communicates himself to the lovers, the more their liberty grows.

To express this on the metaphysical level, the more dependent the lovers are upon the unchosen absolute, the more independently they act. The more deeply they experience the dependent relativity of their essence, the more fully they express the independent absolute of their assertive existence. Concretely, the more people they love and the more they share the burdens of these beloved people, the more their liberty to accept these burdens generously must be supported by the unchosen absolute. The essence-relativity of the lover's being grows only if the existence-independence of this being is asserted to promote and sustain this growth. The lover's essence expands and becomes liberated in new developmental activity only if the lover's act of existence is free or independent enough to move out through the essence in ever expanding acts of love towards more and more people according to the latter's very different needs.

Thus, inasmuch as the unchosen absolute supports the growth of the lovers' liberty, it works within their very act of existence so that they can perform acts of absolute love. Hence they can assert their independence, within their dependent relativity, towards their fellowmen, their world, and their unchosen absolute. This does not mean that the lover's substantial existence changes in each act of love. On that score, the lover's radical person or basic continuous identity would be broken. Rather, the full power of the lover's independent existence is released in a new way through her or his dependent essence and organizes the latter to a new level of humanity. But the strength for the release is precisely the support of the unchosen absolute which is thus constantly endeavoring to help a person to expand his or her being to that greater fullness called human liberty. This expansive liberty shows itself precisely in the lover's greater faithfulness to the beloved, more intelligent trust of the beloved, greater readiness to increase the beloved's wholesome freedom, and deeper willingness to sacrifice everything for the beloved. Since it is the lover's existence which empowers all the acts of love, accumulates them, and integrates them into the whole of the person, this same existence is the root of the lover's person and liberty.

It is this same act of existence which the lover seems called upon to surrender to death when and if the ultimate sacrifice of life is required in order to save the beloved. Paradoxically, the lover's act of existence must be independent enough for him or her to value the beloved more than the whole world and to value the beloved's act of existence even more than the lover's own act of existence. For example, the engineer sacrificed his career in order to nurse his wife back to mental wholeness. Paradoxically, the lover's fullest act of liberty and personhood can at times appear to require the loss of that existence which is the root of liberty and personhood. Only the unchosen absolute could give sufficient strength to the lover's liberty for such a sacrifice and could call sovereignly for the free use of this strength.

How magnificent the support of the unchosen absolute is can be measured by the lover's freedom from hubris, from recrimination, and from self-deprecation in the midst of the ultimate sacrifice. This is truly a divine act and 'beyond the human' yet done by a human. In the lover's final freedom for generosity is mirrored the unchosen absolute's full communication of itself to the lover.

But the unchosen absolute reveals itself even more clearly in a further reach of man's liberty beyond this ultimate sacrifice. Once the lover has attained this ultimate level of liberty in personhood, he or she at last becomes fully capable of rejecting or accepting the unchosen absolute for itself. The ultimate sacrifice, which seems to leave the beloved and the whole universe behind, thrusts the lover into full confrontation with the unchosen absolute which alone remains. At this point, if the unchosen absolute is not to rescind its support, it must let the lover use this support to reject or to accept it. The lover, knowing the extent of this freedom and recognizing the unchosen absolute's noble generosity, is fully aware that he or she has the liberty, if not the intent, to reject the unchosen absolute now clearly seen as ultimate value. Truly the negative final measure of a man's freedom is his ability to reject the unchosen absolute, if this must be.

On the other hand, the positive measure of the unchosen

absolute's freedom is its willingness to risk this rejection by supporting the lover's dependence so absolutely that the beloved's reciprocation, strengthened by the unchosen absolute, gives the lover strength to resist even the unchosen absolute. The unchosen absolute's willingness to risk everything points unmistakably to its totally other-centered love and to its deep respect for the individual lover. On the one hand, the unchosen absolute's total communication of itself to the liberty of the lover shows its remarkable devotion to the latter and to the liberation of humankind. On the other hand, the lover's liberty finally to reject the unchosen absolute forever by reason of the latter's total self-communication to this lover is a negative demonstration and measure of the unchosen absolute's unbelievably generous desire to promote human liberty at any cost.

This absolute unselfishness, this total communication of the unchosen absolute to lovers, offers a small window upon its fullness of being. Its ontological resources are such that it does support any lover, even all lovers, without demanding return. Its support in each lover is not dependent upon return from the lover and it goes all the way up to and past, if needs be, the final rejection of itself. Further, it not only loves the lover into existence through interior strengthening of the latter but also loves the lover through the beloved whom it is also strengthening to return love generously and other-centeredly to the lover. Thus, in a strange dependence upon both lover and beloved, the unchosen absolute expresses its love for both through each of them. It is not satisfied with directly loving them both into existence as individuals. It feels the need to love the lover through the beloved and the beloved through the lover so that it also loves them into existence as social beings. In this way, it liberates them not only directly through its immediate support of their individual existences but also indirectly through their mutual or social act of love. This operative characteristic best typifies the unchosen absolute in the other-centered act of love: the expansion of human liberty by direct support to the individual and by indirect support through the beloved and the community.

7. The Unchosen Absolute as Rendering Human Love Eternal (See pp. 241–43)

If one is to see the full splendor of the unchosen absolute's action in the other-centered act of love, one must note the full psychological and historical context of its occurrence. The observer will then view the unchosen absolute's support of other-centered love as the central meaning of the universe and the ultimate value of humankind's ongoing historical life. Under these two aspects, it becomes clear how the unchosen absolute renders a person's other-centered love eternal not by a vague poetic metaphor but through the definite events of world history. In this way the magnificent destiny offered to each individual person will dramatically portray the hidden beauty and unfailing love of the unchosen absolute for each person and for the family of humankind.

Let us consider first how the unchosen absolute's support of other-centered love provides the central meaning of the universe, and gives humankind an unbounded intelligent vision of the universe. Recall how the unchosen absolute, immanent to both lover and beloved in their act of other-centered love, strengthens them to accept the whole truth, both the good and the bad, about each other and their situation. Insofar as the lovers cooperated in this, their love of each other became wholesome, that is, it formed a community of liberated persons. Now the very wholesomeness of this particular love is also openness to other loves. It is a ready willingness to love and to be loved by other people so long as in-jury is not done to the original love and so long as the resultant obligations can be physically and psychologically borne by the two original lovers.

The example of the grandparents glancing over their children's children at the fiftieth wedding anniversary comes to mind. This wholesomeness of the original family stretches out to embrace the children's and grandchildren's families whose number is large enough to constitute a neighborhood and widely enough distributed to span a city. But when other-centered love, rooted in the deep affection of definite families, spreads out over the city, its exuberance begins to extend over many cities and the entire nation through other families touched deeply by the original families. It becomes a health-giving patriotism.

It is not even limited to a nation. When cooperation among nations (and even among planetary peoples) is seen to be the best way to love one's own nation other-centeredly, this wholesome love becomes international. Before the time of intercontinental ballistic missiles and worldwide satellite communication, the above sentence would have seemed ridiculously idealistic. Now it is recognized as a necessity that the other-centered love between lover and beloved be ready to stretch its wholesomeness as wide as the world, if not yet as wide as the planetary universe. Nothing less than the taproot of other-centered love can nourish the great tree of life burgeoning out into our wide world and into the universe. There is no more basic and powerful source for the wholesomeness which is needed to heal our torn world and our broken universe.

The total truth, good and bad, of this family, this city, this nation, this international world, and this interplanetary community, will never be accepted unless other-centered love operates at the heart of these communities. If one becomes content with the half-truths generated and sustained by self-centered love, then one must resign oneself to the consequent violence, divisiveness, oppressed freedom, and routinized boredom of domineering 'love', to say nothing of the chaos due to malicious falsehood. Each person each day of his or her life is making decisions which cumulate into a choice of life—either a self-centered or an other-centered life of love. On the one hand, self-centered love provides a life of merely temporary commitment, broken amical relationships, fragmented families, narrowing liberty, despair of national and international community, and the final alienation of total loneliness.

Other-centered love, on the other hand, enables a person to participate fully in the unchosen absolute's life of eternal commitment, perduring friendships, wholesome families and nations, expanding liberty, solid hope for international peace, and final fullness of community. In other words, the other-centered lover lives the continuity or foreverness of the unchosen absolute. As a result, this lover becomes dynamically engaged in the whole truth of the developing universe, finds himself or herself centered within the international human family, and discovers the eternity of other-centered love amid all the beloveds. The foreverness of sacrifical love now has as much meaning as the whole universe—and more, because it includes that unchosen absolute who is beyond, yet within, the universe and who makes this vision first possible and later actual.

A. Operative Characteristics of the Unchosen Absolute

The mention of sacrificial love, however, throws a disturbing, if not contradictory, shadow upon this bright vision which is contained within the ambit of other-centered love. For the whole vision becomes a mocking delusion if a person is annihilated by the very act of other-centered love within which this vision is found. For this reason, let us look at the second aspect of the unchosen absolute's eternal support of other-centered love: the ongoing historical life of this love.

When the unchosen absolute gives strength to the unlimited, yet definite, growth of a particular other-centered love and when it makes sure that this strength is interpreted as a sovereign call to a potential ultimate sacrifice on behalf of the beloved, it implicitly warrants the future worthwhileness of the sacrificial love. If this love is reciprocal and if its future is guaranteed as worthwhile, then it must continue to exist after the sacrificial act. Otherwise, if the lover is completely annihilated in death by his or her sacrificial act, no reciprocity is possible, no love is possible, and hence no future can be guaranteed to this love. The unchosen absolute would be perversely luring the lover into a totally self-destructive act with the false promise of a future life of love and of community.

This is the same unchosen absolute who supports the lover to accept and to live the total truth of the beloved and their situation even to the extremes of the universe; who is constantly urging the lover never to stop building the liberty of other persons and hence the lover's own liberty; who is ever requesting the lover never to limit the other-centered love but to let it expand steadily to as many people as the lover can sustain. Suddenly, then, the unchosen absolute would seem to trap the other-centered lover into an act of love whose very expansiveness narrows life and liberty to nothing, whose future-thrust of foreverness smashes the present millisecond's duration, whose drive to the fullness of total truth leads abruptly to vast emptiness; whose sacrifice is really suicide.

The absurdity of these conclusions, together with the hard factualness of the six phenomena constituting the other-centered act of love, points to a single conclusion: the unchosen absolute works so that, even after an ultimate sacrifice requiring death of the lover, the latter's love and person nevertheless continue on and continue to grow. Somehow death does not lift lovers out from the flow of history and separate them from their beloveds. Instead, if their love is to grow (and this is the promise contained implicitly in the sovereign call), they must still be able to give and to receive love from the beloveds. Further these acts of love must be historical or serially cumulative, and must contain new life events, be spontaneously inventive, move to closer union, and be able to freely develop in depth and breadth.

To conclude otherwise is to accept either Sartre's absurd human or Spencer's inhuman human. For each, at either end of the spectrum of love, loudly affirms the absurdity of other-centered love and the lethal delusions of its practice. Consequently, if the unchosen absolute sovereignly calls the lover to ultimate sacrifice within the act of other-centered love, this absolute likewise implicitly calls the lover to a fuller life of love and of liberty after death. The unchosen absolute also implicitly warrants that it will absolutely support such a future life. The destiny of the other-centered lover is, then, immortal life.

These two aspects of the unchosen absolute's cooperation in the act of other-centered love, namely,

1. its centering of the lover in the total meaning of the universe, and
2. its giving of a historically and forever-growing ultimate value to the lover's other-centered love,

induce the conclusion that the unchosen absolute intends the lover's seemingly temporary and tightly circumscribed love act to be an eternal source of growth. Here, in the act of other-centered love, the unchosen absolute reveals much more than its immanent presence. It also discloses to our minds and hearts what the medievals called God's wisdom and providence. For these are the constituents of God's eternity seen historically and concretely in man's cooperation with God and, more specifically, in man's drive to express love eternally with the total gift of self.

8. The Unchosen Absolute as Other-centered Lover (See pages 243–48)

We have already noted that the unchosen absolute is nothing if not a lover. It starts all loves, sustains each of them, helps them grow, and makes up for their inadequacies; in all these, it delicately balances and blends between lovers their strengths and weaknesses as though it were Love Itself. By reason of its immanence, the unchosen absolute's cooperation with the lover and beloved is the most intimate, creatively adaptive, intelligently realistic, deeply compassionate, closely unitive, and immortally liberative of all activities. If this is not love, what is? If the unchosen absolute is not a lover, who is? Therefore, at this point, it is time to let the personal pronoun *he* stand for the unchosen absolute. We use the masculine form here only because of scriptural tradition; no personal pronoun fits the secular transcendent since the latter includes and is beyond all genders.[54]

He is also the most other-centered of all lovers. In providing the deepest common basis for the love between lover and beloved and in letting them freely set the limits to how much of him they will accept, the unchosen absolute becomes totally communicative of himself. This complete self-gifting reaches its deepest level when the unchosen absolute takes the ultimate gamble of strengthening human freedom so that the humankind has the fullest capability of rejecting or accepting him. Paradoxically, humankind's capability is built out of the intelligent vision and the providential warranty present, in its other-centered love, as gifts from the unchosen absolute's wisdom and providence. These gifts are the dynamisms whereby human other-centered love takes on the unlimitedness of forever commitment and yet expresses this commitment in definite historical events towards a definite growing community of beloveds. In this we glimpse the unchosen absolute's infinite fecundity as he supports human growth unendingly.

Such unconditional gifting, which necessitates no return yet deeply desires loving response, displays an absolute other-centeredness based radically on the unchosen and underived absolute's total independence. He is not derived from any other being but they are all derived from him. Only a divinely poised freedom could gladly risk so much and then sovereignly call every lover to do the same for the beloved. This call centers the lover's life in the beloved and in the latter's community with total truth in love and with total love in truth. It involves a total devotion to the human universe through very definite beloveds and their historical communities. Therefore, the truly other-centered lover, like the unchosen absolute, is secular in the sense that he or she loves the unchosen absolute's world. To reject the world of the unchosen absolute is to reject the unchosen absolute immanent in and loving of that world. The lover, then, is worldly if he or she is truly a lover. For this reason, the unchosen absolute is truly the secular transcendent towards whom we have been approaching.

And yet the unchosen absolute calls the lover to be ready to sacrifice this world, the beloveds, their communities, and life itself. In fact, he makes this call within the lover's deeply creative and deeply secular act of other-centered love. And the only reason given to the lover for this total stripping is the loving wish of the unchosen absolute. In this dark night of decision, only one light shines: the unchosen absolute, the secular transcendent. Here, within the act of other-centered love, the unchosen absolute is at last revealed as the ultimate total object who lies behind and within the proximate total object, the beloved, of human other-centered love. Is this not also to say that the unchosen absolute is the ultimate beloved? Is this not to reveal the beauty of human death as the stripping away of all supports except the unchosen absolute so that man can give himself totally to the beloved unchosen absolute in total trust?

Thus other-centered love is the most secular of loves in its proximate total object and the most transcendent of loves in its ultimate total object. Because these two objects compenetrate in the single act of other-centered love, the reciprocal action between them never ends and man's growth can continue forever. This mysterious compenetration demands further investigation. For it not only discloses a new characteristic in the unchosen absolute but also implies that the first and second of the great commandments found in the Judaeo-Christian tradition compenetrate within the single act of other-centered love.

Conclusion

By delving into the six characteristic phenomena of human other-centered love we have discovered their causes, the eight operative characteristics of the unchosen absolute, by which one can go 'beyond the human' in one's love. Because one can reject or modify this support, one's freedom is not lost and one's love remains as human as seeing and thinking. Nevertheless, this presence of the unchosen absolute within the human act of love must be immediate to and compenetrate the lover's being since it adapts so quickly and delicately to the slightest changes in love between lover and beloved. This dynamic cooperative immanence must also be continuously present if the love is to be constant—and deeply present if the lover is to be able to shoulder the growing obligations of loving more generously and widely.

Further, the reciprocity of love demands that the unchosen absolute operate simultaneously in both lover and beloved as their common possession. In thus quietly mediating between them, the unchosen absolute acts as their compassionate companion. But because loving is such a stop-and-go, up-and-down experience, love risks diminishment, sometimes sudden loss, unless the unchosen absolute furnishes anticipatory reciprocation in both lover and beloved to keep the love somewhat constant and growing. Such anticipation at times takes the form of a sovereign calling of the lover to continual sacrifice for the beloved, to self-transcendence. This is the lover's gamble on the beloved's faithfulness which is warranted by the unchosen absolute's support. Such instant and yet supple adaptation on the part of the unchosen absolute demands of him an inventive intelligence which, as in the lover and the beloved, affirms the whole truth about them and their situation. Consequently, their now more wholesome love can build a more wholesome community. Thus the unchosen absolute's anticipatory support spans not only the past and the present of lover and beloved but also their future and their community's future.

Such total communication, by strengthening the lover and beloved for more and more responsible loves in their community, also gradually expands their independent existence to higher levels of personal integration and liberty—yet all this is crowned by a paradoxical call to give up their existence in self-sacrifice for others. At this point a mysterious event occurs. The lover finds the self being stripped of all chosen absolutes so that only the solitary unchosen absolute remains. Ironically, the lover can then reject the unchosen absolute with the support of the unchosen absolute. This great risk-taking of the unchosen absolute reveals his confidence in his own attractiveness and in his own personal resources of totally achieved being. It further discloses his respect for human liberty and loyalty as well as his confidence in man's basic goodness and generosity. Consequently, the unchosen absolute unites all the other-centered lovers and beloveds throughout the world with absolute generosity whereas grasping self-centered lovers and beloveds separate in anguish.

The unchosen absolute's love, then, spans not only families, neighborhoods, nations, and world, but also all lovers of the past, present, and future in a life-beyond-death where the community ever expands in wisdom, love, and joy. Because the unchosen absolute so totally communicates himself to the human world, he is the ultimate lover; because he works towards fuller love between lover and beloved, they, in turn, through their constant and generous love for each other, make the unchosen absolute the great beloved, the total ultimate object of their other-centered love. This last sentence demands an explanation; it will be attempted immediately in the next section.

B. The Unchosen Absolute, as Ultimate Total Object of Human Other-centered Love

When we say that the unchosen absolute is the ultimate total object, the ultimate beloved, of the act of other-centered love, does this mean merely that each other-centered love has the unchosen absolute forever operative deep within it as its ultimate support? What do *total* and *ultimate* mean here? How is it possible for one act of love to have simultaneously two objects, two beloveds? Would not one beloved distract from the other? From these new angles, let us reconsider the unchosen absolute's operative characteristics and the six phenomena which constitute the act of other-centered love. We hope to discover some new facets of the unchosen absolute and to indicate more precisely the manner in which the unchosen absolute operates within the act of other-centered love.

The Unchosen Absolute: Faithful Face Forever

Any lover who tries to love the beloved other-centeredly must face towards the beloved and concentrate full attention on the latter. As we have already seen, this full attention draws upon all four levels of the lover's experience: the biological, the psychological, the moral, and the metaphysical. With the totality of the self, the lover faces the beloved at every matching level of the latter's experience. In this the lover is totally other-centered, that is, totally devoted to the beloved.

But to perdure in this total self-gifting, the lover needs the unchosen absolute's strengthening presence discovered both within the lover's faithful loving of the beloved and within the beloved's trusting response to this lover. The lover, therefore, in facing the beloved during their mutual and total self-giving, must simultaneously face the unchosen absolute. This happens in such a way that the perduring fidelity with which the lover faces the beloved will be as strong as the confidence with which the lover experiences the support of the unchosen absolute both directly in the self and indirectly in the faithful response of the beloved. Reciprocally, too, the lover's perduring faithfulness to the unchosen absolute's support will be measurable by this lover's constant devotion to the beloved.

Though the beloved and the unchosen absolute are quite distinct realities for the lover, still the lover cannot be faithful to one without being faithful to the other. There is a perfect compenetration of interests and intents within the single act of other-centered love. Instead of distracting the lover from the beloved, the unchosen absolute's support within the love directly thrusts the lover towards the beloved and indirectly, through the beloved's response, lures the lover to the beloved. At the same time the lover is aware that only through the unchosen absolute is the lover's faithfulness to the beloved and the latter's faithfulness to the lover made possible and actual. As a result, the lover cannot help but experience a deep gratefulness towards the unchosen absolute for making possible this great joy of mutual gifting between the self and the beloved.

Of course, the unchosen absolute strengthens lover and beloved for this perduring faithfulness, this 'forever' commitment, through his own constant immanent presence of total self-gift. Without his supportive presence, the foreverness would go out of their love; he is the ultimate basis for their eternal commitment to each other. Insofar as they gratefully acknowledge their complete dependence on him and on his total self-gift to them, they make him the total ultimate object of their love by making each other the total proximate object of this love. In loving each other proximately and totally, that is, directly with all four levels of their experience and with perduring faithfulness, they inevitably love the unchosen absolute totally in and through this same act of love, that is, indirectly and ultimately, since their total or 'forever' devotion to each other, is ultimately made possible by his total self-gift in his immanent presence to them both. Because they totally love the unchosen absolute through their total act of love for each other, he becomes the ultimate total object of this same act of love.

We can better appreciate this fact with a contrary example. The self-centered lover does not give over the total self in total trust forever since this lover continually reflects back upon personal self-interests and implicitly sets time conditions instead of giving full attention to the beloved. Naturally, in this instance the lover is depending mainly on personal strength to be faithful to the beloved and on personal cunning to elicit trusting response from the latter. The conditions introduced into this self-centered love can make it either overly relative to the beloved's demands and thus drown the lover's independence in the world of the beloved or contrarily overly absolute and thus isolate the lover from the beloved because of domineering demands made upon the latter. In either case, fidelity, although weak and relative at best, would be bought at a self-destructive cost; only a partial self-gift is possible.

Furthermore, the unchosen absolute's assistance is left relatively unused and therefore less recognized. Here either the lover or the beloved tends to become not only the total proximate object but also the total ultimate object of the love—depending on which of them conquers the other through cunning strategy. In this way, the foreverness of love becomes as temporary as the strength of weak men and women in a totally relativistic world of broken families, divorce, violence, manipulation and final isolation. This is the price of not facing the unchosen absolute in his faithful immanent presence.

The Unchosen Absolute: the Alpha and Omega of Love

Further, this immanent presence does more than merely cooperate with loves already in progress. As we noted earlier, the unchosen absolute instigates all other-centered loves, sustains them during periods of languishing, and supplies for their inadequacies. Because other-centered love is so difficult a feat for humankind, and because its reciprocal nature demands simultaneity of somewhat equal initiative and response between lover and beloved, it can simply never begin, much less continue to grow, without some assistance from the unchosen absolute. Nevertheless, because of the lover's and the beloved's freedom, this assistance can be refused and self-centered love be attempted. Indeed, no love will occur, unless the human lover freely chooses the beloved and freely chooses how he will love the latter—self-centeredly or other-centeredly.

Yet in his freedom, the lover cannot begin to give full other-centered attention to the beloved unless the lover has the unchosen absolute's instigating assurance that even unrequited love is worthwhile. In this way, the unchosen absolute's assisting presence calls attention to itself by enabling the lover freely to continue this love even when the lover knows that the beloved's response is qualitatively far less than total self-gift and will very likely never be equal to the lover's self-gift. The unchosen absolute, then, supplies for the beloved's deficiencies without obscuring their existence and without attempting to substitute himself for the beloved. For the unchosen absolute's assurance is experienced by the lover not merely in the latter's own act of love but in the very response of the beloved whose weakness pleads for the lover's strength. The lover, aware that some of this strength is not his or her own, is not inclined to pity the beloved or to vaunt the self. Thus in protecting the beloved daughter's fragility, the loving mother relives her own weakness. Consequently, precisely because the unchosen absolute supports a mother's self-trust, she focuses her attention compassionately on the needs and beauty of the beloved daughter. The latter, as the freely chosen beloved, then becomes the loving mother's proximate object.

But the totalness of this love will be dependent on the lover's ability to recognize within the beloved's response a potential for reciprocal total giving—a potential compounded out of the beloved's generosity and the unchosen absolute's supportive presence. Thus the lover trusts and gives the self more totally to the beloved precisely in proportion as the lover becomes more alert to the unchosen absolute's support within the beloved's response. Such alertness occurs, however, only because of the lover's previous recognition that the beloved's response is in itself only a potentially total self-giving. Later the lover recognizes and accepts the unchosen absolute as the ultimate total support of this love and, therefore, as its ultimate total object.

When this last recognition reaches the full awareness that the unchosen absolute is responsible for the beginning of reciprocity in this love, for its continual growth, and for its support during periods of languishing, then the lover knows that the unchosen absolute is supplying for deficiencies not only in the beloved but also in the lover by blending their complementary strengths and weaknesses into a wholesomeness. Through his immanent presence, the unchosen absolute fills the emptiness of each so that each may minister the resultant fullness to the needs of the other. He cheers the loneliness of each so that each may give companionship to the other. Because no love is perfectly matched, he thus helps lover and beloved attain some balanced wholesomeness. Their recognition that his total self-gift to them enables them to be totally devoted to each other makes him the ultimate total object of their gratefulness.

But all of this does not deny that the beloved is the proximate total object of the love since the unchosen absolute initiates, supports, and completes this love through the lover's daring initiative, through the beloved's trusting response to the initiative, and through the growing freedom of their reactions to each other. For this reason, the unchosen absolute, by supporting the self-trust and the other-trust in each, is never guilty of substituting himself for one or the other. Instead, he instigates the lover and lures the beloved into producing their own act of mutual love so that eventually each can freely make a total self-giving to the other forever.

However, this total and proximate self-giving cannot come to exist, nor, existent, continue to grow, unless the unchosen absolute, immanent to both lover and beloved, instigate, support, and complete their act of love with his assurance to both lover and beloved that this act of love is worthy of each. He does this precisely through his own self-gift of immanent presence as total ultimate object of that love. For both the lover and the beloved are very much aware, as their love matures in suffering and in joy, that alone—without the unchosen absolute's total self-gift to them—they could not intelligently trust themselves to a 'forever' relationship. In other words, the proximate total devotion between lovers happens only because of the unchosen absolute's ultimate total devotion to them. Perhaps this is why elderly lovers wonder at their daring to take 'forever' vows to each other four decades previously.

For this reason, the unchosen absolute is clearly the alpha and the omega of love, the source and the term of all other-centered loves. In this sense he is Love Itself. Yet without the free cooperation and contributions of the lover and the beloved in their act of love, the unchosen absolute could not be known through their love. And without the lovers' free pursuit of each other's beauty as total proximate object, the marvelous quality of beauty in the unchosen lover as total ultimate object would never be recognized.

Fourth Step

The Unchosen Absolute: Vital Center of All World's Loves

Because the unchosen absolute, through his immanence, can alone be simultaneously present and operative within lover and beloved to initiate, sustain, and promote their other-centered love, he alone is the ultimate mediator who is forming all communities founded by other-centered loves.[55] He not only unites the individual lover and beloved; but also, with his gift of anticipatory strength, he enables these two original lovers to open their radical love out in branchings to many other people—without diminishing their original love but rather increasing it. This readiness to suffer love under the accumulation of new obligations enables these lovers to stretch their love over a neighborhood, even over a city.

Now, running through the trunk of that original love and through all its branchings is the anticipatory strength given by the unchosen absolute who thus reveals himself to be the unifying animator of community. If no other being can unify either a lover and a beloved or the many families of a community by his simultaneous promotive immanent presence, then the unchosen absolute becomes the total object of these loves and not solely the ultimate object. For, as the sole immanent initiator and completer of loves, the unchosen absolute becomes the personal reason why there is a single universe of loves, a single family of humankind. Just as his singly immanent presence at all four levels of the individual human (biological, psychological, moral, and metaphysical) draws the latter into a total giving of herself or himself to the beloved in order to form a community; so the unchosen absolute's single immanent presence in every other-centered love draws all families, neighborhoods, cities, and nations to give themselves to each other in order to form the total family of humankind.

The unchosen absolute, then, become the single ultimate source of all ecumenism insofar as he is the single vital center of all other-centered loves and thus becomes the single total source of all communities through his total self-giving. It may be that the lover fastens total attention and devotion on the beloved and on the communities resultant from their original love as proximate total object of his love. Nevertheless, in this devotion to the beloved and the communities, the lover finds the unchosen absolute pulsing this love from beginning to end and down to its final depths, so that the universe of loves can come into being and grow widely despite all the violent attacks from self-centered lovers. No matter where the lover focuses love, each new beloved and each new community reveal the fundamental presence of the supportive unchosen absolute unifying all these loves. The latter is, then, the ultimate object of other-centered love because he makes it possible for the proximate object, namely, the beloved and the beloved community, to be worthy of total regard by the lover. He is the ultimate *total* object because no part of any other-centered love escapes his support and because he makes it possible for the beloved and the community to be the proximate total object.

From all this, someone might conclude that the atheist and the agnostic cannot offer or receive other-centered love and, further, that they cannot found community. Such a conclusion would deny the evident facts that Marxist martyrs die for the community and agnostic secularists sacrifice their lives for the advance of science and medicine. Nor is such a conclusion to be derived from our previous discoveries about other-centered love. For the ultimate total object of other-centered love, while immediately present to the lover's act of love, is not immediate to the lover's awareness. If the lover were directly aware of the unchosen absolute's action within him, then this present book would be unnecessary for the most part.

Rather, the unchosen absolute is experienced as the 'more' or is felt as the strengthening assurance for heroic action or is heard as the sovereign call to generous decision or is sensed as the deep serenity amid challenging events. Yet without careful analysis of these experiences, the unchosen absolute would not be clearly recognized for himself, nor would he be well appreciated as a distinct presence within the lover's act of other-centered love. Such clear recognition and explicit appreciation is not needed for the existence of this act of other-centered love even if these qualities would enrich and intensify this love for the Marxist or the agnostic secularist. Even if the Marxist or the agnostic were to deny explicitly the existence of the unchosen absolute, the latter's patient generosity would continue to initiate, support and enrich the beautiful acts of other-centered love elicited by the atheist and the secularist. For the unchosen absolute desires and rewards explicit recognition and appreciation without making them the absolute condition for his cooperation within the act of other-centered love. Thus Marxist and agnostic are not excluded from building the great community of the great tomorrow with their self-sacrificing loves. In fact, ironically, this may be the very lure which makes Marxism and Secularism so attractive to many.

The Unchosen Absolute: Builder of the Future

For every other-centered love there comes a time when the lover willingly risks everything in order to give the beloved complete freedom to leave him or her for another. Here is the discipline of liberation. At this point, in granting the beloved total freedom, the lover discovers a personally greater freedom from final possessiveness. The lover-mother is not only wishing to give 'more' to the beloved son; she is also desiring his greater growth in personhood, his 'more' as a person. But the courage to give him complete freedom to leave home comes from a 'more' beyond the lover, beyond the beloved, beyond the present community. Again, as we saw earlier, only the unchosen absolute lures the lover to take risks for the future by warranting the future worthwhileness of the present risk. Somehow the unchosen absolute promises an even greater love in the future even if the present beloved should turn away from the risking lover.

Contained in this first promise is a second one, that this great future love will certainly fit into the developing community's future way of life, that it will build a wholesome neighborhood community. Without these two promises, the risk would not be warranted and the encouragement from the unchosen absolute would be a mockery of the lover. Consequently, by taking the proximate total risk of granting complete freedom to the beloved, the lover can then discover the 'more' of the unchosen absolute. For the unchosen absolute's warranty found in this act of other-centered love is the final reason for taking the risk.

Now this divine ultimate object becomes also the total object of the lover's other-centered love; just as the human beloved, in receiving the total person of the lover, had become the proximate total object of that love—whether the beloved be a single person, a family, or a larger community. For no individual other-centered love escapes this stage of granting total freedom to the beloved on the ultimate trustful guarantee of the unchosen absolute. Further, the unchosen absolute is the only one who can make such a guarantee for a future love and for a future community composed of free persons. No easy determinism achieves this warrant of the lover's risking trust. The unchosen absolute must be already present in the future love and the future community if he is to guarantee the risk. This great community of the great tomorrow is not a deterministic Marxist proletariat state since it is constituted of free persons. Nor is it an impractical, Walden-Woods experiment since it is guaranteed to exist in the future. Nor is it an idealistic, Thomas More Utopia since it must be an historical community.

Because the unchosen absolute alone can warrant this future love and this great community of the great tomorrow, he is the total as well as the ultimate object of every such other-centered love. He is the builder of the future with humankind—a liberated future of expanded freedom in lover, beloved, and their community, because of the lover's risk of total freedom on behalf of the beloved. For the ultimate total object is attained only through the proximate total object of the beloved's total freedom and through the lover's ready willingness to risk totally. Thus with humans the unchosen absolute builds a future community of free persons through the loving risk of final divorce between lover and beloved. This is not the final irony of other-centered love.

The Unchosen Absolute: Beauty of Transcendent Value

The final irony occurs when man, in his dynamic drive to build the city of man, to live beyond death in the life of that city, and thus to preserve and develop the future life of the beloveds in that community, hears himself called to die for these life values. Strangely, the heroine of the French underground who suffers final torture to get her to reveal the identity of her beloved, is being asked within her other-centered love seemingly to destroy the physical and psychological world which she has so beautifully built around the beloved. In fact, she is asked to do this for the future sake of the beloved and the latter's world. In thus stripping herself of all chosen absolutes, the heroine faces the unchosen absolute alone—this absolute who has spoken reassuringly to her within her other-centered love, who has given her a remarkable sense of imperturbable serenity and who then, having helped her achieve wholesome womanhood, faces her at this precise moment with the chaotic and frightful fragmentation of death. Implicit in this request from the unchosen absolute is the absolute promise of a new and better existence for this lover if she can make this supreme act of trust.

Actually, the unchosen absolute, in asking this trust in himself, is clearly establishing himself as a value greater than the beloved, greater than all beloveds, greater than the heroine's total psychological and physical world. He is claiming to be 'more' than these and indicating that his immanent presence to the world reveals only a part of his value. In fact, at the moment of the heroine's ultimate sacrifice, the unchosen absolute offers himself as taking the place of all these other values and as totally satisfying all human desires. In the experience of a Catherine of Siena offering her life to restore European peace, he claims to be the transcendent value or the final beauty. Indeed, since the chosen absolutes, which lay claim to ultimate secular beauty and attractiveness, have derived these qualities from the unchosen absolute, it becomes clear that the unchosen absolute is at least as beautiful and attractive as the collectivity of these derived absolutes. This points to the unchosen absolute as the greatest of lovers and of beloveds and as the secular transcendent itself.

Unless the unchosen absolute were the transcendent value which contains all other values and more, he could not request this ultimate sacrifice without demanding meaningless self-destruction. But as transcendent value, he clearly is the ultimate object of every other-centered love; he is that center to which all loves tend, through which they dedicate themselves to the world's weal, and in which they discover the final worthwhileness of all their efforts and sufferings. Without the unchosen absolute there is nothing; and compared to him all things appear insignificant. Since no other-centered love escapes this powerful presence of the unchosen absolute, and since this presence is worthy of total devotion even to the ultimate sacrifice of all else, the unchosen absolute is evidently the ultimate total object of all other-centered loves. This means that his value is such that he is more than capable of satisfying the cumulative hungers and desires of all men for all time. He is the ultimate beloved.

B. The Unchosen Absolute, as Ultimate Total Object

Sometimes the unchosen absolute's request for ultimate sacrifice is interpreted as totalitarian manipulation of helpless humankind. Nothing could literally be further from the truth. For the ultimate sacrifice is the person's greatest act of love, most free decision, most human moment. The lover intelligently estimates that the only way open to promote a much fuller life and liberty for the beloved and the community is through actions sacrificial of life. It is out of the deepest love for beloved, community, and world that the lover seemingly leaves them—*seemingly* because actually the unchosen absolute's request contains the implicit but absolute promise of a higher existence. Otherwise, his request is self-annihilation for the hero or heroine.

But what could this higher existence be if not a life after death? Indeed, it must be a life of greater union with the unchosen absolute since this ultimate sacrifice has enabled the lover to leave behind—no matter how reluctantly—all other absolutes in order to embrace the unchosen one. Thus, given the incarnate growth of human spirit in developing body, in expanding psychological personality, and in deepening moral strength, this afterlife must include all the lover's past loves now enhanced by ultimate sacrifice for them. If this be life after death, it must also include growth in these loves. This would be an indefinitely perduring, yet historical, growth through definite love activities, since the human to be human must grow and must grow historically through the highest activities such as love. If this be human life, it must be the life of incarnate person or spirit; that is, it must include a reunion with the body and hence with the incarnate beloved and the incarnate community. What is the reason for this reincarnation unless to rejoin an incarnate community? This would be the great community of the great tomorrow formed principally out of those who dared to make the ultimate sacrifice or who were willing to do so if called to this. At its center would be the unchosen absolute in all his beautiful attractiveness.

Thus the unchosen absolute as transcendent value does not deny the existence or beauty of other values. Indeed, he gives existence to these values, namely, other-centered lovers and beloveds. Then he sustains and promotes them until they are ready to expand themselves greatly in the ultimate sacrifice which leads to higher existence. In fact, when the unchosen absolute operates as transcendent value, his intent is to lead men and women into enhancing all the chosen secular absolutes of life. He does this precisely by exercising his attraction through values such as the beloved, the community, one's career, technology, cultural achievements, animal life, the mineral world, and so on. Thus the unworldly transcendent value is busy working for enhanced secular values through the total lending of his very self to the world of humankind. This is the meaning of his immanent presence to the world. Consequently, the unchosen absolute, in the role of transcendent value, exercises his attraction as the ultimate total object of other-centered love in order to enhance the value of the proximate total object, namely, the beloved in the community. Because of this dialectic between the proximate and ultimate total objects of other-centered love, the beloved and the lover have the potential for indefinite growth in value as they become more and more aware of each other's value and of the transcendent value.

The Unchosen Absolute: Person at the Heart of the Universe

To think with some clarity about the unchosen absolute as personal transcendent value, one needs to appreciate three basic qualities of personhood: uniqueness, wholesomeness, and self-communication, and to see them in the operative characteristics of the unchosen absolute. First, whenever personhood is growing, it moves towards greater uniqueness. This remark is not meant to glorify eccentricity, which often enough is more neurotic than wholesome, more introvertive than self-giving, more impersonal than personal. But the more a person tries to make well-informed decisions in a particular life job and the more this person pioneers in work and family life, then the more uniquely the personality will develop because of the unique circumstances which the person must incorporate into work and life decisions.

Secondly, the more truly unique a human being becomes, the more wholesome the person is. For the unique decisions which one makes realistically, daringly, and prudently, must take into account as much information as possible, as much of the decider's own emotional life as possible, as many of the community's needs as possible, and as much of the unchosen absolute's communication as possible. In other words, a person's basic decisions have to draw upon all that the decision maker has in himself or herself, upon all that the situation offers, and upon all that the beloveds and the unchosen absolute can contribute. Thus the balanced decision tends to expand a person in a wholesome way, while the unbalanced, hasty decision is fragmentary and uneven in its results because the decision maker is torn by conflicting emotions arising out of undigested information and out of deep fears about hurting the self and others.

Thirdly, wholesomeness implies that the person is self-communicative or self-giving. The better this person's decision is, and the more deeply the decision maker is identified with the situation, the more thoroughly one both reveals and develops a personal inner life. The president of the United States can hardly escape self-divulging action the more he gives himself to the terrible decisions intrinsic to every large government action. Not merely the United States community but sometimes the whole world is involved in these decisions. This demands of the president a personal decision, that is, a decision unique in its realistic intent, wholesome in the totality of information used, and self-comunicative in its desire to increase the commonweal.

Let us, then, consider these three basic qualities of personhood as they appear in the operative characteristics of the unchosen absolute. We hope that this will reveal a further dimension of his being at the same time as it clarifies how he is the ultimate total object of other-centered love.

His uniqueness is precisely his transcendence, namely that he alone can start, support, liberate, communally expand, request an ultimate sacrifice, and warrant with final worthwhileness every other-centered love in the whole wide world of love. On him alone do all the chosen absolutes ultimately draw to make themselves more beautifully attractive and to him alone do they finally point as the unchosen source of their present existence and future hopes. Because of him alone, then, our universe is truly a universe, and not a multiverse of possibly horrible conflict. This unification he effects in the midst of the fragmentation caused by self-centered loves. Actually, the fact of our being a universe of loves is emphasized and recognized as mysteriously marvelous because of the explosive qualities of the self-centered loves which tend to destroy this unity.

A single transcendent value must draw us centripetally to communal unity against the centrifugal forces of self-centeredness; otherwise there would be no universe, but simply fragments of what was once a universe. Besides, transcendent value is a contradiction if it is not singly unique: first, the immanent presence of two or more ultimate transcendent values would require our universe also simultaneously to be a multiverse; secondly, one of the two ultimate transcendent values would have to be 'more transcendent' than the other lest neither be ultimately transcendent. But then contradiction and ambivalence would be at the heart of our universe rather than the unique personal mystery of the loving unchosen absolute. To exist at all the unchosen absolute must be unique.

The unchosen absolute's wholesomeness, the second quality of personhood, was first seen by us as he drew the individual human personality into wholesomeness through dedication to the beloved and the latter's community. Then, as in the case of the grandfather or grandmother, he led the lover into expanding that love into the lives of other beloveds and other communities through perduring faithfulness, deep self-trust, expansion of liberty (the lover's fully developed person), discipline of liberation, and readiness for ultimate risk and sacrifice. The unchosen absolute could not support such a wholesome and holistic love unless the support itself had all those wholesome and holistic qualities in all the abundance necessary to operate within all the other-centered loves of the international human family. How could the unchosen absolute be the vital center, the pulsing heart as it were, of this universe of love, how could he be the center of this wholesome community—unless he were the most wholesome and holistic of all beings, unless he were the most personal of beings? On no other grounds could he be the center around whom and because of whom this worldwide human family is formed as the ultimate whole of the universe.

But the uniqueness and the wholesomeness of the unchosen absolute are revealed most strikingly in his self-communication to the universe of man. Thus, because he is the unchosen or underived absolute, he is in no way relative or dependent; and because he therefore requires no return of love in order to remain a lover, he can communicate himself totally, through his immanence, to the world of man without demanding the slightest return. This is true although his very dedication to the world as its supreme lover indicates how much he appreciates a return of love. Further, as the unchosen absolute, he is not lured into love by the need to complete himself in another; rather he completes all other lovers because he himself is already complete when he meets them. Yet the joy he takes in sharing these loves can be measured by his dedication to them from beginning to end at the deepest level allowed him by the lovers. For all these reasons, namely, his freedom from demand, his completeness, and his joy in dedication to the great human family, the unchosen absolute enjoys an absolute freedom in all his loving within every other-centered love.

With such freedom, he can afford to allow each lover and beloved to enjoy the other as proximate total object, that is, with total (unconditional) devotion lover and beloved can focus their love on each other and not through any mediator. Yet because of his immanent self-communication in instigating, supporting, and expanding the lovers' mutual devotion toward the fullest wholesomeness in each other, he becomes the ultimate object of this devotion, the recognized and beloved source of this love. For the aware the lovers become of his assistance, the more they can give themselves freely and deeply to each other. Because lovers have the unchosen absolute as the ultimate object of love, the love between the lovers remains 'total', and becomes even greater. For each lover has a new confidence in self and in the other, a new confidence in their future hopes, and a new confidence in the family of mankind precisely bcause of the unfailing support of the unchosen absolute.

As the lover and beloved gradually liberate each other through their love, their increase of freedom naturally renders them more sensitive to its source in their every act of love. Their growing liberty, their enhanced personhood, is a constant living with the unchosen absolute, liberty itself, in each other and in all their communities. For this reason, the unchosen absolute becomes the beloved ultimate total object of their love. Paradoxically, as their liberty grows, they become aware of their growing capacity to reject him or to accept him precisely because he has communicated himself more and more generously to their love in living their life with them at a deeper and deeper level of intimacy. The lovers' very growth in liberty is actually an ever deeper acceptance of the unchosen absolute into their lives of love. Indeed, their ever growing interdependence on each other's affection is the opportunity for the unchosen absolute to increase their independent liberty and to live in expectancy of their increased return of love to each other and hence to himself.

Consequently, the unchosen absolute could not possibly communicate himself more freely or more totally to the lovers. He comes to them out of his absolute freedom to give himself to them unconditionally so that they, in turn, out of their strengthened freedom, can give themselves more freely and unconditionally to each other. He waits on their freedom which sets the limits for his self-communication. Could he give himself more totally than this—especially when each new level of communication increases the freedom of the lovers to open themselves more wisely and widely for the next higher level?

The unchosen absolute, therefore, in his uniqueness, his wholesomeness, and his free self-giving, reveals the unlimited personalness of his being whereby he enables persons to be and to grow through the creativity of other-centered love. Truly he is the heart of the family of man, the heart of hearts, the lover of all lovers. He is certainly the most secular of beings in his immanence and at the same time the most unsecular of beings in his transcendence. He is paradoxically the secular transcendent. Thus when we glance into other-centered love, his mystery is not dissipated but is found to be more vast and more complex than we had suspected. At the mysterious heart of the universe one finds the most personal of beings, the heart of the matter.

C. Conclusion to the Fourth Step

As we have just seen, when the unchosen absolute is named the ultimate total object of the human lover, much is claimed. It means that when the other-centered lover and beloved face each other and draw upon all four levels of their being in an act of total devotion, they are simultaneously facing the unchosen absolute whose support is making their full devotion to each other possible. He does this by a total gifting of himself within their very acts of existence and within their other-centered love. This instills confidence in both lover and beloved to give more of themselves to each other. Then, by thus becoming more aware of the presence and influence of the unchosen absolute, each can more faithfully give the self to the unchosen absolute. Here is a remarkable compenetration of intents and interests without any confusion among them. This is quite different from the reaction of the self-centered lover whose self-interests distract him or her not only from the beloved but also from the unchosen absolute; inevitably, this love decays.

With the reassuring support of the unchosen absolute, the lover can endure unrequited love or weak return from the beloved over many years. During this time, the lover can gradually come to know that this strong resolve to keep on loving is not simply his or her own strength and that as a result he or she has little reason to be condescending or pitying towards the beloved. Indeed, the lover becomes more and more aware that the unchosen absolute's support is total self-gift and, out of gratefulness, he or she responds to the chosen absolute as the ultimate total object, the ultimate beloved who may well fulfill all that the lover has ever needed or wanted. But since this assuring support occurs only through the lover's daring initiative, only through the beloved's trustful acceptance and only through their mutual act of love, each is always the proximate total object for the other. The chosen absolute's support is no substitute for the other, no distraction from the other; rather he is a stimulus for the growth of each in their mutual love. In this sense the unchosen absolute is Love Itself.

When this support is seen to occur in all other-centered lovers, then one begins to see how the anticipatory and compensating strength of the unchosen absolute which is found in every love renders the unchosen absolute the unifying animator of all communities, indeed of the whole worldwide human family. This picture is extended through all time when one notes that the ultimate sacrifice asked of each lover and guaranteed to be worthwhile by the unchosen absolute extends beyond the grave far into the future. For the unchosen absolute has guaranteed that there will be future great loves for the self-sacrificing hero or heroine to make the sacrifice worthwhile. This clearly points to a future great community of tomorrow as well as to a continuous support of all other-centered lovers of the past million years. Thus the unchosen absolute is seen to span not only all communities of the present but all those of the past and the future. Truly he is the transcendent value, the ultimate beloved, the final beauty of life. Such communities would naturally be continuous with their past and with each other and would be, therefore, enjoying the friendships, knowledges, arts, and skills of their past now growing into greater finesse and beauty in this present and future universe of lovers, this growing intercentury and international human family. Thus the finest secular values, the chosen absolutes, would be instigated, pursued and developed forever under the influence of the unchosen absolute who would then fittingly be named: the secular transcendent.

On these counts the personhood of the unchosen absolute is evident. For he is unique in his transcendent presence which forms the universe of lovers; he is wholesome in his total self-gift which inspires the other-centered lovers to build the family of man in their mutual self-gifting; he is fully self-communicative in his liberty which enables all lovers to liberate their beloveds with total self-sacrifice and thus to make their beloveds the total proximate object of their devotion. This they have the confidence to do because they experience the total liberty given them by the unchosen absolute—a liberty to reject him for the world or, if needs be, to lay aside the world for him. As a result, his generosity leads the lover into making the unchosen absolute the ultimate total object of his or her love without diminishing, but rather increasing, love for the human beloved.

Study of the operative characteristics of the unchosen absolute has thus revealed that he is the ultimate total object of other-centered love. In this study we seem, however, to have learned more about human conversion to the divine lover than about the nature of the divine lover himself. Still, a person has explored no small mystery when one comes upon the fact that loving the ultimate total object through the proximate total object, and accepting such love from the beloved, is really the observance of the first and the second great commandments within a single act of other-centered love.[56]

Yet how can one hold back from trying to penetrate further into the mystery of the unchosen absolute? Given the fact that the unchosen absolute is such an ultimate and total self-communicator, one wonders how this fact can be possible. In totally lending himself to lovers, he helps them expand their existence. How can he expand an existence already possessed by each? If he can do this, would this not change their existence, their radical person, so that a different personal identity would result? This would hardly be conducive to perduring faithfulness. If the reader is intrigued by this question, he or she might consider the unchosen absolute as the expander of man's existence and hope that some new inkling of his personal being will be revealed in the appendix to this fourth step.

Appendix to the Fourth Step

(For Those Who Wish to Explore More Deeply the Being and Meaning of the Unchosen Absolute)

The Unchosen Absolute as Existence Itself

To fully realize that the unchosen absolute is the ultimate total object of all man's other-centered loves is to understand that the unchosen absolute is existence itself,[57] that is, he is totally and only existence and is the source of all else that exists. Let us strip this fat statement to its skeletal structure and state the two basic reasons why the ultimate total object of other-centered love must be existence itself. First, the unchosen absolute is the ultimate object of other-centered love because he gives existence to each other-centered act of love, because he does this through the lover's very act of existence which is empowering the act of love, and because he alone can so empower the human act of existence to produce such an act of love.

Further, the unchosen absolute is the *total* ultimate object of every other-centered act of love because no part of this act escapes his giving of existence, because all four levels of the lover's being are completely involved in producing this act of other-centered love, and because the unchosen absolute is sole ultimate animator of such love and its resultant community. Thus the total being of the lover is supported by the unchosen absolute when the lover sums up his or her being in an act of other-centered love to form a radical community. This cannot occur unless the lover's substantial existence, in its support of every level of the lover's being and in its luring of the beloved's response, is supported in turn by the unchosen absolute. The latter, then, must be existence itself if his support of the lover's existence is actually the expanding of this existence and if this expanding could not occur unless the unchosen absolute was the original donor of this lover's substantial existence. For one can give another being existence, and not merely modify what is already existent, only if one is existence and only existence; that is, only if it is one's nature to be existence. For one can cause only according to what one is; the donkey cannot give birth to a Kentucky Derby colt; nor can the porcupine produce rabbits or violets. Thus only a being whose nature is solely existence can give existence. Donkeys produce donkeys; porcupines generate porcupines; the total existence which is the unchosen absolute produces acts of existence in all beings.

There is a second skeletal reason for stating that the unchosen absolute is existence itself. This reason is found at the base of one's mysterious personhood. For how can the absolute independence of a person, one's assertive existence, assert itself through this person's dependent relational essence without ending in absurd contradiction? Clearly, one is held in existence by all one receives into one's essence from the environment; as we saw earlier, the human being is a relational substance. Consequently, since no part of this totality escapes being relative, the person would seem quite capable of being the beloved, that is, of totally accepting the lover in body, mind, and heart, but quite incapable of being the lover or expanding existence beyond essence in self and in the beloved. For when the human lover wishes to assert absolute independence, his or her assertive act of existence must arise out of his or her limiting and restrictive relational essence as the latter arises, in total dependence, out of the community and its tradition. Only with the support of the unchosen absolute can one operate beyond one's limiting essential past and beyond one's restrictive community environment at the same time as one draws strength from them. Otherwise, the human self is trying to lift itself out of itself. In other words, radically new growth in a person would have no cause and therefore no explanation if there were no unchosen absolute whose nature is solely existence.

In addition, since the human being's act of other-centered love draws upon its human totality at every level of its being—especially when the act of total sacrifice is being asked—the unchosen absolute must work at both the level of operations and the level of the person's substantial act of existence. For the latter is the final source for one's deepest operations. But only existence unlimited by a dependent essence, the existence which characterizes the unchosen or underived absolute, can directly cause others' existence, such as the existence possessed by the other-centered lover. This last is true because only a being that is solely existence without a limiting essence can give existence to other beings of all specific types. All other existents, being limited by an essence, can bring into existence only beings of their own type of essence; greyhounds cannot bring humans into existence any more than humans can bring greyhounds into existence—they only attend, cherish and modify the already existent other.

These two reasons, though basic, are nevertheless skeletal. They must be fleshed out with more demonstrative analysis of previously discovered phenomenological data. Therefore, we will reconsider the eight operative characteristics discovered in the unchosen absolute's cooperation with the other-centered lover.[58] Taking them one by one, stage by stage, we will try to sound out this cooperation in order to find out how the unchosen absolute deals with a person's substantial act of existence and whether or not his procedures require us to admit that he is truly existence itself. If the unchosen absolute is found to be existence itself, then it will be much clearer why he is the ultimate total object of all other-centered loves and how his operative characteristics are possible.

1st Stage: The Unchosen Absolute Is Continuously and Deeply Immanent (See pp. 181–84)

As we have seen, the absolute character of the other-centered act of love, that is, the six characteristic phenomena which mark the presence of the absolute in the very structure of this love act, is caused by the unchosen absolute as much as by the human lover. Since the lover's assertive act of existence expresses one's independent freedom through a historically cumulative essence, it gives specific structure to this absolute love act. It is definitely Herman Jordan's act of love and no one else's. Yet these absolute characteristics cannot occur without the support of the unchosen absolute and thus the other-centered love cannot exist without this support. For this reason, the unchosen absolute must cooperate with Herman Jordan's act of existence in the production of this absolute act of other-centered love. This is simply the radical immanence of the unchosen absolute within Herman Jordan and within the latter's act of love, just as the specification of this love act is thoroughly the cumulative history of Herman Jordan's life up to the point of his act of other-centered love.

This immanent cooperation with the lover's act of existence is also continuous. For moment-by-moment the act of other-centered love must be adaptively modulated to the needs of the beloved and of the latter's situation if only because of the constancy or foreverness of other-centered love. The human essence, built out of its historical encounters with the environment, constantly changes its relationship to surrounding beings so that man's radical principle of continuity is his act of existence. Consequently, the unchosen absolute's immanent constancy of cooperation with the lover occurs more fully and directly in the latter's act of existence rather than in his ever newly relationed essence.

Indeed, as this immanent presence offers more and more support to the lover whose love-obligations are gradually accumulating, it works at ever deeper levels of the lover's being. This means that the unchosen absolute works with the lover's substantial act of existence—especially if the lover is seemingly about to sacrifice this existence for another's sake.

Yet the immanent cooperation of the unchosen absolute with the lover's act of existence does not deny the distinct independence of the lover. In fact, the more the lover becomes aware of the unchosen absolute's presence, the more distinctly she or he feels personal identity. This is the case because the very strength of the unchosen absolute's presence gives the lover a new sense

1. of being able to refuse the latter's support,
2. of going beyond the self in accepting this support,
3. of being loved by the absolute,
4. of being shamefully ungrateful in refusing the support.

In this way, the continuous and deep immanence of the unchosen absolute to the lover's act of existence not only shows that the unchosen absolute cooperates with the lover's act of existence but also results in the lover becoming more, rather than less, aware of distinct personal existence. Thus, as a truly distinct operator, the unchosen absolute works along with the lover's substantial act of existence so that the operational act of other-centered love can occur. In other words, Herman Jordan brings his history, at all four levels of his being, to specify and to structure the new act of love, while the unchosen absolute brings support to Herman's existence so that this existence is given to this particular historical act of love.

2nd Stage: The Unchosen Absolute Is Unitive and Companionate (See pp. 184–185)

There is good reason to think that the unchosen absolute not only supportively accompanies the lover's act of existence in the production of the act of other-centered love but also gives existence to this act. In order to understand why this is so, one must consider the double reciprocity, exterior and interior, which operates in every act of other-centered love.

The exterior reciprocity is the very structure of mutual support within the single act of other-centered love between the lover and beloved. Recall that, for the act of other-centered love even to exist, the lover and the beloved must somehow offer to each other simultaneously and proportionately a dependent and accepting trust together with a mutually independent allowance and promotion of liberty in the other. This highly intricate act, we discovered, could never occur if the unchosen absolute, present in both lover and beloved, did not compensate for the weaknesses of both in a magnificently orchestrated adaptation to their ever-changing needs and to the constantly changing demands of the environment. Without this compensation, the act would hardly be reciprocal, to say nothing of other-centered. Since only the unchosen absolute can be so immanently present simultaneously and adaptively in both lover and beloved and since without this presence there would exist no act of other-centered love, it becomes clear that the underived absolute is responsible for the very existence of this act.

This seems to imply that the lover and beloved contribute nothing to the act of other-centered love. Such an implication is false. Without the human lovers, the act of love could not exist as the act of, for example, Helen and James Hendricks on the afternoon of their twenty-fifth wedding anniversary following upon a quarrel over who was responsible for failure to pay last month's electric bill. For the act of other-centered love gets its concrete meaning or historical structure from the lovers even though the possibility of its existence is due to the support of the unchosen absolute. Besides, this act of love is freely given because the unchosen absolute's support is freely accepted or rejected by both lover and beloved. Of course, the outright refusal of support by only one of the parties makes the single reciprocal act of love almost impossible. Thus the unchosen absolute's support must adapt to the assertive freedom of both lover and beloved if it is to give existence to their act of other-centered love.

The remarkable immanent activity of the unchosen absolute within the exterior reciprocity of the other-centered love act must, of course, be meshed with the interior reciprocity between essence and existence within both the lover and the beloved. For the interior reciprocity between one's relational-dependent essence and absolute-independent existence, which constitute the single dynamic human being, makes possible the exterior reciprocity of mutual trust and assertive liberty between lover and beloved in the act of love. It also explains why and how this single act of love, on the part of either or both lover and beloved, can be at once relative and absolute, dependent and independent, receiving and giving, trusting and free. In other words, the six phenomenal characteristics of other-centered love lead us back into the very interior essence and existence of lover or beloved as these two principles reciprocally effect the more exterior reciprocal act of love.

What becomes clear from this is that the unchosen absolute cannot support the operational exterior reciprocity without being also anteriorly the support of the substantial interior reciprocity. If the unchosen absolute is responsible for the existence of the exterior reciprocity that constitutes the act of other-centered love, he can exercise this responsibility only if and when he operates at the level of the individual person's essence and existence. This becomes more clear when one reflects that the deepest reality to be found in the other-centered act of love and to be commonly possessed as ultimate total object by lover and beloved is the mediating unchosen absolute. He is the radical source of their unity of mind, heart, and body; he is their call to deeper union. Thus his compassionate and companionate adaptation to their changing needs and hopes is his contant cooperation at the substantial level of the lovers' essences and acts of existence. In this way, the unchosen absolute is the ultimate reason why the act of other-centered love exists although the lover and the beloved give the definite meaning and specific historical structure to that love.

3rd Stage: The Unchosen Absolute Is Faithfully Creative of Other-centered Love (See pp. 185-86)

But how does the unchosen absolute work at the level of essence and existence in lover and beloved? We know that the unchosen absolute both initiates the act of other-centered love and sustains it when it languishes. This he does through anticipatory reciprocation which we now recognize as his giving of existence to the love act by way of the lover's act of existence or radical person. His sustaining of a languishing love or his blending of an uneven love relationship with another form of reciprocation called compensatory indicates that he continually gives existence to habitual love or friendship. This fits the constancy of his immanent presence just reviewed.

But to accomplish this feat, the unchosen absolute must totally know lover and beloved and must totally operate within both. For the blending of this single reciprocal act between the complexly developed lover and beloved demands an intimate and total knowledge of them both if the immanent unchosen absolute is to adapt this blending of compensatory reciprocation to the constantly changing needs and hopes of both lover and beloved in their constantly changing environment and community. Now the success of the unchosen absolute's blending is measured by the unobtrusiveness of his mediation. Since he is the ultimate total object of the other-centered love and not the proximate total object, he cannot be a third party to this love so as to supplant lover or beloved. Rather, he must render each more attractive and devoted to the other through his mediation of anticipatory and compensatory reciprocation, through his constant adaptive presence as the ultimate total object of their love.

A second reason for stating that the unchosen absolute must cause the existence of the other-centered act of love through the existences of lover and beloved is simply the fact that the act of other-centered love draws on and draws together all four levels of a lover's being (biological, psychological, moral, and metaphysical) since this fullest and deepest act of a person's life demands the focusing of all the lover's powers, knowledges, emotions, and physical resources.[59] Therefore, if the unchosen absolute is to cooperate with the lover and the beloved in the producing of the act of other-centered love, then he must be cooperating throughout the being of both the lover and the beloved. He must be working through each one's substantial act of existence as it lends itself, at all four levels, to the new operational act of other-centered love. For it is the lover's substantial act of existence which asserts the absolute characteristics within the operational act of other-centered love. In fact, this act of love seeks to be a total gift of the lover's total being to the beloved; it is the bestowal of the lover's substantial act of existence upon the beloved—a matter which becomes very clear should the lover have to shorten or give up life for the sake of the beloved. Thus, if the unchosen absolute is to support such a gifting act of love, he must support the total substantial act of existence of the lover. Thus, he must cause the existence of the operational act of other-centered love through the lover's and through the beloved's substantial acts of existence which consequently expand with each new operational act of love.

4th Stage: The Unchosen Absolute Sovereignly Calls for Personal Sacrifice (See pp. 186-87)

This expansion of the lover's and the beloved's acts of existence is clearly seen when they feel themselves sovereignly called to an act of sacrifice by the unchosen absolute. At this time a person feels most deeply the pulse of the assertive act of existence and knows most surely that one dominatively possesses this existence and is therefore a free person. For this reason, the sovereign call or strengthening presence of the unchosen absolute within a person's experience of freedom reveals the personal freedom of the unchosen absolute. In other words, the free self-transcendence of the lover and beloved in the sacrificial act of other-centered love unveils the free supportive presence of the transcendent unchosen absolute. Because so much is condensed into the above statements, it would pay us to expand them for more leisurely consideration.

First, it should be noted that not a few people would be surprised that the unchosen absolute is deeply involved in expanding the free personhood of human beings precisely when he calls the latter to the seeming sacrifice or restriction of their human existence. To understand this, one must recall that a person's assertive existence is revealed

1. biologically when one successfully adapts the challenging thrusts of the environment to one's own survival,
2. psychologically when, in an inventive and disciplined manner, one integrates one's personality through a balanced dialectic of the community tradition with one's own individual independent decisions,

3. morally when one attempts, even at the cost of one's life, to maximize the good of the community by quietly revolutionary decisions,
4. metaphysically when one acts as a substantial relation, that is, when, being held in existence by all that one receives from the environment and community, one nevertheless asserts one's independent existence by introducing novelty and continuity into the moral, psychological, and biological levels of one's being through sacrificial decisions for the greater good of the community.

This is how the act of other-centered love, in its spontaneous novelty, expands the existences of both lover and beloved. There is a 'new existence' in lover and beloved when the lover trusts himself to the beloved with an inventive act of love which takes the chance of pioneering. It may be that the lover husband decides at fifty years of age to leave a lucrative law career to become the minister of a small congregation. He then asks his beloved wife and children to share the consequent deprivations with him. After the first shock, the initial conflicts of misunderstanding, and much anxious soul-searching, their generous and trustful response expands his and their existences to new depths of mutual affection, to new people, to new ideas, to new hopes. But the lover and his beloveds are also entrusting their futures to the unchosen absolute's guarantee which supports the lover's existence in his decision. If a person were only a relational essence and were totally dependent on the environment, as Herbert Spencer would have it, such a decision would be impossible. But, as a matter of fact, the human being is also assertive existence supported by the unchosen absolute. As a result the novelty of true personhood becomes possible and eventually actual.

Out of such novelty or 'new existence' issues the uniqueness of love characteristic of personhood. For the growth of mutual trust from a sacrificial decision between lover, beloved, and community makes all the involved loves less self-centered. Thus they are less routinized, less reduplicative of the past self. The novelty of the decision is demanding a unique reintegration of the person. In this way, the uniqueness of the love-act and of the loving persons is also seen as 'new existence', as a new expansion of the original substantial acts of existence into new operational decisions arising out of new understandings, new hopes, and even new friendships.

Clearly this uniqueness is highly personal. How personal it is, can be estimated from these facts:

1. the lover such as the husband and father just mentioned does not demand that his beloveds return his love by trusting their futures with his new future; he leaves them completely free, although, in trust of their faithfulness, he expects and hopes for their free return of love expressed in their readiness to gamble their lives with his;

2. the husband and father's trust in his beloved is a building of new liberty in them and in himself so long as each person does what he or she considers best for the group;

3. the sovereign call to heroic decision experienced first by the husband-father and secondly by the beloveds strengthens him to make the decision and to leave the beloveds totally free to refuse the unchosen absolute's support.

In this extreme and highly simplified example, one can see more clearly the principles which operate within similar, but murkier, decisions and situations.

On this basis, the sovereign call offers to all concerned an increase of liberty, not a contraction. It is a companionate and compassionate offer rather than an iron-clad demand. Thus the novel and unique act of other-centered love well expresses both the assertive existence of each person but also his or her independent personhood. This new expansion of each person's substantial act of existence is in this sense a 'new existence' in complete continuity with the person's past existence. To put it in Augustine's words, the developing person is a substantial relation. The father-husband's steadfast constancy is maintained at the same time as he assumes new dynamic relations with his beloveds and his community. From this it is evident how the unchosen absolute's sovereign call and supportive presence works at the level of every person's existence in such a way as to enhance the novelty, uniqueness, and liberty of each one's personhood. For the unchosen absolute's allowance and promotion of the lover's and the beloved's liberty reveal his own freedom in giving or not giving support to them in their other-centered love. The unchosen absolute must be richly personal and free to support so many people in their attempts at such free other-centered love.

The extent of this richness becomes clearer as one contemplates the strongest form of uniqueness and personal liberty: the sacrificial act of other-centered love which gambles the lover's total existence. The doctor who in mid-career gives six years of her life to practicing medicine at an African mission station gambles more than the psychological world of her practice, family life, and leisure companions; she may lose her physical life as well. This heroine who prudently gambles her total existence in order to protect the beloved's existence (the African village) sums up her whole life in this new act of demanding a 'new existence' for herself and her beloved. This is a transcendent act, for it goes beyond all the past decisions of this lover to gamble her total future. She would be foolish to do this unless she had some guarantee of the future worthwhileness of this sacrificial love act—a guarantee which only the unchosen absolute could offer her. Certainly such a terminal act, summing up a person's past and future existence, is a unique act and the freest of acts; it is, then, the most personal of acts. For it is the sacrifice of the lover's personal existence for the sake of the beloved's personal existence.

Such metaphysical compassion for the beloved, such self-transcendence, is the mark of maturely free personhood. But it would be an absurd gesture if it were not based on the sovereign call of the unchosen absolute (who alone can guarantee the future), and if it did not contain the implicit promise of an expanded existence for the lover even beyond death. Then both the heroism of the lover and this immanent promise of the unchosen absolute open the beloved's crushed person to a future healing expansion of existence. Possessed of such beauty, this heroism becomes contagious for the beloved and for all those surrounding the beloved.

In this way, lover and beloved are corresponsible with the unchosen absolute for the sacrificial act of other-centered love. But the unchosen absolute takes the largest gamble since he furnishes the strength to both lover and beloved. With this strength either one or both can follow through with the act of love or can paradoxically use the strength to refuse the love act. Here the unchosen absolute supports the lover's and the beloved's acts of existence so that these substantial acts can expand the whole operational personality of each with this total act of sacrificial love.

From this it is evident that the unchosen absolute freely supports the substantial act of existence in lover and beloved so that, through this act of existence, the unchosen absolute can give existence to each one's free act of other-centered love. It is, then, the freedom of the unchosen absolute which causes the existence of the other-centered love and thus enables the lover and the beloved to freely give specific meaning or historical structure to this love act. This unique, free, and sacrificial act is not just a momentarily high expression of personhood. It is also personhood achieving its ultimate growth before death by trusting in the unchosen absolute's promise that after death the person will continue to grow in an ever more expansive existence. Such growth in free personhood is clearly the aim and the result of the unchosen absolute's supportive immanence within the lover's substantial act of existence.

5th Stage: The Unchosen Absolute Is Totally Communicative (See pp. 187–89)

But how deeply radical is this existence-influence of the unchosen absolute and how widely does it extend? Certainly the unchosen absolute must be intelligently aware of the total present states of lover, beloved, and their situation if he is to cooperate in the total giving of lover and beloved towards each other and towards their community. The unchosen absolute must know the complete truth of the present situation if his support is going to be truly promotive of the lovers' and the community's future good. In addition, he must thoroughly love the lover, the beloved and their community since, in the act of other-centered love, the lovers are gambling their existence for each other unconditionally, that is, without any limits. This total human love must be matched by the unchosen absolute's loving support.[60] Otherwise, the unchosen absolute unreasonably limits the lovers' personal growth, while supposedly at the same time he reasonably promotes it. His generosity is limited, therefore, only by the limits constituting the lovers and their situation and by the limits which they may freely set for the use of his support.

Thus the complete truth and the complete love which the unchosen absolute exerts within the lovers' total being promote their other-centered love. Hence by this total communication of himself, he becomes the present basis for that future complete life which he guarantees to the other-centered lovers. If the unchosen absolute is to support the sacrificial act of other-centered love, he must not only know the lovers in their present state but must make sure that his support does not deny their past nor preclude their future growth. In other words, although his support is occurring at the present moment of time, it must span in knowledge and in loving intent both the past and the future of the lovers. His creative immanence is then a sustained responsibility towards the lovers' total life; it is as much future oriented as it is traditional and contemporary.

Such a total communication of the unchosen absolute to the lovers could only occur at the existential level because the substantial act of existence of the lover is the continuity which first integrates all past personal achievements and which then asserts itself into the future through present decisions on behalf of the beloved and the community. But such development, as we have seen, is radically the integral expansion of a person's existence into new experiences, new knowledge, new love, and new hopes.

This expansion within the person and the community is not a wild thrashing about in all directions but rather a unifying integration of previous achievements through the new decision. Here growth does not mean rampant stretching but cohesive expansion of the totality of person and community. Since the unchosen absolute is working radically through the existences of all the persons involved, his total self-communication to them through his dynamic immanence tends to unify the world of humans and to move it towards increased wholesomeness—despite all the conflicts within individuals and communities. In other words, the unchosen absolute supports human assertive or independent existence so that one can subordinate the self to the good of the community at the same time as one is acting in a quietly revolutionary way to enrich the community. In this way, the existence of each person escapes the Sartrean assertion of total domination over the other and yet acts absolutely or independently on behalf of the community. This is possible only because the unchosen absolute's support takes into account the future of both lover and community and urges the lover towards action which will ultimately benefit all participants and not just the lover.

Since the unchosen absolute totally gives existence to the activity of lover and community through their acts of existence, he implicitly accepts this world and its future destiny in its totality according to a complete truth and a complete love. To put this more actively, the unchosen absolute totally dedicates himself at the existential level to the human world and hence to the universe surrounding and influencing this world. This giving of existence, according to the limits set by the constitution of things and by the free wills of humans, is the unchosen absolute's total self-communication, his metaphysical generosity.[61]

From the other side, it indicates how totally and continually dependent are humans and their world upon the unchosen absolute's support of their existence. Here it becomes clear that the total growth of the human world, as it evolves slowly through the eons, is a gradual revelation of the riches contained in the unchosen absolute's act of existence whereby he works within the individual acts of existence constituting this universe. Indeed, the very variety of beings and the deep mystery of their involutions within this freely developing human world indicate the magnificent inventiveness and freedom of the unchosen absolute. Through the centuries the latter has freely supported individual acts of existence as their development evolved inventively up through higher and higher beings until they finally mounted to the level of radical human persons. He freely supported these same acts of existence taken socially until they formed schools, flocks, herds, even species, and finally human communities. For his responsibility spans past, present, and future as he unifies in its radical existence not only the human world but also the universe out of which this human world arises.

Thus the unchosen absolute's total communication of himself at the existential level of man enables the latter to be truly a substantial relation, truly a person. For, in supporting the human past, present, and future, the unchosen absolute's total communication enables a person to be fully substantial and fully expansive. This means that the person is immortal, can be perduringly loyal to beloved and community, can be freely and continuously creative of liberty in both. Further, the unchosen absolute's total communication, in supporting human understanding of self, of the beloved, and of the community, and in energizing a person's free decisions for good, has enabled the latter to be fully relational that is, to be more and more fully responsible for and responsive to the needs of the whole universe. To put this succinctly, the unchosen absolute has helped the human person to achieve more and more wholesomeness precisely through the community's growing wholesomeness which he reciprocally promotes. This wholesomeness is the person's assertive act of existence as it expands through the totality of his or her essence in new integrative activities which are aimed to increase the commonweal. Thus one's very being becomes intrinsically and ever more deeply related to all the beings of the universe.

But this can happen only if one recognizes and exploits one's total dependence upon the unchosen absolute. One must understand that one is totally relational, that is, totally at the mercy of one's environment and community, unless one's act of existence is supported in its independent substantiality by the unchosen absolute. Here dependent human substance is seen to be essentially a *relatio ad extra* (that is, dependency); while the supportive and supremely independent unchosen absolute is recognized to be essentially a *relatio ad intra* (that is, independency).

But, then, how can human existence bring us to understanding of the unchosen absolute if the two are so diverse? One possible answer: taken individually, the dependent-independent act of human existence is hard put to lead us into intimate knowledge of the unchosen absolute's existence; but viewed in its community, or taken socially, the human act of existence can reveal something about the *relatio ad intra* or independence of the personal unchosen absolute's existence. For, in a sense, the act of human other-centered love towards the beloved within the latter's community is something like a *relatio ad intra*. This means that the act, in its total communication of self to the other, is contained within the community, enriches principally the community, and is accomplished largely through the expansion of existence within all the members of the community. Here the rich variety of communal growth expresses better than the smallness of individual personal growth the magnificent dynamism within the unchosen absolute.

Further, the collective independence and continuity of the community better exemplifies the absolute independence and perduring faithfulness or eternal constancy of the unchosen absolute. Then, too, the very fact that expansion of the same existence (not the change between diverse existences) is the principal focus of attention enables the observer to better appreciate the unchanging yet creative dynamism of the unchosen absolute's act of existence. Finally, while the total communication of the lover remains within the community, it nevertheless introduces spontaneous novelty, uniqueness, and personal development at the level of communal existence. For this reason, it more adequately expresses the freshness, total satisfaction, and independence of the unchosen absolute in his own act of existence. Yet, at the same time, it also images well his relational concern for the universe which he freely supports in existence since any human community which expands its own existence interiorly also exteriorly contributes to other human communities in freedom.

Clearly, then, the unchosen absolute does not lose his independence by expressing it in total communicative dedication to the world of man, but he does allow the world of man to represent somewhat the deep inner riches and exuberance of the unchosen absolute's act of existence. Indeed the collective existence of world community becomes the more adequate way of illustrating this unchosen existence in its independence or *relatio ad intra*. For the human community's existence is greater than the individual person's assertive existence in the latter's dependence or *relatio ad extra*.[62] Thus the unchosen absolute's total satisfaction in his own existence is not seen as a smug isolation from the needs of others, or as narcissistic introspection, or as unfeeling domination of other beings. Rather, through the collective independence of the community, it is recognized to be the fullest exuberance taking joy in itself and wanting to give this joy to others if they so desire. In fact, this may well be one of the best ways of defining existence as it acts in the unchosen absolute and expands in the international human family to embrace the world with other-centered love.

6th Stage: The Unchosen Absolute Is Expanding Human Liberty (See pp. 189–92)

It is now rather clear that the unchosen absolute causes the existence of the act of other-centered love through the acts of existence in lover, beloved, and community. Paradoxically, this total communication of the unchosen absolute expands the existence of all concerned while at the same time it better unifies each of the persons and hence the community which they form. But how deeply does the unchosen absolute penetrate the existence of each person? This is the next question to ask. Already we have briefly noted that personhood and liberty expand when the human act of existence is touched by the unchosen absolute. Does this mean that the unchosen absolute's supportive expansion of the individual lover's existence is exactly the same as his expansion of the lover's personhood and that the latter's expansion is the same as the growth of his liberty? Are these just three aspects of the same single process?

To clarify slightly a very mysterious area of reality, let us define what we mean here by *personality, person,* and *liberty.* First, *personality* is taken to be the integrated network of virtues, knowledges, imaginative sets, emotional patterns, and physical routines which arise out of the radical person as the latter adapts to and learns to control the environment. The human personality is the sum total of the radical person's experience in the human world; it is the operational expression of the radical person. The radical person is, of course, the human substantial act of assertive existence which is always expanding and reorganizing its relational essence for better integration with the communal situation. The term, *radical person,* is used here to signify only a part of the human person. For the human person embraces the totality of assertive existence, relational essence, and operative personality. Nothing of the human is outside person.

Now, the liberty of the human must be distinguished from freedom. For *freedom* is simply one's ability to choose from an array of options, both good and bad, for a particular decision; the juvenile delinquent has freedom. But *liberty,* the ability to choose the good consistently in one's decisions, is so characteristic of the mature person that this liberty is seen to be the healthily balanced person in his or her totality.[63] But such liberty cannot occur at all in one unless it is radically based in the independence of one's assertive act of existence. It cannot occur humanly unless it happens through his or her relational dependent essence which set the historical and constitutive limits within which one asserts one's existence. Nor can liberty occur operatively unless one's operations are integrative, that is, unless the acts of understanding, the past willed decisions, the emotional drives, the imaginative sets, and the physical routines are coordinated in a balanced and supple unity so that one can make free decisions consistently creative of communal good.

Now, the act of existence expands in accord with, and yet beyond, the essence whenever it gives existence to new operations which carry it to higher levels of integration or humaneness. If these new operations are to be integrated with the previous operations, the act of existence must give existence to the operations in accord with the relational essence. But if the operations are to go beyond the past in order to dominate the physical situation or to create new liberty in the beloved and in the community, then the act of existence without contradicting the past must go beyond the previous organization of the relational essence, that is, beyond the previous unity of the personality.

In addition to this, the operation given existence by the radical act of existence should contribute to a new and better unity of the personality and thus offer a new and better unity of the total person. It is precisely through the other-centered act of love that this unity is most thoroughly and deeply achieved since, as we previously noted, it draws upon all four levels of a person's being in a total commitment of the lover's being to the beloved and to their community. The act of other-centered love is the *forma virtutum* in the words of Aquinas, that is, it is the basic unifier of the human personality and it enables the personality to express the radical unity of the freely expanding existence in one's essence. This act of other-centered love done on a large scale is called *conversion*.

For these reasons, the more balanced the personality and the more unified the essence and the existence of the human being, the more liberty one has; rather—to paraphrase the insight of Sartre—the more liberty one is. Thus freedom (the ability to choose or not to choose, to choose this or that option) finds its full maturity in liberty, the ability to decide for the good consistently. For the assertive substantial act of existence, the root of liberty, causes the free-choice operation by way of the limiting relational essence and then supports, accumulates, and integrates this operation along with other operations to form the free personality rooted in virtuous living. Thus liberty, as the fully and beautifully balanced personality, is the crown of freedom.

This is how the assertive act of existence expands through the limiting essence by way of these integrative operations so that the total person is better organized, more closely unified, more truly authentic, and more fully possessive of liberty. Thus paradoxically the all-embracing, essential relativity of man to the universe grows so long as the independently assertive act of existence is expanding through better and better integrated operations to form the maturely free human personality. In this sense, one is one's liberty.

This is seen most dramatically in the act of other-centered love with its six phenomenological effects of the unchosen absolute. Through these six phenomena one best expresses one's liberty, uniqueness, and dynamic integrity. For the marks of the unchosen absolute's presence in this act of other-centered love—namely one's perduring faithfulness, intelligent self-trust, expansive freedom, disciplined liberation, imperturbable wholesomeness, ultimate self-sacrifice—demonstrate how all-embracing, how deep, how lasting is one's person in its liberty if one allows existence to expand fully in a totally other-centered dedication to the beloveds and to their community. At this point, the human person possesses existence so dominatively that he or she can use the strength lent by the unchosen absolute to defy the latter if the person should so wish.

But, as we have also noted, this premier personal decision cannot occur unless the unchosen absolute as a cooperating cause supports it through the lover's very act of existence, that is, through the lover's radical person. So present is the unchosen absolute to the radical person in communicating himself totally to the latter that this absolute may call upon the radical person freely to sacrifice himself or herself on behalf of the beloved and the community. In this strange relationship the unchosen absolute is so dominative over the existence of the human person that he can give the latter a sovereign call seemingly to self-destruct for the sake of bettering the existence of other persons. Yet man so dominatively possesses his existence that he can use the unchosen absolute's strength to refuse the call.

On the other hand, so dominative is the unchosen absolute that he can promise something beyond self-destruction. For example, to the French Resistance heroine he can promise that the seeming destruction of her own existence actually will lead into a higher type of life for that same existence. The heroic act will not destroy but elevate the heroine's existence. How could the unchosen absolute exercise such dominance and make such a warranty unless he were able to cause the assertive human existence, the heroine's radical personhood and the root of her liberty? Moreover, only one who possesses existence in such a way that he could control the giving of existence to future events could give such a guarantee to the heroic lover. And only one who had originally given the act of existence to the heroine could ask her now to seemingly relinquish it in death or at least to risk it for a higher type of living not yet experienced. Finally, only one supremely confident about his gifts of existence to others could afford to support the latter even in their refusal of his sovereign call. Would such confidence be reasonable if the unchosen absolute did not have a conviction both of the goodness of human existence and even more of his own power to draw goodness out of all existence? Are we not facing here the fact that the unchosen absolute possesses his own existence in such a way that he can bring other existences into being out of non-being and then support them in such a way that their expansion ultimately builds a more and more beautiful human world—despite humankind's frequent refusals to expand its own liberty?

The unchosen absolute, then, in an ongoing creation of novelty freely responds to all the beneficent activity in the human world. He does this by using anticipatory reciprocation to initiate this activity and compensatory reciprocation to render it as vigorous as man will allow. For man's liberty can refuse this reciprocation or, using it, can inventively specify it. The more dependent the lover, the beloved, and their community become upon the unchosen absolute, the more independent each becomes. This happens because within their dependent essences they find their acts of existence expanding more and more successfully in higher integration of personality and in consequent growth of liberty. For the act of existence gives fuller and fuller support to the human operations which ordinately accumulate into virtues, knowledges, emotional disciplines, imaginative sets and physical routines—the constituents of the integrated personality. For this reason the other-centered love of these persons enjoys increasing fidelity, trust, freedom, total concern for the other, and readiness to suffer deeply for the loved ones. Because this happens in the community, the lover draws strength both directly from rapport with the unchosen absolute and indirectly from the beloved's response. Thus wholesome existence expands radically throughout the community.

In order to understand more fully how completely the unchosen absolute dominates a person's own act of existence, it should be recalled that this anticipatory response of the unchosen absolute to the world of man is done with absolute freedom. The unchosen absolute can work or not work at the level of radical existence, can give life or not give life, since as related *ad intra*, as totally independent, he in no way needs the universe in order to exist or in order to love. As a result the unchosen absolute's constant support of community and world indicates a free faithfulness of remarkable continuity. This constant support also reveals an amazing wealth of free actuality in the unchosen absolute as he gives existence to many new beings and expands consistently the acts of existence already long ago given.

Unlike a human whose dominative possession of the self's existence does not allow one to bring anything into existence out of nothing but only to modify the already existent, the unchosen absolute's dominative possession of existence is such that he can give original existence to beings and then continue to support this existence in its expansion; otherwise, he could not guarantee the future by his control of what is to exist or not to exist. Thus he must have existence as his very nature. In other words, his existence must not be restricted by an essence and must be the totality of his person. This is to say that he must have existence so that it is all that he is. Thus he would be existence itself and this way of possessing existence would be his uniqueness, his richness of person. It would also be his metaphysical generosity whereby he alone can give existence to all others since he alone has no essence to limit his support of other beings in their existence.

Because of being existence and of being only existence, the unchosen absolute is dependent on nothing else for existence. Only the unchosen absolute is totally free to love or not to love, to love temporarily or to love forever. On this score of being totally existence and nothing else, the unchosen absolute is totally free not to demand a return of love yet also free to be totally desirous of, and responsive to, any return of love. Such existence, however, because of its totalness, is exuberant in the gifting of existence to others. His deepest joy is to give of his abundance so that others may be finally overjoyed.

The human world, then, reveals in its other-centered loves the unchosen absolute as existence itself, the sole being who is only existence with no limiting factor. It also shows that the unchosen absolute exuberantly gives existence at the center of the human world, at the radical personhood of all men and women. Clearly, because he is existence itself, the unchosen absolute can be immanent to all existents, simultaneously present to the total continuity of human history, unitive and companionate of all other existents, faithfully creative of them, most radically personal of all beings, sovereignly calling to the seemingly ultimate sacrifice of existence, totally communicative and expansive of human liberty.

7th Stage: The Unchosen Absolute Renders Human Love Eternal (See pp. 192–96)

The panoramic view of how the unchosen absolute gives existence to community members is attained only when one realizes what *forever* means in the act of other-centered love. For the human lover to declare that his or her love for the beloved is forever, would be foolish if the unchosen absolute were not promising that his absolute support of this lover was forever. This is exactly what the unchosen absolute does when he guarantees the future worthwhileness of the lover's final act of sacrifice on behalf of the beloved and their community. If the unchosen absolute did not provide a future good worthy of the sacrificial act and if he did not intend that the heroic lover was to exist in a higher life after sacrificial death, the act would then be more suicidal than heroic, more foolish than wise.

We have already seen that this higher life must be a continuation of the previous life if it is to give meaning to the latter. It was also clear that this continued life would be senseless unless it meant a continuation of the sacrificial love at a higher level of liberty. Thus a future community of love is promised to the heroic lover when the unchosen absolute sovereignly calls him or her to the final sacrifice. Otherwise, there would be no continuity of the previous communal life which made the hero or heroine's other-centered love first possible, then actual, finally expansive, and ultimately eternal.

The unchosen absolute, then, reveals that he is the giver of future existence forever not merely to the other-centered lover but to the lover's beloved and to their community—provided they freely accept this gift. Because he spans the past, present, and future with his act of existence, the unchosen absolute's perduring fidelity to the human world points to the unlimited fecundity of this act since he must be supporting now at this moment not only the contemporary twentieth-century world of human beings but also all those other-centered lovers who are now presently loving forever in the great community of their once future. Further, this perduring faithfulness, this continuous dedication of his act of existence (or radical person) to the ongoing human world, establishes the unchosen absolute's continuing identity. It shows him as initiating all change while himself remaining unchanged; as expanding all other existences, especially those of the human world, while his own existence remains unexpanded in its dynamic singleness, in its infinite fecundity.

The unchosen absolute is, then, the source of all changes since all change arises from the act of existence when the latter supports operations demanding change in the operator and in the effect operated upon. For this reason, it is easy to confuse change with existence and mistakenly to identify the total process of all changes with the unchosen absolute in the manner of Whitehead. Indeed, the more powerful the act of existence, the more change it causes and therefore the more easily it can be mistaken for the mere totality of change.

But change is impossible unless continuity underlies it—either continuity in the agent of change or continuity in the effect changed. Change has to occur in, or in accord with, something that is antecedent to and consequent to the changing. Otherwise the chaos of uncaused changes occurs. For this reason all changes that occur in the human world can occur only because all the acts of existence (or radical persons) which constitute the world of humankind support them. But then, as we have discovered, all these acts of existence expand through operational changes only because of the unchosen absolute's continuous support of each person and of the consequent community of humankind.[64]

The unchosen absolute, then, because his act of existence spans past, present, and future with complete truth and with complete love, enables the world of humankind to be a single developing world and the universe of humankind to be truly a developing universe and not a fragmentary multiverse. In fact the continuity of the unchosen absolute's dedication to the human world and to the universe enables humans to have a history (a conscious awareness of cumulative human development) and enables the living universe truly to evolve (to accumulate perfection in speciation from a single original source). Because the unchosen absolute is unchanging existence itself, he can be the infinitely fertile source of all changes and of every development in the world and universe of humans. Moreover, for the same reason he is the ultimate cause for their unity, continuity, and destiny.

The unchosen absolute, then, in establishing the present world of humankind and in expanding it continuously and forever into the future, displays his own inner psychology better and better in the developing history of humankind, shows the intricacy of his providence in the free and sophisticated planning done by humankind, and offers humankind the opportunity to return love to him either directly in prayer or indirectly through loving service to the beloved and the community. At this point it becomes clear that the central value and meaning of humankind's life is the beloved in the community (the proximate total object) and the unchosen absolute (the ultimate total object and final beloved).

Evidently, too, this other-centered love is meant to grow forever as the human act of existence continues to expand through its relational essence by way of ever new operations. To be truly human is to grow eternally by way of other-centered love, which draws upon all humankind's powers and resources, and assures it of balanced growth throughout its total being before, during, and after death. Again, to be truly human is to never stop giving the totality of one's personal being in other-centered love to the beloved and to the community, and finally to the unchosen absolute. Thus the human being's foreverness is seen in its radical person and in its union with existence itself, the unchosen absolute, as together they build, before and after death, that great community of the great tomorrow.

8th Stage: The Unchosen Absolute Is Other-centered Love Itself (See pp. 196–98)

Once other-centered love is seen to be the central and everlasting value of humankind's world and universe,[65] then the next step is to observe how the unchosen absolute loves other-centeredly. This is to show how the latter is Other-centered Love itself. For other-centered love in human beings is godlike because the absolute Other-centered Love operates in humankind to make such love possible and actual. But what is this absolute Other-centered Love as revealed in human love?

First of all, it is absolute generosity. It gives existence to all men and women; it gives them existence to the degree that their structure and their freedom allows; it gives existence by offering its own immanent presence in total self-communication without diminishing, but rather enhancing, humankind's distinct autonomy; it gives to humankind without diminshing itself, without losing its own existence in any way.

On this last point, note that if the unchosen absolute's generosity were to diminish his existence, it would change his identity since his radical personhood is his act of existence as infinite, that is, as without any restrictive, specifying essence. Any loss of existence, in turn, would render the unchosen absolute less and less able to be generous, to be independent, to be adaptive to humankind's needs, to be faithful in establishing the continuity of its history and of the universe's evolution, and to be worthy of being humankind's ultimate total object and ultimate beloved. In other words, this deepest of all self-giving, if it meant some loss of existence, would be self-defeating and would induce such self-defeat into all human acts of other-centered love. The devaluation and disintegration of the world of humankind would then ensue. Thus, to explain the continued development of the human world and the eternal intrinsic unity of the unchosen absolute, the unchosen absolute must be recognized as exercising absolute generosity without the slightest personal loss. This is the first characteristic of absolute Other-centered Love.

The second characteristic of Other-centered Love itself is its unconditional giving. The unchosen absolute simply refuses to demand a return of love for his absolute generosity. This is possible for him because he is never diminished by his giving of existence to the other. Nor is his existence diminished or threatened if return of love is not made since his act of existence is not derived from another and is not therefore conditioned by another's gift or refusal of existence to him. However, this should not be taken to mean that he is unconcerned about humankind's return of love to him or that he does not expectantly hope for this return. If the central meaning and value of the universe is reciprocal other-centered love, then failure to return love is the greatest tragedy and futility in the world of humankind and of the underived and unchosen absolute. For the return of love is what enables the lover to enter more deeply into the life of its beloved and of the community (proximate total object) and consequently to live more fully within the life of the unchosen absolute (ultimate total object). Neither purpose is possible without the other since the one act of other-centered love touches simultaneously both beloved and unchosen absolute. Evidently, then, the unchosen absolute is deeply concerned over the success or failure of other-centered love insofar as he loves humankind and its world. Nonetheless he would not be diminished in existence even should the world of humankind totally collapse through self-centered rejection of love's return on a worldwide scale.

This last point is seen more clearly in the third characteristic of Other-centered Love itself: the absolute freedom of its gifting. Because the unchosen absolute depends on no one for existence or operations, he can, as so underived, support the lover to such an extent that the latter is able to give away the whole world and even the beloved. Because of his absolute worth, the unchosen absolute can offer himself to the lover in place, as it were, of the beloved and of the total universe. This gives the lover an almost immeasurable liberty with which to measure the liberty of his or her benefactor, the unchosen absolute.

And yet there is even a better measure of the latter's absolute liberty: his willingness to give humankind the strength to reject him forever by choosing the world or the beloved in his place. Only absolute freedom could afford to risk the loss of all lovers and of the whole universe in absolute trust of humankind's free goodness and its general readiness to return love for love given. He could risk this only if he prized humankind's liberty and freely given love as the highest value in others and only if he wanted to crown human liberty divinely, no matter the cost. The absoluteness in this gift of liberty is the measure of the absoluteness of the unchosen absolute's personal liberty, the third characteristic of

Other-centered Love itself. It could also be an expression of his absolute trust in humankind and in its destiny.

In this sense, the unchosen absolute's love for humankind is nondominative even though—indeed because—he exercises total dominion over his own act of existence. His absolute liberty, therefore, enables humankind's other-centered love also to be nondominative—unlike the absolute dominative freedom of Sartre's lover. This nondominative quality arises out of humankind's metaphysical gratefulness for its own liberty which, as radically its own act of assertive existence, has been received from the unchosen absolute and which, as relational essence, has expanded by way of its community. For the experience of human liberty makes one aware that the unchosen absolute is free not to give existence to humankind and, having given existence, not to return humankind's love since the unchosen absolute alone would not be diminished by failure to return love. Yet because the unchosen absolute is so fully personal, so richly free and inventive, and so deeply gladdened by humankind's return of love, he would find no reason not to respond. After all, he is the ultimate reason why every act of other-centered love carries within it the ultimate basis for any return of love, namely, complete dedication to the other, the fourth characteristic of Other-centered Love itself.

For when the unchosen absolute sponsors foreverness in the human act of other-centered love, he implies his own pledge never to abandon the world of humankind. And such a pledge would make little sense unless the unchosen absolute intended to love this world of humankind forever by always doing more than merely returning its love for him. For this reason, each other-centered lover is forever expanding beyond previous experience and going beyond the self because of the unchosen absolute's increased support or manifest love for the lover.

But the absolute generosity, unconditional giving, total liberty, and complete dedication of the unchosen absolute as Other-centered Love itself are dynamisms radically appreciated only in his fifth characteristic: absolute domination of his own existence. For, since the unchosen absolute as underived owes his existence to no one except himself, he precedes in existence all other existents. Since all other existents are derived and dependent, the unchosen absolute must be the one to give them existence. But to give them existence, he must possess existence in a giveable way, that is, without any limitation. Therefore he can give existence in any way he wishes, at any time he wishes, to whomsoever and to whatsoever he wishes. If he gives existence without diminishing his own act of existence, then 'in the beginning' he must create the existence of others out of nothing. His self-sufficiency then is his omnipotence because he is without limits.

Due to this total domination of his own existence, the underived and unchosen absolute can be so metaphysically generous that everything existent is totally and continuously related to him as long as it exists since he alone is the radical source of each one's dynamic existence. He can be so metaphysically unselfish in his giving that he receives nothing for himself simply because he bestows existence on others unconditionally, that is, without demands other than those composing the being's very nature, namely, the being's own needs for growth. This is possible for the underived and unchosen absolute since, unlike all human beings, he is never dependent for his own existence on the return of love from others.

Because of this total domination of his own existence, the underived and unchosen absolute can be so free metaphysically that he is willing to risk total loss of the human world and even of the universe in order to affirm humankind's free autonomy. In this way his love demonstrates his deep respect for humankind. For he would not be diminished in his personal existence by such a catastrophic loss even though he would be deeply aware of its tragedy for humankind.

Because of this total domination of his own existence, the underived and unchosen absolute can be so dedicated metaphysically to the world and to the universe of humankind that he can promise to give himself forever to them. For his existence, the most personal and perduring of all existences, is not limited to a particular time span, nor to the influencing of only a particular range of beings, nor to merely reciprocal and proportionate return of love. Just as Kristen Jones and Pete Smith are related to each other even before they ever meet because they are persons or members of the human race, so the underived and unchosen absolute is related to all beings as creative existence because they are all members of the existents' race, that is, because they are existents only through his single creative act giving them existence. This is why all existents form the household of God and why all existent men and women form the family of God.

The underived and unchosen absolute, then, considered as Existence itself is truly Other-centered Love itself, the total giver of life and liberty forever in creative fidelity. Here at last we come upon the secular transcendent in its transcendency. To put it inadequately yet succinctly, the underived and unchosen absolute is humankind's deepest friend forever and yet so much more than this. For he is also humankind's God who alone is worthy of our finest loyalty, our warmest worship, our highest hope.

EPILOGUE

The Mystery, Problem, and Search of Love Revisited

When we first began this search into the limits, if not ecstasy, of human love, we secretly wondered whether the cold light of philosophy might not freeze hard the warm supple mystery of love and whether, like some laser beam, its clinical touch might not even kill life by dissecting love into neat concepts.

But actually the pencil light of philosophy only made us aware of the vast reaches in the mystery of love. Where it cast its slim beam, new shadows appeared such as the complexity of reciprocal love or the seeming impossibility of continual sacrifice for the beloved. Yet the pulse of divine life within people's reciprocal efforts to love each other worthily could nevertheless be felt. For within the loyal foreverness of deep human love, within its anticipatory strength for future loves and responsibilities, within its intelligent trusting, within its warm hope that generous sacrifice is the central joy of life, one feels the more than human support—stubbornly and graciously present. One reads every so often of a mother and father who, in addition to their own family, regularly board and room court-protected children in such a warmhearted and thoughtful way that these same children return confidently to this home as though they were the blood members of the family. What enables a man and a woman so to expand their hearts and minds as to include all these tortuous and tortured lives day after day till decades of years pass and some of these fifteen children, in turn, give full love and life to their children?

Nevertheless, even if one has become somewhat enlightened about the dark mystery of love, the latter remains a problem. Man has still to live with the unexpectedness of love, its ecstacies and tragedies, its humdrum quality and its simple joys. In the instance of the philosopher, love yields the least of all life-phenomena to all challenging hypotheses, to all attempts to probe its depths, and to all measurings of its meaning. Love resiliently refuses to be rationalized though it is filled with tough intelligence. Indeed, love is the despair of the philosopher—a fact to which this book well attests.

But then have all our searching efforts been in vain? Yes, if we had hoped to neatly catalogue, control, and predict the serene depths of the storm center of life. However, if all we had hoped for was a deeper sensitivity to the mystery, to the tender power, and to the hopeful future of our loves, then perhaps our search has not been foolish. If only for a second or two we glimpsed Other-centered Love Himself and saw the great tomorrow awaiting us, that splendid life after life, then the confidence generated by this glimpse could well encourage each of us to risk deep love just once more and to rediscover the beautiful, life-giving mystery at the heart of reality. After all, what else is more worthy of our sufferings, our lives, our selves, and our God?

NOTES

These notes do not constitute a bibliography; many significant works on the theory of love are not mentioned. Nor, for the most part, are these notes to be considered documentation for the statements made in the text itself. Rather these entries simply indicate other writers who may develop a common point far more adequately than the present author or who may take a viewpoint opposed to his. These notes merely single out some of the people who have influenced the author's thinking.

1. Robert G. Hazo's *The Idea of Love* (New York: Frederick A. Praeger, 1967), already something of a classic on its own account, outlines some forty diverse doctrines on love.

In his controversial *Love in the Western World* (Princeton University Press, Princeton, N.J., 1982, enlarged edition), Denis de Rougemont traces the proliferating theories about romantic love (impassioned desire or eros) from roots in the twelfth century troubadours of Languedoc up to the twentieth century women's liberation movement. Carefully distinguishing romantic love from true or active love (agape), he discovers that the fidelity at the dynamic core of agape is the single most important element for stabilizing modern marriage. For fidelity enables the lover to accept the beloved's gifts and limitations and to discover one's own true self precisely while the lover and beloved grapple with the real world of daily routines, joys, and sufferings. Thus the free creativity of faithful marriage has as its goal, not the control of others, but rather the mutually full and authentic liberty of each other.

2. Despite its title, *The Friendship Game* (Garden City: Doubleday-Image, 1970) by Andrew Greeley offers no little wisdom in its concrete style and practical advice about friendship and married love, though its psychological and sociological approach does not allow it to say much about the mystery of this love.

3. In *Human Love* (Chicago: Regnery, 1967; also, Chicago: Franciscan Herald Press) by Jean Guitton, one finds a strikingly deep and orderly humanistic treatment of love in its mystery, stages of development, and sexual meaning. The first section considers the mystery of love: its elements and the various historical attempts at rendering it more open to intelligent analysis.

4. In Part II of *Man's Search for Meaning* (New York: Washington Square Press, 1963). Viktor E. Frankl indicates that every man has a will to meaning (154), a desire to detect ultimate value and not merely to project it (156–57, 175). Every man wants to affirm meaning freely (158) in his unique life-decisions (154), even at the cost of death (155).

5. Before exploring the meaning of various loves—affection, friendship, eros, and charity—C. S. Lewis (*The Four Loves*, New York: Harcourt, Brace, Jovanovich, 1977) observes perceptively that our gift loves, unlike our need-loves, lend themselves to idolatry and that they do so the more easily in proportion to their beauty (19–20).

6. In *The Problem of Pain* (New York: Macmillan, 1975), C. S. Lewis distinguishes carefully between love and kindness. Love wants the best for the beloved even if it is to be achieved through suffering. But kindness wishes only the comfort of the other and tends to be more superficial (37–40).

7. Harvey Cox's "Sex and Secularization" (*The Secular City*, New York: Macmillan, 1966, 192–216) sketches with acid how the chosen absolute of Venus and Adonis (Miss America and the cool man of *Playboy* magazine) are carefully built up by advertising and then dismantled by the rigors of everyday life.

8. Thomas Aquinas was convinced that true self-love rooted and shaped friendship (*Summa Theologiae*, II-II, q. 25, a. 4, corpus; Ottawa: Medieval Institute. 2nd ed., 1941). Indeed, on the score that one may not do evil to oneself in order to do good for

another, Aquinas held that one must love oneself more than one's neighbor (II-II, q. 26, a. 4, corpus). According to Etienne Gilson (*The Christian Philosophy of Saint Augustine*, New York: Random House, 1960), Augustine held that love of another always involved love of one's own good (love of one's self) because love is reciprocal, a mutual gift-giving (138). In his *De Trinitate* (Bk XIV, chap. 14, 18) Augustine even says: The person who knows how to love himself loves God (*Qui ergo se deligere novit, Deum diligit*). See Oliver O'Donovan's *The Problem of Self-Love in Saint Augustine* (New Haven: Yale University Press, 1980) for additional information on this.

Strikingly, the thought of Erich Fromm (*Man For Himself*, Greenwich, Conn.: Fawcett Publications, 1967, 134–42) is not totally alien to these ideas of Aquinas and Augustine. Fromm distinguishes true self-love from selfishness and sees in self-love the conjunctive basis for loving others since the affirmation of one's own life is an affirmation of life for others. But he sees selfishness as an attack on the self because it gradually throttles one's power to love. However, he fails to indicate how self-love operates in heroic self-sacrificing love.

The relevance of this perennial problem is seen in two companion articles in *America* magazine June 4, 1977: (vol. 136, 22, 498–503. Donald Heinz in "The Consuming Self" believes that the present emphasis on self-actualization is excessive. He sees it as a late bourgeois individualism which is finally breaking its covenant with society, world, and human condition. On the other hand, John Giles Milhaven in his "Love: Giving of Self or Meeting the Self's Needs?" feels that the only way to love realistically is to meet one's own needs first.

In contrast, John Macmurray, (*Persons in Relation*, London: Faber and Faber, 1961, 94) finds the notion of self-love contradictory since it would mean only self-alienation if love is essentially 'being for the other'. This stand makes sense if, as Macmurray holds, persons are truly constituted by their mutual relations to one another (17, 24, 27–28, 95), that is, if a person exists only insofar as he is related to others (211). See notes 24 and 27, however, for remarks directly opposed to this purely relational doctrine of person.

For Bernard Lonergan (*Insight,* New York: Philosophical Library, 1957), on the other hand, egoism or ultimate self-centeredness is an incomplete development of intelligence because it fails in the self-abnegation required for the free play of intelligent inquiry. Inevitably it excludes certain correct understandings (220). In his opinion, tension between self-centeredness and detachment is never eliminated no matter how high one's personality integration reaches (474-75). Thus the suffering of other-centered love is never finished.

John M. McDermott, S.J. in *Love and Understanding,* (Rome: Analecta Gregoriana, vol. 229, 1983), his study of Pierre Rousselot, S.J., who began transcendental Thomism with Pierre Scheuer, S.J. and Joseph Maréchal, S.J., discovers:

1) to love God and oneself is the same thing (49);
2) the duality of independently existing individuals is incapable of grounding the unity of love; but since all beings are united in their love for infinite being, a relationship as among members of a physical body ensues and each part can be drawn to sacrifice itself for the other parts, if they are judged more necessary for the good of the totality (47-48);
3) human persons can recognize the divine love as the ultimate sense of reality even in the midst of innocent suffering (301). Rousselot himself considered this to be a derivation' from Thomas Aquinas.

9. In *Before Philosophy* (Baltimore: Penguin Books, 1967) Henri Frankfort *et al.* develop a definition of myth (15–16) which shows the latter to be a dramatic form of poetry elicited by and pointing to mystery. With this definition in mind, one can say that love is a mystery which transcends the poetry stimulated by it, which is far greater than the reasoning meant to comprehend it, and which is far more beautiful than the ritual celebrating it.

Steven David Ross explains in *Philosophical Mysteries* (Albany, N.Y.: State University of New York Press, 1981) that mystery is inherent not only in the nature of things but also in the very nature of rationality (1). This he applies to all knowledges (including science) and especially to philosophy. There is no fundamental or ultimate or supreme mystery at the heart of all mysteries (132) except the mystery of the indeterminateness of mystery—though

God is a great mystery. Ross contends that only an ordinal metaphysics can adequately explain the qualities of mystery (66). Ross outlines such a metaphysics in *Transition to an Ordinal Metaphysics* (Albany, N.Y.: University of New York Press, 1981) in which he pays homage to Justus Buchler's *Metaphysics of Natural Complexes* (New York: Columbia University Press, 1966).

10. Spencer's total material determinism is described well in *Masterpieces of World Philosophy* (edited by Frank N. Magill. New York: Harper and Row, 1961, especially 652, col. 2–653. col. 1) where there is a neat condensation of *First Principles*, the introductory study to his *Synthetic Philosophy*.

11. Ayn Rand in *The Virtue of Selfishness* (New York: New American Library, 1964) establishes her philosophy of individualism on the principle that love is the expression of one's own self-esteem. Thus love is a response to one's own values as seen in the other person. For this reason. disinterested or other-centered love is a contradiction (44) since man's self-interest, that is, his survival precisely as man, can be served only by a non-sacrifical relationship with the other (31). In this way, man grants values to others as extended or secondary values of his own primary values, namely, himself (47). Ayn Rand considers John Galt of her *Atlas Shrugged* (New York: Random House, 1957) the best representative of her objectivist ethics (13).

Frederick Copleston, in *A History of Philosophy*, vol. 6, *Wolff to Kant* (Westminster Md.: Newman Press, 1960) has noted that Rousseau's occasionally paradoxical use of the term *freedom* (91–92) and his developing doctrine of the state (82) make it difficult to understand how man's freedom can be his specific difference from the infrahuman (66). For self-love is man's fundamental impulse (67) and all else, such as compassion and justice for others, is a mere modification of this impulsive self-love (75-76). Indeed, all moral development is merely an extension of this self-love to the love of all mankind (77). This remains true even though a higher form of liberty is generated in society (than in man's natural state) when a man identifies his will with the general will in society (82).

For Nietzsche, the mythic ideal of the superman offers the aristocrats of life a model for the self-legislation of values (see James Collins, *A History of Modern European Philosophy*, Milwaukee: Bruce, 1956, 800). This legislation is carried out through decisions much resembling Sartre's projects (790). The exceptionally gifted man is encouraged to fabricate out of his own freedom his own moral norms even if this means, as it inevitably does, the use of the mass of men as an instrument for the superman's drive to full power and to full manhood (801). After all, the universe is only a meaningless river of becoming until the exceptional man molds it to his own meanings and values (802).

12. Since the main intent of this book is not a treatise on Sartre's thought, I attempt no detailed analysis, but only a general interpretation. Therefore, only key loci will be cited with no attempt to provide extensive documentation and analyses of texts. Occasionally, I elaborate conclusions which I consider implicit in Sartre, and support them with loci—again without argument. I am using Sartre here merely to exemplify an extreme position directly opposed to that of Herbert Spencer on the doctrinal spectrum of man's freedom to love. For this same reason, I quote only *Being and Nothingness,* never the *Critique of Dialectical Reason* (*Critique de la Raison dialectique, précédé de Question de Methode,* Paris: Gallimard, 1960). At any rate, Alfred Stern (New York: Dell Publishing, 1967, 2nd ed.) finds that this last book does not change significantly Sartre's earlier existentalist philosophy (252).

13. William Barrett (*Irrational Man*, Garden City, Doubleday-Anchor, 1962) finds that Sartre's dialectic between sadism and masochism, used excessively, calls into doubt the very possibility of love since there is an unbridgeable chasm between the subject, being-for-itself, and the object, being-in-itself (257). Alfred Stern's *Sartre* (New York: Dell Publishing, 1967, 2nd ed.) argues that, in making existence precede essence, Sartre creates a man with total interior freedom and, consequently, with total responsibility (50–52, 75–77). Hence, 'the absolute' in each lover demands that the beloved's freedom be possessed or enslaved as soon as the love becomes more than physical—this is the inner contradiction of love (154–55). For this reason a positive sense of community

becomes impossible and alienation is the inevitable fate of every love (*Masterpieces of World Philosophy*, Condensation of *Being and Nothingness*, edited by Frank N. Magill, New York: Harper and Row, 1961, especially p. 1086, col. 2 and p. 1088, col. 1).

14. Sartre himself (*Being and Nothingness*, translated by Hazel E. Barnes, New York: Washington Square Press, 1966) states that the fundamental act of freedom is one's choice of oneself in the world (a fundamental option), and that this choice is the conscious foundation for all future deliberations (564–65). A person's freedom is identical with one's existence (542) because to choose oneself is to be (537). This freedom is an unavoidable annihilation of the in-itself by the for-itself. One is condemned to be free, that is, to exist beyond one's essence, beyond the causes and motives of one's choice (537). There is no middle ground between a totally determined person and a totally free person (541). No factual state (such as an economic or political or psychological situation) can motivate any act or determine consciousness (532) since motives have meaning only as present within one's original self-project or fundamental choice of oneself as transcendence (534). Thus one's original choice creates all one's motives and sets up one's world with all its meaning (568). Indeed, the free person chooses his past in terms of his future (554). In this way one 'creates' oneself as an absolute that takes precedence over all other beings. (See Alfred Stern's *Sartre*, 29, 51–52, 75.)

Against the more common opinion of Sartrean experts, Thomas C. Anderson takes the position (*The Foundation and Structure of Sartrean Ethics*, Lawrence, Kansas: The Regents Press of Kansas, 1979) that a coherent Sartrean ethics does exist in general form and that it is not relativistic, nor totally subjective, nor nihilistic.

15. Sartre is convinced that freedom cannot be something like a pre-existing choice. For one knows oneself only as choosing. Thus freedom must be the fact that this choice is always unconditioned (586). Changes in one's environment cannot of themselves force one to abandon one's project or decision (619) since by choosing an end, a person chooses to have relations with all the existents constituting his environment (621). In other words a person's freedom not only distinguishes him from his environment but also

causes the hard fact that things are there in all their unpredictability and adverseness. This is why man is both absolutely free and, consequently, absolutely responsible for his situation (623). (See Stern's *Sartre*, 77, 146–47, 75).

16. Sartre feels that the other's freedom is untouchable because the other always remains being-as-object under my attempts to influence him or her. I cannot increase or diminish the other's freedom: I can only offer the other occasions for exercising freedom (501).

17. Clearly, Sartre's process-philosophy, in which being is behaviors or actions or doings (582), cannot abide anything resembling substance (101, 175, 569). The latter taken as essence, he thinks, would render a person totally necessitated (572–73). Stern has noted (*Sartre, loc. cit.,*) the intrinsic contradiction of something being without being something (51) or of mere nothingness undergoing an action (59). But if there is no God to introduce novelty into the universe of persons and if the environment cannot interiorly modify a person's inner free choices or decisions, then there is no source of these free actions except the free existent self, which must therefore pre-contain its future free decisions or actions. Otherwise, the free actions have no source; further, any connection between successive decisive actions would be impossible. This would be a universe of unconnected events: chaos itself.

18. It would be calumnious to assert that Sartre would want to hold or to practice the implications which I find in his thought. For example, he himself would be horrified by enslavement of the beloved. Nevertheless the implications are there and render his ethics difficult, if not impossible, of achievement. A Sartrean, however, could countercharge that the infinite Creator-God, if he is absolute, would be caught in the same net of critiques brought against the absolute Sartrean man. But believers in the infinite God could reply that Sartre's man *claims* to be ultimately absolute, when *de facto* he is at best derivatively absolute; while the infinite God of believers is truly ultimately absolute. Because Sartre's man is not ultimately absolute, he must continually reassert

his false claim to ultimate absoluteness—and hence must forever domineer over the beloved—in order to keep growing at the expense of the beloved. But the God of the believers is *de facto* ultimately absolute and therefore need not *demand* obedience so that he can grow, even though he must *desire* obedience of man since all creatures' fuller development requires such obedience. This obedience is, however, never slavish subservience since this would be a denial of the autonomy given man by the creating God and would be a contradiction of God's creative act.

19. Note that all citations are from Herbert Spencer's multi-volumed *The Synthetic Philosophy*, (New York: Appleton, 1910): each citation gives the volume number and title of each book within the series before citing the page—except for volume 1 which is *First Principles*.

20. Herbert Spencer's philosophy exhibits a remarkable split between its principles and its conclusions. For example, the ultimate of religion (the unknowable Force) and the ultimates of science (matter, space, time) cannot be conceived or known in any way (*First Principles*, 56–57). We can only be conscious of their existence (*First Principles*, 109) by an indefinite consciousness which is the abstract, not of a series of thoughts or ideas, but of all thoughts and ideas (*First Principles*, 81). In other words, even though all knowledge of its very nature is relative (*First Principles*, 68), still this total relativity forces us to recognize the absolute (*First Principles*, 82, 109). Appearance or phenomenon forces us to be aware of reality or noumenon, although we cannot conceive even a connection between them (*First Principles*, 108). Spencer asks us to believe that despite our having no idea of the connection between the absolute and the relative (between the noumenon and the phenomenon), nevertheless the relative or phenomenal demands the existence of the absolute or the noumenal. The knowable forces us to accept the unknowable as unknowable in every way.

21. When one studies Spencer's Humean explanation of cognition, the gulf between his principles and his conclusions gapes more widely. He speaks of two sets of manifestations, the more vivid being sensations of presentation and the more faint being

ideas of representation (*First Principles*, 128–29). The first type of continuous manifestations are the object or non-ego: the second type are the subject or ego (*First Principles*, 137). On this basis, it is no surprise to discover that for Spencer 'reality' means simply persistence in consciousness (*First Principles*, 143). In fact, this reality ultimately is Absolute Force or Unconditioned Reality which has no beginning or end (*First Principles*, 176); it is also the Indestructibility of Matter always pressing in upon us (*First Principles*. 159). Here the Unknowable Force suddenly has attributes which make it known.

22. There is a more disturbing element in Spencer's theory of cognition. Unable to distinguish that thought is reflective or self-aware even as it lives its content or object, (vol. 1, *Principles of Psychology*, 148), Spencer is convinced that the substance of the mind (the self), though existent, is totally unknowable (vol. 1. *Principles of Psychology*, 146–47, 156–57). In this way, he sets man at the mercy of his totally relative thinking and sensing. Though Spencer clearly wishes to rescue the universe and man from relativity, his basic metaphysical principles condemn man to unmitigated relativity since no ultimate reality is in any way knowable (*First Principles*, 56). Without absolutes, there is no way to establish continuity in the universe known or in the knowing subject. Without continuity, there is no way to compare two things or events: they are simply disconnected and incomparable. This leaves us with both a universe and a knower atomized into unconnected parts.

23. Again, it should be no surprise to find that Spencer reduces the universe simply to physical forces. For these powers move into vegetal, animal, and human levels of being and, sheerly by their growing complexity, differentiate these diverse types of being (*First Principles*, 190–95) through what Spencer calls the transformation of forces from physical to vital, from vital to mental, from mental to social. Although Spencer speaks of the correlations between the mental and physical as though they were truly qualitatively different levels of being (*First Principles*, 195–200), still the mental level is ultimately reducible to the physical by transformation. Of course, he finds these transformations just as unknowable as the ultimate causes (*First Principles* 200–206). Because of this

alleged continuity between all levels of being and of activity, Spencer feels free to surmount and to describe these levels by way of greater and greater generalizations which eventually become the laws of evolution. For example, his generalization on the direction of motion (*First Principles*, 207–27) moves up from physical movement to include eventually even voluntary actions (219) and social activities (221). For this reason, it is quite difficult, if not impossible, to distinguish scientific generalizations from philosophic principles in Spencer's thought.

24. On this score one has reason to doubt that liberty is possible under Spencer's philosophy of first principles, cognition theory, and cosmology. For liberty expresses itself through a unique decision which therefore cannot be merely the product of determining universal laws. Further, liberty can be an expression of the self only if the self is able to reorchestrate all its energies to its own unique purpose. But this requires a permanent self, a substance reflectively knowledgeable of itself—the very factors denied by Spencer. The atomizing of society is further assured when Spencer subordinates the altruistic to the egoistic ultimately (vol. 2. *Principles of Psychology*, 595, 612–13, 617) because the altruistic always envisions ulterior benefits for the self, the egoistic. Despite, then, Spencer's own inclinations and experience, his first principles inevitably interpret the world and man atomically so that the dissolution of the world becomes as inevitable as its evolution. A Greek necessity subtly dominates his philosophy so that only illogically could he find place for liberty and love in his philosophic system.

25. Fundamentally, then, Spencer's thought becomes a materialistic process-philosophy since, in his opinion, a person cannot know his own permanent being but only his atomistic activities. (For an illustration of this, see vol. 1, *Principles of Psychology*, 150–62). If man cannot know his own substance, certainly he cannot know the noumenon, the absolute Unknowable Force, behind the relative phenomena-process. This is why man, according to the first principles of Spencer (and not according to Spencer's conclusions and inclinations), is simply the sum of his environmental influences, nothing more. Frederick Copleston (*A History of*

261

Philosophy vol. 8, Part 1, Garden City: Doubleday-Image, 142–68) takes a much more benevolent view of Herbert Spencer's philosophy by emphasizing its conclusions more than its first principles. On the other hand, the Spencerian philosopher, Hugh Elliot, in his *Herbert Spencer* (New York: Henry Holt Co., 1917) develops a picture of Spencerian philosophy which much resembles the one detailed above (222–23, 238, 268, 274–78).

26. A careful statement of man's counterbalancing complexity of body-soul, matter-spirit, determinism-freedom, temporal-eternal, independence-dependence, occurs in Jean Mouroux's *The Meaning of Man* (translated by A. H. G. Downes, Garden City: Doubleday-Image, 1961) where he shows the resultant paradoxes within human love (182–209). Mouroux's method of antinomies undergoes critique from Jules Toner in the *The Experience of Love* (Washington: Corpus Books, 1968, 94).

27. This paradox becomes understandable if one accepts the ontological principle neatly enunciated by Frederick D. Wilhelmsen (*The Metaphysics of Love*, New York: Sheed and Ward, 1962) namely, that being loved is what makes being be (84, 139). However, Wilhelmsen does not thus reduce being to simply the relational (38–40). Rather, with Aquinas, he sees being as both standing constituted outside of its causes and tending towards its end—by the very fact of its being (86). Thus in eros, the lover stands out of himself towards the other for the sake of his own perfection; but in agape the lover simply affirms his own richness of existence in giving it to others (73). In loving oneself, one tends to love the whole of being (152), like God who loves man into completeness (23).

28. Frank M. Oppenheim in his article "A Roycean Road to Community" (*Proceedings of the Jesuit Philosophical Association*, East Dubuque: Tel Graphics, 1969, 54–60) sketches, within Royce's five conditions for community, the dialectic of dependence and independence which eventually results in loyal love.

29. Anders Nygren (*Agape and Eros*, translated by Philip S. Watson, 2 vols., Philadelphia: Westminster, 1953) distinguishes

pagan eros (desire for the best, even for divinization) from Christian agape (the gift and sacrifice of self for the beloved without consideration of the beloved's excellence). But in doing so, he splits man into two divergent forces, natural and supernatural. Evidently, this result runs counter to the unity of man uncovered in this book. Maurice Nédoncelle (*Love and the Person*, translated by Sr. Ruth Adelaide, S.C., New York: Sheed and Ward. 1966, 13–19) and Martin D'Arcy (*The Mind and Heart of Love*, New York: Meridian Books, 1956, 80–81 and 354) criticize Nygren's theory on this score.

30. In *The Mind and Heart of Love* (New York: Meridian Books; Cleveland: The World Publishing Co., 1956) Martin D'Arcy makes much of essence as the masculine, rational-assimilative, self-interested aspect of love and much of existence as the feminine, ecstatic, self-giving aspect of love (343–44); of course, he states this in a formalistic manner (331, 341, 344). The synthesis of essence (source of self-regarding love) and existence (the source of self-sacrificing love) is in Existence Itself, God (370, 342).

31. A hint of how and why this dominative self-possession is found in one's act of existence is given by Maurice Holloway in his article "Towards the Fullness of Being" (*Proceedings of the Jesuit Philosophical Association*, Woodstock Md.: Woodstock Press, 1962, 15–37). Here he shows that for Thomas Aquinas the act of existence is act for all other elements in man and is therefore open to indefinite growth so long as it is in union with Existence Itself. This is further developed by Frederick D. Wilhelmsen (*The Metaphysics of Love*, New York: Sheed and Ward, 1962) when he distinguishes the tragic and the ecstatic aspects of the act of existence (140–55).

32. In Sartre's *Being and Nothingness*, (*op. cit.*), love is a constant conflict during which the lover tries to absorb the beloved as both try to enslave each other (445). The agony is that, if one does successfully enslave the other, the love is killed. So both try to possess the freedom of the other (448), that is, the lover seeks to be the object in which the beloved loses freedom (449). This means that the lover tries to force the beloved to re-create the lover in the

latter's freedom (450). Because of this inner contradiction within the act of love, the lover must use the beloved as an instrument subordinated perpetually to the lover's uses; nor can the lover, therefore, ever increase or diminish the liberty of the beloved (501, 458, 461). Thus the lover must make the self the absolute end, the unsurpassable one, to whom all things and all others bow as pure means to the lover's aggrandizement (451). For this reason, the lover must always be the seducer, must continually remind the beloved of the latter's nothingness at the same time as the lover establishes the self in fullness of being through the beloved's seduction (454–55). The Sartrean lover is condemned to play the God whose existence he or she is condemned to deny. Thus the Sartrean person's total interior liberty appears to be finally controlled by an inevitable Greek fate. Is this the basic absurdity sundering Sartrean being?

33. Robert O. Johann notes (*The Meaning of Love*, Glen Rock, New Jersey: Paulist Press, 1966), in following Louis Lavelle and Thomas Aquinas, that only insofar as I love another, do I truly love myself and that in thus breaking out of the narrow circle of my own existence, I open myself to the Absolute Value (50–53). Thus the direct love of the other is derived from direct love of oneself (30) and in this community of selves a special unity is discovered which is the unique source of all being and of all being loved (38–39).

34. That man merely projects his religious ideals (his God) out of his mind without any experience of these ideals in the real world of everyday, is a theory advanced by Freud. It has been taken up and expanded by F. Sierksma. William A. Luijpen, in his book *Phenomenology and Atheism* (Pittsburgh: Duquesne University Press, 1964) has discussed and criticized the positions of both Freud (202–11) and Sierksma (211–24).

35. When Ernest Becker reflects the psychology of Otto Rank for us (*The Denial of Death*, New York: Macmillan, 1973), he notes how psychological frustration tortures us when we try to establish

the human beloved as God in our loves and how eventually our cosmic heroism must go beyond all human relationships (167–69).

36. Maurice Nédoncelle, in *God's Encounter with Man* (New York: Sheed and Ward, 1964) spends almost half of his book describing the prayer between human persons in order to show the beauty of their trusting dependence on each other.

37. In *The Art of Loving* (New York: Harper and Row Bantam, 1963), Erich Fromm describes mature love as a union which, rather than depleting one's individuality and integrity, preserves and enhances them. Jules Toner in *Experience of Love* (Washington: Corpus Books, 1968) gives an appreciative critique of Fromm's theory of love (54–56, 111–15).

38. Throughout his *Love and Person* (translated by Sr. Ruth Adelaide, New York: Sheed and Ward, 1966) Maurice Nédoncelle stresses the reciprocity between centers of consciousness. He finds this reciprocity present in every relation between any I and Thou and essentially constituting the act of love. He makes such reciprocity the philosophic center of his personalism and describes it in some metaphysical detail (215–33).

Taking a somewhat different tack, Ignace Lepp (*The Psychology of Loving*, translated by Bernard B. Gilligan, Baltimore: Helicon Press, 1964, 32) finds that theoretically reciprocity can be absent and yet love can be present. However, in his experience, love of this kind is quite exceptional, since love can fully promote the existences of the lovers only through their communion or reciprocity. Indeed, unrequited love often ends in the disillusionment of the loving one (33).

Amaury de Riencourt, in his *Sex and Power in History* (New York: Dell Publishing Co., 1974) offers an all-inclusive historical and pre-historical study of the biosocial interplay of forces between man and woman. His description of human evolution, in a pioneering effort, focuses primarily on the female. As a result, he comes to the conclusion that progress in human evolution has been stimulated by the increase of sexual differentiation and inhibited by unisexual values or by the dominance of one sex over the other.

39. Etienne Gilson, (*The Christian Philosophy of Saint Augustine*, New York: Random House, 1960, 138) finds that Augustine makes all love between persons reciprocal and that he thus founds a union between persons which makes it possible for a man to love his neighbor as his own self. On the other hand, John O. Evoy and Maureen O'Keefe *The Man and the Woman*, New York: Sheed and Ward, 1968, 86) distinguish fulfilling love from complementary love; they state that fulfilling love can be nonreciprocal and thus becomes salvific love. The latter remains love although it lacks reciprocity.

40. One of the deepest probes into the very structure of love is Jules Toner's *The Experience of Love* (Washington: Corpus Books, 1968). There he discovers that radical love is a way of joining the acts of being of both lover and beloved in active co-being (163).

41. Gerald G. May, the psychiatrist, takes a daring stand in his *Will and Spirit* (New York, Harper and Row, 1982). He not only sees agape love as the root of narcissistic, erotic (romantic), and filial (compassionate) love (132), but he also finds agape love to be a permanent, eternal, serene, and alone fully satisfying communion with the other person (131). For agape love is not merely human; it has divine qualities (132). Not to understand this, he claims, is to risk being filled with guilt at one's always conditional love and, hence, to be angry with God since he seems to demand of us a divine, unconditional love beyond our powers. Thus the need for God's assistance in any act of agape love. This is precisely the central focus of this search for the limits of love.

42. Adrian van Kaam and Kathleen Healy in *The Demon and the Dove* (Pittsburgh: Duquesne University Press, 1967, especially 46–49) explore famous literary case histories in *Anna Karenina, A Burnt-out Case,* and *The Fall.* The authors discover that each man's selfishness reveals the destructive demon, while his self-transcendence discloses the constructive dove. For this last reason, the person who receives love finds that his potentialty to love the other is liberated, that he is freed from the prison of mere self-centeredness, that he is called to go beyond himself for the other.

By relativizing the relativizers, Peter Berger (*A Rumor of Angels* Garden City: Doubleday-Anchor, 1970) establishes that without absolutes one cannot measure passing events nor can one move reasonably from one set of values to another set (40–45). He then points out five occasions when signals of transcendence from the absolute can be clearly heard (52–72).

43. Gabriel Marcel connects immortality intimately with love. In *The Mystery of Being* (vol. 2, *Faith and Reality*, translated by René Hague, Chicago: Regnery-Gateway, 1960, 69) he contends that to affirm another with trusting resignation of oneself into the hands of the other is to love the other. Such love asserts that the other can never be totally extinguished by death. Marcel finds that all values would be annihilated if death were the ultimate event of life. For him value is genuine only if it is accompanied by the consciousness of one's immortal destiny (*Homo Viator*, translated by E. Crawford, New York: Harper and Row, 1962, 182–83). In *Creative Fidelity* (translated by R. Rosthal, New York: The Noonday Press, 1964, 149) he tells us that communion between friends is eternal.

44. Gabriel Marcel uses a banking term to speak of this divine assurance within human love (*Creative Fidelity*, translated by R. Rosthal, New York: Noonday Press. 1964). He speaks of God issuing infinite credit which one friend extends to another, and vice versa, so that friendship becomes possible (167). This interpenetration of each other by mutual affirmation leaves the friends free and able to grow (40–43) since this receptivity is a co-existence (12, 89, 91).

45. Paul Tillich's *My Search for Absolutes* (New York: Simon and Schuster, 1967) investigates the destructive tendencies of relativistic approaches to truth and calls for an experience of the absolute, the holy. Again, Viktor E. Frankl (*The Unconscious God*, New York, Simon and Schuster, 1975, 61) claims that existential analysis has discovered a latent relation to transcendence inherent in man. This is not a mental projection created by man

but something in man's very being which refers to something other than man, the God of the unconscious.

John M. McDermott, S.J., in a very compact, yet metaphysically wide-ranging article ("A New Approach to God's Existence," *The Thomist*, vol. 44, 2 (April, 1980) pp. 219–50) shows how the moral imperative contained in a heroic decision to die for the beloved certainly indicates the existence of an independent absolute, namely God. This proof presupposes one's basic act of faith in the validity of human reason. But it argues further that such a faith in reason escapes contradictions and chaos only if it is joined by a greater faith in love and in the God of love. Thus the reasonable act of love goes beyond (not contrary to) human reason to reveal God's existence.

46. The argument that follows has a parallel in Josiah Royce's *The Problem of Christianity* (New York: Macmillan, 1913: Chicago: Regnery-Gateway, 1968: Vol. 1, Lecture 4, Part V–VI, 182–87) where he indicates that a community based on loyalty can come into existence only if a supreme Spirit of loyalty first animates it.

47. H. Richard Niebuhr finds relativism and the eventual collapse of all justice inevitable unless the absolute value of God is recognized and lived (*Christ and Culture*, New York: Harper-Torchbooks, 1956, 240).

48. Benjamin S. Llamzon studies in *The Self Beyond* (Chicago: Loyola University Press, 1973) the process of wholing which occurs in love: the individual being tends towards its own wholeness of being through the interpersonal relationships which it enjoys (86). Such lovers, in turn, form the whole of a family, next the whole of friends, then the whole of friends of friends, and finally the whole of world community which ultimately stretches throughout time and beyond the earth (119–34). In more psychological terms, Ignace Lepp (*The Psychology of Loving*, translated by Bernard H. Gilligan, Baltimore: Helicon Press, 1969) shows that the loving couple must never stop eliciting from each other enriching developments of personality, especially through the service of some common goal (188–89). Further he holds that the non-erotic

love offered in friendship is capable of indefinite expansion to multiple friends (200–05).

In his "Graced Communities: A Problem in Living" (*Theological Studies*, 44 (Dec. 1983) 604–24). Frank M. Oppenheim, S.J., recounts Josiah Royce's discovery: when the individual human is transformed from his attitude of isolated self-preference into the attitude of a loyal member of a universal community, he is thus empowered to love his beloved community as a reality distinct from, and higher than, any human individual. Oppenheim then indicates that, in this way, the individual human comes to love every human member, actual and potential, of this community (622–23). Such a community includes all graced families, humankind itself as graced, the Christian community, Jesus Christ, and the Trinity. For this is the way the Holy Spirit loves (620–21) and constitutes these communities.

49. Robert O. Johann finds that unselfcentered love enables a person literally to be and then to share in Being Itself, a limitless abundance. The person draws on this abundance in order to give to others without impoverishing himself (75). This is the achieving of all-inclusive wholeness (166). (See *Building the Human*, New York: Herder and Herder, 1965).

50. Teilhard de Chardin felt that a universal love is not only psychologically possible but also the sole complete and final way to love. He went on to declare that this type of love, in turn, demands some ultimate source and object of love (*The Phenomenon of Man*, New York, Harper Torchbook, 1961, 166-67).

51. Gérard Gilleman has written a classic portrayal of Thomas Aquinas's understanding of other-centered love as *caritas* (*The Primacy of Charity in Moral Theology*, Westminster, Md.: Newman Press, 1961). For Thomas, *caritas* is the source of self-unity, of communion between persons, and of union with God. It gives a healing wholesomeness to a person. For, by way of mediation, *caritas* unites all human virtues within a person so that the latter can enter integrally and benevolently into the lives of others and can simultaneously direct all his actions to God with the deep assurance that his other-centered love is worthwhile despite all the sacrifices entailed (99-188).

52. In *Does God Exist* (translated by Edward Quinn, Garden City, N.Y.: Doubleday, 1980, esp. pp. 564–75), Hans Küng bases his conviction that God exists on the ultimately justified fundamental trust in reality. For this trust cannot reasonably exist unless all reality is grounded ultimately in God. This conviction is discerned within the act of entrusting oneself to belief in God as the ultimate ground, meaning, and purpose of reality. Küng admits that this is not an outward rationality of demonstrated truth forced on the mind. Rather, it is an inward rationality offering a fundamental certainty by the very act or practice of boldly trusting God's reality. In and by this act a person experiences the reasonableness of his or her trust.

But J. L. Mackie in *The Miracle of Theism* (Oxford: Clarendon Press, 1982, esp. pp. 243–48) finds Küng's argument slippery (246) since the latter surreptitiously uses the cosmological and teleological proofs (previously rejected) in an altered form (243), that is, as combined with Kant's moral argument and William James's will-to-believe. Further, Mackie holds that the ultimately fundamental trust in reality is reasonable or justifiable in its own right (247) without the need to postulate God, as the grounding, meaning, and ultimate goal of reality. Thus the very believing in God would not be self-justifying, as Küng seems to think, since this maneuver would be a return to the ontological argument previously rejected by Küng (248).

Our approach in searching the limits of love is similar to Küng's argumentation in that we speak of experiencing the six phenomena or qualities of other-centered love. Yet our approach is different from Küng's in that:

1) these six phenomena are revealed in and by the objective situation wherein the act of other-centered love occurs as part of this situation;

2) therefore these six phenomena of other-centered love are taken as objective effects of a cause immanent to, yet transcendent of, the act of other-centered love. This cause is the unchosen absolute or God. Consequently our approach is impervious to the criticism of J. L. Mackie.

53. In *Love Alone* (New York: Herder and Herder, 1969) Hans Urs von Balthasar warns us that the cosmological and anthropo-

logical methods, when used to explore Christian mystery, lead inevitably to extrinsicism (the world-logos is used to explain all) or to immanentism (man as the epitome of the world explains all). Only agape, totally free love or absolute love, offers hope of recognizing God (8,43,61). This agape is Christ.

54. Clearly, God's mediation between lovers and friends is beyond male and female for three reasons:
1) God's mediation is the unification of male and female by way of their complementary differences; it does not work for the dominance of either.
2) God's mediation between friends of the same sex is within and yet beyond their particular sex, it works towards their psychological and spiritual union without denying the difference between male friendships and female friendships.
3) God's mediation in married love or friendship-love demands that the participants' love go through, and then beyond, each other to a higher level in order to include other humans such as their children, friends, extended family, neighborhood, church, nation, humankind, and finally God.
Thus the use of the pronoun *he* to refer to God is not meant to exclude the feminine in God any more than it is meant to limit the unchosen absolute to maleness—especially when God is so much more than male or female or their union. Popular usage is the main criterion lest one end up calling God It.

55. Robert O. Johann (*The Pragmatic Meaning of God*, Milwaukee: Marquette University Press, 1966) outlines the basic principle that wholeness in man and in his community is not possible without the headship of God who affirms all friendships (44–55).

56. Karl Rahner in his "Reflections on the Unity of the Love of Neighbor and the Love of God" (*Theological Investigations*, vol. 6, translated by Karl-H. and Boniface Kruger, New York: Seabury Press, 1974, 231–49) cautions that charity does not dissolve into nothingness within the love of God. In fact, he holds that these two loves do not operate in independence of each other; rather neither can be understood or even expressed without the other.

271

57. Should one wish to estimate how different one's practical spirituality becomes when one recognizes that God is Existence Itself and the source of all existents (without being identical with any of these existents), one should consult Yves Raguin's *Paths to Contemplation* (translated by Paul Barrett, St. Meinrad, Indiana: Abbey Press, 1974). Raguin not only contrasts the various metaphysics underlying Buddhism, Hinduism. and Christianity, but also shows how the different metaphysical understandings lead to large differences in attitudes and in modes of prayer and of living.

58. In *Love Alone* (New York, Herder and Herder, 1969, 25-50), Hans Urs von Balthasar shows how limited philosophy is in describing the initiatives of God's love since, lacking revelation from God himself, it must work only with the effects of this love on man—effects blurred by the imperfections of the individual man and woman. These are the six phenomena or qualities which are found in and describe other-centered love, and which reveal the eight operative characteristics of the unchosen absolute, God.

59. On the manner in which all the various operations of a human being can be drawn together as one (especially by the wholesome act of love), see George P. Klubertanz, "The Unity of Human Operation" (*The Modern Schoolman*, St. Louis: (1950) 27: 75-108).

60. John C. Haughey explores God's role in promoting intersubjectivity (*The Conspiracy of God*, Garden City: Doubleday Image, 1976, 14-16). He finds that God's dynamic union with man requires and even increases one's ability to relate to others.

Working with the laws of physics, biological evolution, and astronomy in his *Commitment to Care* (Greenwich, Conn.: Devin-Adair, 1978), Dr. Dean Turner develops a total philosophy of care in order to find God. This care is the will to discover, conserve and propagate the intrinsic values and meanings of life (10).

This philosophy, while refuting any explanation of the world through chance, discovers the existence of ultimate purpose in the world and, therefore, finds the existence of God.

61. In *Jesus the Christ* (translated by V. Green, New York: Paulist Press, 1976, 191), Walter Kasper finds that modern society's starting point either in the Western concern with the individual self-interest of man or in the Marxist emphasis on social conflict contrasts sharply with Christ's beginning in the unselfcentered love of God for man and of Christ for both God and man. This love is a totally inclusive embrace. No one is left out of their love ever.

62. The theandrism of Raimundo Pannikar (*The Trinity and the Religious Experience of Man*, New York: Orbis Books, 1973, 71-82) would attempt to explain at a theological level what I am hinting at in this philosophical aside.

The fact that *caritas* opens friendship up to the inclusion of other people is underscored by Edmund J. Fortman, S.J., in *The Triune God, A Historical Study of the Triune God* (Grand Rapids, Mich.: Baker Book House, 1982, pp. 193-94). He remarks that in the unselfish love of friendship whereby one gives oneself totally to another, there can still be a bit of selfishness unless this friendship makes room for a third person. This insight he finds in Richard of St. Victor (d. c. 1173): When two love one another mutually, there is dilection on both sides but not condilection. There is condilection when a third is loved concordantly and socially by two, and the affection of the two flows together in the kindling of a third love (*De Trinitate*, III, 19). Evidently, Richard is slightly in favor of trinitarian life.

63. St. Augustine distinguishes freedom of choice (between good and evil) from liberty which is the capacity to choose the good strongly (*The Enchiridion*, 32. *PL*, vol. 40, col. 247). Etienne Gilson indicates this locus among others and explicates this distinction in some detail (*The Christian Philosophy of Saint Augustine*, New York: Random House, 1960, 143-64, and note 85, 323-24).

64. In *The Person and Love* (Staten Island: Alba House, 1967), John Cowburn, S.J., distinguishes two basic types of love: the cosmic of natures and the ecstatic of persons (234-35). He shows how these loves respectively form society and community not merely for a particular moment of time but for all eternity. This occurs among humans and with the three persons of the divine Trinity (383-416).

65. Hans Urs von Balthasar reminds us (*Prayer*, translated by A. V. Littledale, New York: Paulist Press, 1967) that our everyday world sails along over the boundless love of the Father—without much awareness on our part. Nevertheless the Father is supporting every single existent in one great continuous act.

INDEX

Authors

275

Index

Exempla

Themes

relational substance, 85; moderate h. b., 40; Sartrean h. b., 40; Spencerian h. b., 40, 71
humanity, true, 243
humankind, definition of, 40; h. its own supreme value, 38

ideal, projected, 157
identity, personal, 223
immanence, 216; dynamic cooperative i., 199; dynamic i. of unchosen absolute to lovers, 183
immortality of humankind, 145, 211, 233, 267 n. 43; *see also* death.
imperative, moral 268 n. 45
independence, 25, 29, 88, 92; absolute i., 73; biological i., 73, 75; denial of human i., 159; dependent i., 155; horizontal i. and opportunities for balanced personality, 78; horizontal psychological i., 78; human i., 182; human metaphysical i., 83; human vertical biological i., 76; i. and dependence, 50; i. built out of human dependencies, 81; i. of human person, 48, 53; i. of total giving, 118; i and uniqueness and unity of personality, 53; moral i., 81, 89; moral i. and willingness to suffer, 53; psychologial i., 88; psychological i. and clarity of chosen absolute, 52; radical i., 155; ultimate i., 85; vertical i., 84; vertical moral i., 82; vertical psychological i., 78, 80; vertical i. of speciation, 77
inheritance, genetic, 61
instinct to live on 'beyond' death, 145; *see also* immortality
integration, personal, 199
intelligence, adaptive, 188; cumulative i., 189; holistic i., 189; inventive i., 78
interpersonalism, 103, 109, 116, 152
interpretation, 73
intimacy, continuous, 184
inventiveness, 107

justice, 255 n. 11

kindness, 252 n. 6

leadership, pychological, 85
Leninist-Marxists, 42
liberation, 106; the 'more' in l. of beloved, 169; l. through love 266 n. 42; discipline of l., 143, 151, 172, 208; disciplined l. of other-centered love, 152; loss of expansive l., 159
liberty, 44, 67, 85, 98, 103, 105, 108, 129, 145, 151, 236, 261 n. 24; l. and freedom of choice 273 n. 63; l. as constant living with the unchosen absolute, 215; l. 'beyond' ultimate sacrifice, 191; l. in sacrifice, 148; l. of beloved, 107; l. of moderate person, 50; active l., 82, 83; assertive l., 225; definition of l., 121, 236; deprivation of beloved's l., 159; enlargement of l., 170, 186; full and authentic l., 251 n. 1; fullest act of l. and loss of existence, 191; increase of l., 229; independent l., 116, 117; l. as absolute gift of unchosen absolute, 245; l. as ability to reject or accept the unchosen absolute for itself, 191; new l., 190, 229, 237; passive l., 82; personal l., 83, 90, 143, 149, 199; total l., 218
life-goal, ultimate, 17
limits, setting of, 129
logotherapy, 39
love, acceptance of, 112; act of l., 87, 272 n. 59; active l., 251 n. 1; characteristic phenomena of human other-centered l., 198; continuity of l., 8; creation of l., 112; dominative l., 106, 110, 115; eliciting of, l., 137; free act of l., 161; international l., 194; less self-centered l., 228; love as single cooperative act, 109; l. of another and true self l., 264 n. 33; loyal l., 262 n. 28; original l., 10, 113, 121, 166, 168, 193, 206; other-centeredness of intelligent l., 120; paradoxes of human l., 262 n. 26; personal l. relationship, 70; reciprocity of l. 50, 266 n. 39; radical l., 266; relation between l. of God and l. of neighbor, 271 n. 56; romantic l.,